T0364837

hier werner schmidt bei der arbeit

in memory of Werner's parents
in Erinnerung an die Eltern
von Werner

Andrea Bocco Guarneri

WERNER SCHMIDT
architekt

ECOLOGY CRAFT INVENTION ␣
ÖKOLOGIE HANDWERK ERFINDUNG

with a preface by ␣
mit einem Vorwort von
Gernot Minke

AMBRA | V

Author
Andrea Bocco Guarneri
DIST – Politecnico di Torino

Gedruckt mit freundlicher Unterstützung von ␣ Printed with financial
support of Kulturförderung Kanton Graubünden and ␣ und
Vischnaunca da Trun Cultura

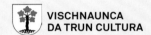

Das Werk ist urheberrechtlich geschützt.
Die dadurch begründeten Rechte, insbesondere die der Übersetzung,
des Nachdruckes, der Entnahme von Abbildungen, der Funksendung,
der Wiedergabe auf photomechanischem oder ähnlichem Wege und
der Speicherung in Datenverarbeitungsanlagen, bleiben, auch bei nur
auszugsweiser Verwertung, vorbehalten.

This work is subject to copyright.
All rights are reserved, whether the whole or part of the material is concerned, specifically those of translation, reprinting, re-use of illustrations, broadcasting, reproduction by photocopying machines or similar
means, and storage in data banks.

© 2013 AMBRA|V
Printed in Austria
AMBRA|V is part of Medecco Holding GmbH, Vienna

Verlag und Herausgeber bitten um Verständnis dafür, dass in Einzelfäl-
len ihre Bemühungen um die Abklärung der Urheberrechte und Textzi-
tate ohne Erfolg geblieben sind.

The publisher and editor kindly wish to inform you that in some cases,
despite efforts to do so, the obtaining of copyright permissions and usage of excerpts of text is not always successful.

Die Wiedergabe von Gebrauchsnamen, Handelsnamen, Warenbe-
zeichnungen usw. in diesem Buch berechtigt auch ohne besondere
Kennzeichnung nicht zu der Annahme, dass solche Namen im Sinne der
Warenzeichen- und Markenschutz-Gesetzgebung als frei zu betrachten
wären und daher von jedermann benutzt werden dürfen.

Product liability: The publisher can give no guarantee for the information contained in this book. The use of registered names, trademarks,
etc. in this publication does not imply, even in the absence of a specific
statement, that such names are exempt from the relevant protective
laws and regulations and are therefore free for general use.

Layout, Cover design: Bellissimo & the Beast, I–Torino
Übersetzung ␣ Translation: Atelier Werner Schmidt, CH–Trun
Lektorat ␣ Proofreading: Andrea Lyman, Alun Brown, A-Wien,␣Vienna
Druck ␣ Printing: Holzhausen Druck GmbH, A–Wien,␣Vienna

Gedruckt auf säurefreiem, chlorfrei gebleichtem Papier – TCF
Printed on acid-free and chlorine-free bleached paper

Mit 616 Abbildungen
With 616 illustrations

Bibliografische Informationen der Deutschen Nationalbibliothek
Die Deutsche Nationalbibliothek verzeichnet diese Publikation in der
Deutschen Nationalbibliografie; detaillierte bibliografische Daten sind
im Internet über <http://dnb.ddb.de> abrufbar.

ISBN 978-3-99043-505-2 AMBRA|V

TABLE OF CONTENTS

INHALT

PREFACE

001

002

Werner Schmidt is known as the pioneer of straw bale building in Europe.

His first building with straw bales dates from 2002, and stands as an example of his creativity, his courage and his perseverance. The novelty of this building was its multi-storey load-bearing walls made of jumbo bales, which support the entire roof and snow loads (over 100 tons), and which (together with lime-cement plaster) also withstand the horizontal forces generated by wind. Werner Schmidt was authorized to construct such a building thanks to his perseverance, and this turned out to be a stroke of luck for him. So far, twenty straw-bale buildings which he designed were built, and seven more are planned.

Werner Schmidt's work is remarkable not only because of his pioneering of straw bale building, but also for his apparent creative will and experimentation with different materials, as well as his quest for new building solutions. To me, this is most obvious when I look at the following four domed buildings:

• the church in Cazis of 1997, a bare concrete shell structure, (→■001)

• the 1997 extension of a house in Trun, a wooden grid shell with wood shingle covering, (→■002)

• the 2010 training pavilion in Oensingen, a wooden-ribbed dome with straw-bale infill, where the problem of weatherproofing is ingeniously solved by a curved roof membrane stretched over it, (→■003)

• the hill house in Amden currently under construction, where different dome shapes are merged, creating a sculpture made of shotcrete, covered with a green roof. (→■004)

I hope that Werner Schmidt's enthusiasm and creative urge do not fade away, and he continues to bless the building world with many groundbreaking buildings.

Gernot Minke

Kassel, May 2013

Werner Schmidt ist als Pionier des Strohballenbaus in Europa bekannt.

Sein erstes Gebäude, das aus Strohballen errichtet wurde, entstand 2002, ein Beispiel für seine Kreativität, seinen Mut und sein Durchsetzungsvermögen. Neu war dabei die Ausbildung mehrgeschossiger Wände aus lasttragenden Jumbo-Ballen, die allein die Dach- und Schneelasten von über 100 Tonnen abtragen und die zusammen mit dem Kalk-Zement-Putz die Horizontalkräfte aus der Wind-Last aufnehmen. Dass dies baurechtlich genehmigt wurde, ist seinem Durchsetzungsvermögen geschuldet und war ein besonderer Glücksfall für Werner Schmidt. Seit dieser Zeit bis zum Sommer 2013 sind zwanzig der von ihm entworfenen Strohballenbauten fertiggestellt, und sieben mehr sind in der Planung.

003

Aus seinem Werk wird nicht nur seine Pioniertätigkeit im Strohballenbau deutlich sondern auch sein ausgeprägter Gestaltungswillen und seine Experimentierfreudigkeit mit den unterschiedlichsten Materialien sowie sein Streben nach immer neuen konstruktiven Lösungen. Am deutlichsten wird dies für mich wenn man die folgenden vier Gewölbebauten betrachtet:

• die Kirche in Cazis von 1997, eine nackte Betonschalenkonstruktion, (→■001)

• der Anbau eines Wohnhauses in Trun von 1997, eine Holzgitterschale mit Holzschindel-Abdeckung, (→■002)

• der Schulungspavillon in Oensingen von 2010, eine Holzrippen-Kuppel mit Strohballen-Ausfachung, bei der das Problem der wetterfesten Abdeckung durch ein darüber gespanntes geschwungenes Membrandach genial gelöst ist, (→■003)

004

• das Hügelhaus in Amden, das zurzeit im Bau ist und eine Verschmelzung unterschiedlicher Kuppelformen darstellt, eine Skulptur aus Spritzbeton erstellt, die mit einem Gründach abgedeckt wird. (→■004)

Es ist zu wünschen, dass Werner Schmidts Begeisterungsfähigkeit und sein Schaffensdrang nicht nachlassen und er die Bauwelt weiterhin mit vielen wegweisenden Bauten beglückt.

Gernot Minke

Kassel, Mai 2013

"the most accessible form of freedom, the most subjectively enjoyed, and the most useful to human society consists of being good at your job and therefore taking pleasure in doing it"

(Primo Levi, 139) (→**B072:139**)

Heritage and training.

Werner Schmidt was born in Trübbach/SG, on 24 June 1953. Among his ancestors there were people of many trades: his grand-grandfather Jakob was a shipwright from Lohr am Main, Germany, who moved to Switzerland to escape the consequences of a fight; his son Jakob was a carpenter whose son Jakob (again) – Werner's father – was a master builder. On his mother's side (Hartmann family), his grand-grandfather was a blacksmith; his son a coppersmith who ended up working for the Rhätische Bahn (Rhaetian Railway) in the early 20th century.

Schmidt likes to think that such family traditions have instilled handicraft and an interest in Stirling and steam engines into him. This is not just speculation; in 1969-72 Schmidt was an apprentice mason, then in 1973-78 he studied at the Höhere Technische Lehranstalt (HTL) – an engineering college – in Winterthur. While on holidays he worked as a mason, sometimes with his father, and collaborated with architect Walter Schlegel. One year he went to Brighton to practise his English, then moved on to Carrbridge, Scotland, where he was employed as a ski instructor. In winter 1978-79 Schmidt was again a ski instructor in Disentis, where he met Lisa Candinas, who

„die größtmöglich erreichbare Form von Freiheit, meist subjektiv empfunden und für die Gesellschaft am nützlichsten, besteht darin, in seinem Beruf gut zu sein und wahre Freude daran zu haben"

(Primo Levi, 139) (→**B072:139**)

Erbe und Ausbildung.

Werner Schmidt wurde am 24. Juni 1953 in Trübbach/SG geboren. Unter seinen Vorfahren finden sich Menschen verschiedener Handwerksberufe: sein Urgroßvater Jakob Schmidt war ein deutscher Schiffsbauer aus Lohr am Main, der in die Schweiz kam, um den Konsequenzen einer Auseinandersetzung zu entkommen. Sein Sohn Jakob war gelernter Zimmermann, und dessen Sohn – Werner Schmidts Vater – trug ebenfalls den Namen Jakob und arbeitete als Baumeister. Auf mütterlicher Seite (Familienname Hartmann) gab es seinen Urgroßvater, der gelernter Hufschmied war, und dessen Sohn ein Kupferschmied, der zu Beginn des 20. Jahrhunderts Dampfmaschinen für die Rhätische Bahn instand hielt.

Schmidt ist überzeugt, dass diese Familientraditionen ihm das Handwerk eingeflößt und in ihm das Interesse für Dampfmaschinen und Stirling Motoren geweckt haben. Dies ist nicht nur eine Vermutung; denn in den Jahren 1969–72 absolvierte Schmidt eine Ausbildung zum Maurer, von 1973–78 studierte er an der Höheren Technischen Lehranstalt (HTL) in Winterthur. Und während seiner Semesterferien arbeitete er als Maurer, manchmal bei seinem Vater, und arbeitete an Projekten für den Architekten Walter Schlegel mit.

later became his wife and mother of their children. In 1979 he moved there, and obtained his first commission as a site engineer for the new municipal sports centre. Soon afterwards he began working as a site engineer at the Disentis abbey too: (→■031,032,093,094) one of his longest and most fruitful professional relationships was born.

Schmidt wanted to refine his architectural education and Schlegel suggested that he study abroad. He considered various options including Berkeley, but chose the Vienna Hochschule für angewandte Kunst (now, University of Applied Arts) where no further examination was required to validate his diploma. He was selected in 1981 but began his studies one year later. In Vienna, he was a student of Hans Hollein, and enjoyed a sense of freedom compared to the educational regimentation he perceived at the ETHZ (Swiss Federal Institute of Technology Zurich). A few minor design assignments and the job at the abbey museum allowed him to pay for his studies. Schmidt graduated in 1989 when he was already 36, and father of three children. Subsequently, he established his professional practice in Disentis.

A "hands-on" approach.

Werner Schmidt's training as a mason has deeply influenced his later work. In contrast with many fellow architects, his approach appears outstandingly rooted in practicality and feasibility. In Schmidt one finds an obvious continuity between formation and professional practice. He relishes in 'getting his hands dirty' both metaphorically – i.e., dealing with the building site problems and minutiae during the design phase – and literally – actively participating in the construction of his buildings. This is very evident by just seeing one of the short films he has produced to document the making of his buildings; while you learn more directly than through a handbook or a lecture how to erect a straw-bale building, you can perceive the significance of physical, direct agency in architecture.

True, the architect's direct involvement in the building work

Er ging für einen Monat nach Brighton, um sein Englisch aufzufrischen, dann zog er nach Carrbridge in Schottland, wo er als Skilehrer eine Anstellung fand. Im Winter 1978–79 kam er nach Disentis und arbeitete dort ebenfalls als Skilehrer und lernte Lisa Candinas kennen, die später seine Frau und Mutter ihrer Kinder wurde. 1979 zog er nach Disentis und erhielt seinen ersten Auftrag als Bauleiter für das neue Sportzentrum der Gemeinde. Kurze Zeit später begann er für das Kloster Disentis ebenfalls als Bauleiter zu arbeiten: (→■031,032,093,094) eine seiner längsten und fruchtbarsten beruflichen Beziehungen war geboren.

Schmidt wollte seine architektonische Ausbildung verfeinern, worauf Walter Schlegel ihm empfahl, im Ausland zu studieren. Er betrachtete verschiedene Optionen, aber entschied sich schließlich für die Hochschule für Angewandte Künste in Wien (heute Universität für Angewandte Kunst), wo sein Diplom anerkannt wurde und es keiner weiteren Prüfungen bedurfte. Er wurde 1981 angenommen, begann sein Studium aber erst ein Jahr später, als Schüler in der Meisterklasse von Hans Hollein. In Wien verspürte er Freiheit, im Gegensatz zu den allgemein bekannten Reglementierungen der ETH Zürich. Einige kleinere Designaufträge sowie ein Auftrag im Klostermuseum erlaubten ihm die Finanzierung seines Studiums. 1989 absolvierte Schmidt erfolgreich sein Studium. Zu diesem Zeitpunkt war er bereits 36 Jahre alt und Vater dreier Kinder. Nach und nach baute er sich sein berufliches Standbein in Disentis auf.

Eine spielerische Annäherung.

Werner Schmidts Ausbildung zum Maurer hat seine spätere Arbeit sehr beeinflusst. Im Gegensatz zu vielen anderen Architekten, ist seine Herangehensweise tief verwurzelt mit der Machbarkeit und Realisierbarkeit.

Bei Schmidt findet man eine sichtbare Kontinuität zwischen dem Entwickeln und der Berufspraxis. Er frönt dem ‚sich-die-Hände-schmutzig-machen' sowohl metaphorisch – zum Beispiel indem er sich mit den Problemen auf der Baustelle

might be the consequence of an uncommon technique. But for Schmidt, conception and manual competence are inseparable, and his work – as shown, for instance, in his sketches – reveals a playful attitude, the activity of a "*homo ludens.*" (→B057)
To comprehend means, literally, 'to take into one's hands.' Cognitive as well as creative processes cannot do without physical acts; before any transformative intervention takes place, to know what surrounds us implies touching this reality.
The Latin word for 'skill', *calliditas*, comes from *callus*, 'corn': implicitly meaning that it can only be the consequence of acquired experience. (→B001) Further – Matthew Crawford thinks that, far from being the result of gratuitous acts of expression, "creativity is a by-product of mastery of the sort that is cultivated through long practice." (→B032:51)
In the contemporary virtuality-driven world, authors like Crawford and Sennett have made a non-negligible effort to rediscover the qualities of hand-working, both for a balanced development of the individual's personality, and for the inherent quality of the outcome produced. Schumacher had already noticed that "the type of work which modern technology is most successful in reducing or even eliminating is skilful, productive work of human hands, in touch with real materials." (→B098:122)
Intelligibility of and familiarity with the physical world are prerequisites for taking responsibility towards it, as Crawford has acutely observed. (→B032:8) Doing manual work, he points out, increases the "sense of agency and competence," (→B032:5) and "gives some independence from the manipulations of marketing." (→B032:17-18)
This said, it has to be clarified that Schmidt's buildings do not exhibit any particular sign of having being 'handcrafted'. Nor are hand-made details to be found, unless creative residents have intervened.

Straw-bale building as a means.
Straw-bale building as a means. In the last decade, the solution Schmidt has most often used to achieve an extremely

und allen Einzelheiten beschäftigt – und wörtlich – indem er aktiv an der Ausführung seiner Gebäude teilnimmt. Dies ist offensichtlich, wenn man einen der Kurzfilme anschaut, die er normalerweise zur Dokumentation während des Errichtens seiner Gebäude produziert. Da man durch Anpacken direkter lernt als durch ein Handbuch oder eine Vorlesung darüber, wie man ein Strohballenhaus errichtet, kann man die Wichtigkeit des physischen und direkten Eingreifens in Architektur verstehen. Das sich Einbringen des Architekten in den Bauprozess könnte eine Konsequenz aus der Anwendung einer ungewöhnlichen Bautechnik sein. Aber für Schmidt sind Konzept und handwerkliches Können untrennbar, und seine Arbeit – wie es sich zum Beispiel in seinen Skizzen zeigt – enthüllt eine spielerische Haltung, die Tätigkeit eines „*homo ludens*". (→B057)
'Begreifen' bedeutet wortwörtlich 'in die Hände nehmen'. Sowohl geistige als auch kreative Prozesse können nicht ohne physische Handlung vollzogen werden. Zu wissen, was uns umgibt, bedingt das Berühren dieser Realität, bevor es zu einem transformierenden Eingreifen kommt. Der lateinische Begriff für 'Fähigkeit', *calliditas*, stammt von *callus*, 'Schwielen': dies bedeutet im Prinzip, dass das Verständnis von Dingen nur eine Folge aus sich angeeigneten Erfahrungen sein kann. (→B001) Des weiteren formuliert es Matthew Crawford so, „Kreativität ist ein Nebenprodukt der Meisterhaftigkeit, die sich durch lange praktische Erfahrung entwickelt", (→B032:51) und viel weniger nur das Ergebnis grundloser Ausdrucksarten ist.
In der zeitgenössischen, virtuell-getriebenen Welt haben Autoren wie Crawford und Sennett einen nicht zu vernachlässigenden Versuch gestartet, die Qualitäten des Handwerks wieder zu entdecken, sowohl in Bezug auf eine ausgeglichene Entwicklung der Persönlichkeit des Individuums, als auch für die inhärente Qualität des daraus resultierenden Produktes. Schumacher hatte bereits erkannt, dass „die Art von Arbeit, die moderne Technologien erfolgreich zu dezimieren oder beinahe auszumerzen wissen, ist die geschickte, produktive Arbeit menschlicher Hände, in Berührung mit echten Materialien". (→B098:122)

high insulation performance of the building envelope is the employment of straw bales; although this can obviously be attained with other materials. For instance, in the Maissen extension (1997), (→p40-43) a 60-cm cellulose insulation was used; house Schmid-Cavegn (1998) (→■006) is almost identical to the houses Schmidt designs today – I am referring, among other things, to prefabricated timber structure, spatial concept, and positioning of rooms – but for the insulation used. More complex and unique in his oeuvre is house Gartmann (2000), (→p120-123) where the insulation is EPS and XPS panels. Schmidt's interest in straw-bale construction dates from about 1995, when an acquaintance told him about the Steens book. (→B107) In 1997 or 1998 he built a 1:1 prototype in the yard of his father's workshop – a corner-shaped straw-bale wall, 4 x 5 x 2.5 m, with a window and a door. The final comment of his initially sceptical father – "not bad!" – confirmed he had passed one of most difficult tests. In 2001 he resolved to make a study trip to New Mexico, where he attended a course in natural building and permaculture at the Lama Foundation. He also visited a number of straw-bale buildings in the region. Soon afterwards, (→§09) he was able to build his first straw-bale house – the much-celebrated and iconic house Braun-Dubuis in Disentis. (→■007;p254-259) After this commission, clients tended to come to him because they were attracted by the advantages of the new material. Since then, the list of Schmidt's straw buildings has been growing quite impressively – it now includes 20 works in three countries – and more are on the way, including an entire development in Lower Austria, in cooperation with GrAT [Group for Appropriate Technology] of the TU Wien [Vienna University of Technology]. (→■008,140-141) In his designs, straw is used in different ways, often with hybrid solutions which make use of structural timber and prefabricated elements. There is no 'typical Werner Schmidt way' of employing straw – on the contrary, every new project is an opportunity for further improvement and experimentation. (→§08) Schmidt gained much of his knowledge about building with

Das Verständnis für und eine Vertrautheit mit der physischen Welt sind Voraussetzung dafür, ihr verantwortungsvoll gegenüber zu treten, wie Crawford scharfsinnig beobachtet hat. (→B032:8) Arbeit mit den Händen auszuführen, steigert den „Sinn für Tätigkeit und Kompetenz", (→B032:5) und „gibt einem eine gewisse Unabhängigkeit von der Manipulation des Marktes". (→B032:17-18) Es ist klar, dass Schmidts Gebäude keine speziellen Kennzeichen aufweisen, 'handgemacht' zu sein. Überdies sind keine handgemachten Details zu finden, es sei denn, die Besitzer haben selbst Hand angelegt.

Strohbauten als ein Mittel.
In den letzten zehn Jahren war die von Schmidt meist gewählte Lösung der Einsatz von Strohballen, um eine extrem gute Isolierung der Gebäudehülle zu erreichen, obwohl dies offensichtlich auch mit anderen Materialien erreicht werden kann. Zum Beispiel bei dem Erweiterungsbau Maissen-Petschen (1997), (→S.40-43) wo eine 60 cm dicke Zellulosedämmung verwendet wurde; das Haus Schmidt-Cavegn (1998) (→■006) entspricht bis auf die verwendete Isolierung beinahe dem Design von Schmidts heutigen Wohnbauten – ich beziehe mich unter anderem auf die vorfabrizierten Holzelemente, das Raumkonzept, und die Anordnung der Räume. Komplexer und einzigartiger in seinem Werk ist das Haus Gartmann-Sgier (2000), (→S.120-123) wo die Isolierung aus EPS und XPS Platten besteht. Schmidts Interesse an Strohballenkonstruktionen reicht bis ins Jahr 1995 zurück, als ihm ein Bekannter von Steens Buch berichtete. (→B107) Im Jahre 1997 oder 1998 baute er einen 1:1 Prototyp im Hinterhof der Werkstatt seines Vaters – die Eckkonstruktion einer Strohballenwand, 4x5x2,5 m mit einem Fenster und einer Türe. Der Kommentar „nicht schlecht!" seines anfangs sehr skeptischen Vaters bestätigte ihm das Bestehen der wohl schwierigsten Prüfung. Im Jahre 2001 konnte er eine Studienreise nach New Mexico antreten, während die-

006

007

ser er an der Lama Foundation an einem Kurs zu natürlichem Bauen und Permakultur teilnahm. Er besuchte auch in der Umgebung dort eine Vielzahl von Strohballenhäusern. Kurze Zeit darauf konnte er (→§09) sein erstes Strohballenhaus bauen – das ikonenhafte und vielfach zelebrierte Haus Braun-Dubuis in Disentis. (→■007;p254-259) Nach diesem Auftrag kamen weitere Bauherren zu ihm, die durch die Vorzüge des neuen Materials angezogen wurden. Seit damals ist die Zahl der Schmidt'schen Strohballenhäuser beträchtlich angestiegen – sie umfasst mittlerweile 20 Arbeiten in drei verschiedenen Ländern und weitere sind in Planung; unter anderem ein ganzes Siedlungsprojekt in Niederösterreich, in Zusammenarbeit mit der GrAT, Gruppe für angepasste Technologie der TU Wien. (→■008,140-141) In seinen Arbeiten wird das Stroh auf verschiedene Arten verwendet, oftmals in kombinierten Hybrid-Konstruktionen, die den Vorzug von Leimholz und vorfabrizierten Elementen nutzen. Es gibt keinen typischen Werner Schmidt Stil für den Einsatz des Strohs. Auf der anderen Seite ist jedes neue Projekt eine Möglichkeit weiterer Verbesserungen und des Experiments. (→§08) Schmidt erlangte einen Großteil seines Wissens über den Strohballenbau durch direkte Erfahrung, aber es sei auch erwähnt, dass er schon früh Kontakt zur GrAT herstellte, die seit 2000 Materialtests durchführt, und dass er mit der HTW Chur in Kooperation stand, wo Tests zum Druckverhalten durchgeführt wurden. Werner Schmidts internationaler Ruf nahm rasch zu, auf Grund seiner Konsequenz als ‚grüner' Architekt und der Qualität seiner Bauten, aber auch durch eine Art Modeerscheinung des Strohballenbaus – trotz der noch immer schwindend geringen Zahl an Strohballenbauten und die gravierenden Restriktionen und Vorurteile gegenüber dieser Bauweise. Neben dieser Modeerscheinung ist es vor allem einer seiner Bauherren, Beat Küng, der diese Schlüsselfaktoren von Schmidts Erfolg und Einzigartigkeit am treffendsten formuliert: er ist in der Lage, Kompetenz und Leidenschaft für ein Bauen basierend auf einer breiten, ökologischen Vision zu vereinen.

straw bales through direct experience, but it is also worth mentioning that he connected quite early with GrAT – which since 2000 has been conducting tests on this material – and that he co-operated with the HTW [University of Applied Sciences] Chur, where further tests were conducted on compressive strength.

The international repute Werner Schmidt quickly gained relies on his inherent consistency as a 'green' architect and the quality of his designs, but also on some kind of current vogue for straw-bale building – in spite of the still relatively negligible number of houses built and the heavy constraints and prejudices affecting this technique.

Besides this current vogue, it is one of his clients, Beat Küng, who best captures the key factor of Schmidt's success and uniqueness: he is able to marry competence and passion for actual building with a wide ecological vision.

Innovation grows in niches.

Ecosystemic and social niches are the places where variety originates. (→B100:110) Such a statement encompasses that particular kind of social innovation which goes under the label of 'techn(olog)ical innovation'. Niches can be literally secluded places, but also special groups of people, trades, and income brackets.

Obviously, the survival of a niche relies on environmental (local) conditions and resources. These may also include awareness. According to Leopold Kohr's theory of size, (→B065) Switzerland may be one of the few countries where democracy is still exerted on a proximity basis. One could wonder if her being a political cluster of niches has in some way helped the development of places such as Graubünden, which can be described as niches of good architecture (to mention but a few contemporary architects, see the work of Bearth & Deplazes, Caminada, Clavuot, Olgiati, Zumthor). (→B031,033,034,095,128) In niches, bizarre experiments can be made without creating too much fuss. Matter-of-factedness can be established. Like

Innovation wächst in Nischen.

Ökosystemische und soziale Nischen sind die Orte, an denen Vielfalt entsteht. (→B100:110) Eine solche Aussage beinhaltet die spezielle Art der sozialen Innovation, die unter dem Deckmäntelchen der ‚techn(olog)ischen Innovation' steht. Nischen können wortwörtlich abgeschirmte Plätze sein, aber auch aus speziellen Gruppen von Menschen, Märkten oder Verdienstgruppen bestehen.

Offensichtlich hängt das Überleben einer Nische von (lokalen) Umweltbedingungen und Ressourcen ab. Dazu zählt auch das Bewusstsein. Gemäß Leopold Kohrs ‚Theorie der Größe', (→B065) könnte die Schweiz eines der wenigen Länder sein, in der die Demokratie auf einer nachbarschaftlichen Basis praktiziert wird. Man könnte sich sogar fragen, ob sie durch ihre Funktion als einer Art politischen Bündelung von Nischen nicht zur Entwicklung von Orten wie Graubünden, die als Nische der guten Architektur eingestuft werden kann (Bearth & Deplazes, Caminada, Clavuot, Olgiati, Zumthor, (→B031,033,034,095,128) um nur ein paar zeitgenössische Architekten zu nennen), beigetragen hat.

In Nischen können bizarre Experimente durchgeführt werden, ohne zu große Verwirrung zu stiften. Nackte Tatsachen können etabliert und manifestiert werden. Wie in Baumschulen können Innovationen und sogar Häresien herangezogen werden bis sie stark genug sind, um in die weite Welt gelassen zu werden. Ich denke, ich liege keiner bloßen Vermutung auf, wenn ich sage, dass Sepp Holzer oder Werner Schmidt nur an solch abgelegenen Orten ursprüngliche Wege der Landwirtschaft und der Architektur entwickeln konnten. (→§06)

In Richtung eines vegetarischen Hauses.

Sowohl Fachleute als auch Zulassungsstellen „betrachten Materialien, welche über Jahrhunderte eingesetzt wurden, als großes Risiko und setzen ihren Glauben viel lieber in unerprobte Kunststoffe und synthetische Materialien, die vielleicht in zehn Jahren zerfallen werden. (…) Leider ist es relativ schwierig,

GASTRONOMIE

EX10

GEMEINSCHAFTSKÜCHE
CAFE EXTERN

KELTEN + ZCV

konzentrierende Kollektoren
Parabol od Rinne

008

an early sketch of the entrance area of the 'Zero carbon village'

eine frühe Skizze vom Eingangsbereich des 'Zero carbon village'

in nurseries, innovations and even heresies can be cultivated until they are strong enough to be taken to the fore. I do not think I am a victim of suggestion if I say that only in remote places could Sepp Holzer or Werner Schmidt develop original methods in agriculture and architecture. (→§06)

Towards a vegetarian house.
Both professionals and approving bodies "regard materials, which have been used for centuries, as high risk and are much happier to put their faith in unproven modern plastics and synthetic materials that will probably fall apart in ten years. (...) Unfortunately it is hard to certify natural methods which rely on good practice on site and the careful selection of materials; this involves trust and care." (→B126:13)
An unconventional mind and an unusual determination are required to envisage simple building techniques based on local, natural materials – and have them formally approved. (→§09) Often, they are not provided for in environmental assessment methods – or else, their characteristics are underestimated or incompletely covered. Yet this is crucial, since "it will not matter how green or low-impact a method is, if there is no assessment attached to it, then it may be difficult to specify it." (→B126:182) Such cultural bias in favour of industrial products has been cleverly exploited by manufacturers and is more or less explicitly ruled by laws, by-laws and standards. (The fact that much effort is bestowed upon generating energy from renewable sources, instead of reducing consumption, betrays that the interest is more in using the current concern for global warming as a sales opportunity than in decreasing the building sector's footprint.)
Just as 'slow' food is gaining recognition and appreciation, a 'slow building' movement should rise which would employ "good, clean, and fair" materials and techniques. (→B086) At the present time, "laws do not require manufacturers to declare the full constituents of their [building] products, how much energy has been used in their manufacture and whether

natürliche Methoden, die auf guter Erfahrung durch ihren Einsatz gründen und die sorgsame Selektion von Materialien voraussetzen, auf ihre Tauglichkeit zu testen; dies setzt Vertrauen und Sorgfalt voraus." (→B126:13)
Eine unkonventionelle Einstellung und eine ungewöhnliche Entschlossenheit sind notwendig, um sich einfache Bautechniken vorzustellen, die auf den lokalen und natürlichen Materialien basieren – und sie offiziell genehmigen zu lassen. (→§09) Häufig sind sie in den Methoden der Umweltverträglichkeitsprüfung nicht enthalten – oder ihre Eigenschaften werden unterschätzt und unvollständig abgedeckt. Jedoch ist dies entscheidend, da „es nicht von Bedeutung ist, wie grün oder von welch geringer Auswirkung eine Methode ist, wenn es keine entsprechende Einstufung gibt, dann ist es möglicherweise schwierig, sie zu spezifizieren." (→B126:182) Solch kulturelle Voreingenommenheit zugunsten der Industrieprodukte wurde von den Herstellern clever ausgenutzt und wird mehr oder weniger ausdrücklich durch Gesetze, Zusatzverordnungen und Standards gelenkt. (Die Tatsache, dass viele Bemühungen in die Erzeugung von erneuerbaren Energien gesetzt werden, anstatt den Verbrauch zu verringern, verrät, dass das Interesse vielmehr darin besteht, die gegenwärtige Besorgnis zur globalen Erwärmung als Verkaufsstrategie zu nutzen, als den energetischen Fußabdruck in der Baubranche zu verringern.)
Genauso wie ‚slow food' an Anerkennung und Wertschätzung gewinnt, sollte sich eine ‚slow building' Bewegung etablieren, die „gute, saubere und faire" Materialien und Techniken zum Einsatz bringt. (→B086) Zum gegenwärtigen Zeitpunkt „fordern Gesetze von den Herstellern keine Nachweise zur Beschaffenheit ihrer (Bau-)Produkte oder darüber, wie viel Energie in ihrer Fertigung steckt, und ob es irgendwelche Schadstoffbelastungen gibt." (→B126:184) Dies führt zu Entscheidungen aus Unwissenheit und häufig getrieben durch die Macht der Gewohnheit, und zu guter letzt durch den Preis. Nichtsdestotrotz sollte die Wahl auf Materialien und

there are any pollution burdens." (→B126:184) Choices are therefore little informed, and often driven by habit and above all by price. Nonetheless, preference should be accorded to materials and techniques which "need minimal manufacturing and transportation." (→B126:10)

On the other hand, it is true that we do not know much about natural construction materials and techniques. Unfortunately, "natural building possibilities are not glamorous and high-tech, rarely involve computer technology or 'intelligent systems' and are hard to patent and thus create investment opportunities for venture capitalists and merchant bankers." (→B126:186) Moreover, often test protocols have been developed that only suit industrial, standardised products. However, contrary to common belief, "The industrial replacements have typically been developed to reduce the labor and costs of construction, not necessarily to improve the quality or safety of buildings." (→B126:26)

Obviously, we need not refuse the numerous highly useful modern materials and products, nor does Schmidt do this: the remarkable performances of his houses are partly due to windows which need both state-of-the-art machinery and glass panes. Modern products and designs can be coupled with low-energy, minimally processed natural materials. Schmidt's work shows that a natural approach to architecture does not necessarily produce 'hairy' buildings for hippies and drop-outs.

Learning from tradition.
David Eisenberg has noted that "industrial building [has replaced] labor intensity with resource intensity. (…) Indigenous methods [have been] stigmatized by the perception that they are obsolete or used only by an impoverished society." (→B040:23) But, from a holistic point of view, the contrary is true: traditional techniques are more respectful of environmental balance than current building methods. And they are not less durable either: many centuries-old buildings made of

auf Techniken fallen, die „einen minimalen Herstellungs- und Transportaufwand benötigen." (→B126:10)

Andererseits ist es wahr, dass wir nicht viel über natürliche Baumaterialien und Techniken wissen. Leider „sind natürliche Konstruktionsmöglichkeiten nicht glamourös und keine high-tech, selten beziehen sie Computertechnologie oder ‚intelligente Systeme' mit ein und sind schwierig zu patentieren, und sie schaffen dadurch nur schwer günstige Geldanlagebedingungen für Risikokapitalgeber und Handelsbanker." (→B126:186) Außerdem wurden häufig Testprotokolle entwickelt, die nur genau den industriellen, standardisierten Produkten entsprechen. Aber im Gegensatz zur allgemeinen Überzeugung, „wurden die industriellen Ersatzstoffe für gewöhnlich entwickelt, um die Arbeit und die Baukosten zu verringern, nicht zwangsläufig um die Qualität oder die Sicherheit von Gebäuden zu verbessern." (→B126:26)

Offensichtlich müssen wir nicht die zahlreichen, in hohem Grade nützlichen, modernen Materialien und Produkte ablehnen, was auch Schmidt nicht tut: viele bemerkenswerte Merkmale seiner Häuser liegen teilweise den speziellen Fenstern zugrunde, für die man hochmoderne Maschinerie und Glasscheiben benötigt. Moderne Produkte und Entwürfe können mit den niedrigenergetischen, minimal bearbeiteten und natürlichen Materialien verbunden werden. Schmidts Arbeit zeigt, dass eine natürliche Annäherung an Architektur nicht unbedingt ‚haarige' Gebäude für Hippies und Durchgeknallte hervorbringt.

Von der Tradition lernen.
David Eisenberg bemerkte, dass „das das industrielle Bauen die Arbeitsintensität mit Materialintensität (ersetzt hat). (…) Ursprüngliche Methoden wurden durch den Glauben stigmatisiert, dass sie obsolet seien oder nur von einer armen Bevölkerung gebraucht würden". (→B040:23) Aber von diesem umfassenden Standpunkt aus betrachtet, ist das Gegenteil der Fall: traditionelle Techniken gehen respektvoller mit der

straw and earth still stand today. Durability is earned through constant maintenance, not through preservatives and other chemicals, which encourage irresponsible behaviour from the residents and bad design from the architect.

Part of Schmidt's attitude towards architecture derives from a respectful, albeit not conservative nor imitative, relation to tradition; mostly vernacular. (→§07) His references include work on traditional Swiss buildings, information from scholarly sources such as Gschwend's (→B048) and Simonett's (→B102) books, as well as observation of exotic rural houses including trulli. (→■010)

Straw-bale building shows many similarities with traditional methods such as load-bearing masonry or cob; it demonstrates that "alternatives to modern building materials are available." (→B016:xi)

Noble and ecclesiastic masonry buildings used to have walls up to 300 cm thick, as Schmidt noticed when he was refurbishing parts of Disentis abbey; a 120 cm straw-bale wall is therefore not so bulky! Also, if their 'depth' is apparent as it is at openings, walls will perceptually indicate "compactness and thereby inner resistance." (→B108:167)

Neither is the use of vegetal debris for insulation a novelty: in traditional houses where Schmidt happened to work as a mason, he found sawdust in between wooden boards.

Sometimes, newly-introduced regulations seem to defy traditional wisdom: Schmidt ironically reports that a recent increase of the legal snow-load from 450 to 620 kg/m^2 has created trouble in the design of mountain buildings... but traditional houses, unaware of any norms, still stand – even after exceptional snowfalls.

Rural buildings show that in many issues it is not necessary to attain perfection, only reasonably satisfactory performances: not seeking the highest performances allows costs to be kept down, and the focus to be on economic as well as technical efforts for the few elements that really need to be state-of-the-art. (→§08)

Umwelt um als die gängige Bauweise. Und sie sind auch nicht weniger dauerhaft: in Europa und andernorts stehen viele Jahrhunderte alte Gebäude, die aus Stroh und Lehm gebaut sind. Dauerhaftigkeit wird durch das stetige Pflegen erreicht und nicht durch Haltbarmacher und andere chemische Substanzen, die zu unverantwortungsvollem Verhalten der Bewohner und schlechtem Design durch die Architekten führen können.

Ein Teil von Werner Schmidts Haltung gegenüber der Architektur kommt von einem respektvollen, obgleich weder konservativ noch imitierenden Verhältnis zu – meist heimischer – Tradition. (→§07) Sein Wissen basiert auf Arbeiten an traditionellen Schweizer Häusern, Information aus Fachbüchern wie Gschwends (→B048) und Simonetts, (→B102) als auch auf dem Studium von exotischen, ländlichen Häusern, wie zum Beispiel den Trulli. (→■010)

Der Strohballenbau zeigt viele Ähnlichkeiten mit traditionellen Methoden wie dem lasttragenden Mauerwerk oder Stampflehm; er zeigt, dass „Alternativen zu den modernen Baumaterialien verfügbar sind". (→B016:xi)

Herrschaftliche und sakrale Steinbauten hatten für gewöhnlich bis zu 3 m dicke Wände, wie Schmidt bestaunte, als er Teile des Klosters Disentis erneuerte eine 1,20 m starke Strohballenwand ist demnach gar nicht so dick! – und wenn ihre Tiefe so offensichtlich ist, wie in Wandöffnungen, deuten die Wände spürbar „die Kompaktheit und dadurch ihre innere Widerstandsfähigkeit" an. (→B108:167)

Auch ist der Gebrauch von pflanzlichen Abfällen kein Novum: in traditionellen Gebäuden, in denen Schmidt als Maurer tätig war, fand er Sägespäne zwischen den hölzernen Schichten. Manchmal scheinen neu eingeführte Regulierungen das traditionelle Wissen heraus zu fordern: Schmidt bemerkt ironisch, dass die neuerliche Anhebung der gesetzlich zugelassenen Schneelasten von 450 bis 620 kg/m² Schwierigkeiten beim Entwerfen von Häusern in Bergregionen mit sich bringen, während traditionelle Gebäude, jenseits von jeglicher Norm,

009

010

009

the 'Nido' composed of several trulli-like spaces, to host La Donaira
staff

Projekt 'Nido' bestehend aus mehreren trulli-förmigen Volumen,
Unterkünfte für die Mitarbeiter von La Donaira

Form is a consequence.
Although many of Schmidt's early buildings – such as the Cazis church (→■011;p44-49) and the Jacomet (→■013;p263-266) and Maissen extensions – have a striking appearance, his design process is strictly developed from the function to be fulfilled and from constructional principles. Form comes at the end of a creative process based on the interaction with clients and driven by their needs, and is not the primary goal of architectural creativity. Form comes from the inside, except when the historical context calls for respect – in which case Schmidt can be sensible without attempting to be mimetic. In his case, therefore, one cannot really speak of buildings shaped in order to adapt to the site they stand on. In Schmidt's work there is no recognisable 'style' or 'designer label': forms and solutions are born from circumstances; for instance, he chooses alien forms when the context is confused (e.g. vonRoll pavilion). (→■012;p50-55)
His recent work shuns exhibitionism, and avoids adopting a 'green architecture aesthetic'. Many of his houses have simple, cubic volumes, gabled roofs, and plastered walls; nothing in their appearance makes them stand out of their context as 'sustainable' buildings. His adoption of straw-bale construction has somehow entailed a simplification of forms, which have become geometrically essential – creating a new vernacular, as it were. His houses do not lack some restrained elegance; nevertheless such modern vernacular hardly meets the taste of magazine editors and design awards panels. But it is living quality that matters. (→§01,05)

Conclusions.
Werner Schmidt's work shows that high ecological consideration can be coupled with convincing architectural results. The quality of his buildings in term of energy performance, livability, and beautiful form constitutes a good practice promoting new paths to a 'green' architecture.
What is more, the richness and non-reticence of the informa-

noch immer stehen, auch nach außergewöhnlich starker Beanspruchung durch Schneelasten. Ländliche Gebäude zeigen in vielerlei Hinsicht, dass es nicht notwendig ist, Perfektion zu erzielen, sondern vernünftige, befriedigende Ergebnisse: nicht das bestmögliche Ergebnis erzielt zwangsläufig niedrige Kosten, oder richtet den Fokus auf ökonomische und technische Bemühungen hinsichtlich der wenigen Elemente, die auf dem Stand der Technik sein müssen. (→§08)

Form ist eine Konsequenz.
Obgleich viele von Schmidts frühen Gebäuden – wie die Kirche Cazis (→■011;S.44-49) und die Jacomet (→■013;S.263-266) und Maissen-Petschen Erweiterungen – ein auffälliges Erscheinungsbild haben, entwickelt er seinen Designprozess ausschließlich im Hinblick auf die Funktion, die erfüllt werden soll, und die baulichen Prinzipien. Die Form kommt am Ende eines kreativen Prozesses, basierend auf der Interaktion mit dem Kunden und geleitet von ihren Bedürfnissen, und sie ist nicht das primäre Ziel von architektonischer Kreativität. Form entsteht aus dem Inneren heraus, nicht von außen; es sei denn, wenn dem historischen Kontext Respekt erwiesen werden muss – in diesem Fall kann Schmidt achtsam sein, ohne nachzuahmen. Im Fall von Schmidt kann man auch nicht behaupten, dass seine Gebäude derart geformt werden, um sie dem Standort anzupassen, an dem sie errichtet werden. In seinen Arbeiten gibt es keinen erkennbaren ‚Stil' oder ein ‚Designlabel': Formen und Lösungen entstehen aus Umständen heraus; zum Beispiel wählt er fremde Formen, wenn der Kontext durchmischt scheint (z. B. vonRoll Pavillon). (→■012;S.50-55)
Seine aktuellen Arbeiten meiden Exhibitionismus, und weichen einem Adaptieren von ‚grüner Architekturästhetik' aus. Viele seiner Häuser haben ein einfaches, kubisches Volumen, Giebeldächer und verputzte Wände; nichts an ihrem Aussehen lässt sie aus ihrem Kontext heraustreten und als ‚ökologisch nachhaltige' Gebäude erscheinen.
Schmidts Verwendung der Strohballenbauweise hat eine Ver-

011

012

013

tion Schmidt gives in his website are doing much to facilitate the diffusion of more sustainable approaches and techniques, and are totally consistent with the open-source character which (according to many) straw-bale building should retain. Schmidt is very conscious of the importance of high-quality communication: his website couples visual refinement and plain navigation; his video clips are appropriately short, direct and understandable; in the entrance of his atelier a few high-quality photographs showcase his most beautiful accomplishments, without the need for any words; prospective clients and visitors can browse his projects, self-evidently described in A3-portfolios where sketches are richly used to communicate both concept and details.

In sum, if concrete example and direct experience are needed now to give impulse to a wider transformation of our built environment, I believe this is one of the places to look at. Nevertheless, two points remain ambiguous and should be clearly recalled:

- extremely low embodied as well as operating energy in building cannot justify waste in other sectors; (→§04)

014

einfachung der Formen mit sich gebracht, die im wesentlichen geometrisch geworden sind und die ein neues, einheimisches Erscheinungsbild schaffen. Seinen Häusern mangelt es nicht an zurückhaltender Eleganz, nichtsdestotrotz treffen solch neue, einheimische Erscheinungsbilder kaum den Geschmack diverser Herausgeber von Zeitschriften oder Design Award Plattformen. Aber es ist allein die Lebensqualität, die zählt.

Schlussfolgerungen.
Werner Schmidts Arbeit zeigt, dass hohe ökologische Ansprüche mit überzeugenden architektonischen Ergebnissen in Verbindung gebracht werden können. Die Qualität seiner Gebäude im Hinblick auf Energieleistungen, Lebensansprüche und schöne Formen, stellt eine gute Methode dar, um neue Wege zu ‚grüner' Architektur zu fördern.

Noch wichtiger ist der Reichtum an und der offene Umgang mit Informationen, die Schmidt auf seiner Internetseite zur Verfügung stellt, die dabei helfen, die Verbreitung von ökologisch nachhaltigen Ansätzen und Techniken zu fördern, und sie stimmen gänzlich mit dem offenen Charakter, den der Strohballenbau bewahren sollte, überein.

Schmidt ist sich über die Wichtigkeit qualitativ hochwertiger Kommunikation sehr bewusst: seine Internetseite verbindet visuelle Feinheit und einfache Navigation; seine Videoclips sind passend kurz, direkt und verständlich; im Eingangsbereich seines Ateliers stellen einige hochwertige Fotografien seine schönsten Arbeiten dar, ohne den Bedarf irgendwelcher Worte; potenzielle Kunden und Besucher können in seinen Projektzusammenstellungen, in Form von selbsterklärenden A3 Portfolios stöbern, in denen Skizzen zur Vermittlung von Konzept und Details reichlich verwendet werden.

In der Summe betrachtet, wenn jetzt konkrete Beispiele und direkte Erfahrungen benötigt werden, um Impulse an eine weiterführende Umwandlung unserer gebauten Umwelt zu geben, glaube ich, dass hier der geeignete Orte dafür ist, dies zu tun. Dennoch bleiben zwei Punkte mehrdeutig und sollten deutlich

014

the bamboo water-wheel of the
Meranflora exhibition is released
into the Passer water

das Bambuswasserrad auf der
Meranflora Ausstellung wird in
der Passer zu Wasser gelassen

015

a pause during Fliri house
construction works

Pause während der Aufbauarbeiten
beim Haus Fliri

015

in Erinnerung gerufen werden:
- extrem niedrige Graue Energie und Energieverbrauch von
Gebäuden, dürfen die Verschwendung in anderen Bereichen
nicht rechtfertigen; (→§04)
- außerordentlich leistungsstarke Neubauten führen nicht
automatisch auf den Weg in Richtung einer notwendigen Ver-
besserung von Altbauten. (→§10)

Wie man dieses Buch lesen sollte.

Wie man dieses Buch lesen sollte. Dieses Buch befasst sich
mit dem Gesamtwerk von Werner Schmidt, was bedeutet,
dass ich viele Dokumente zu abgeschlossenen Projekten,
sowohl realisierte als auch nicht realisierte Gebäude, ordnen
und neu zusammenfügen musste. Ich habe versucht, Fakten
zu ermitteln, die nicht nur auf solch kostbarer Dokumentation
basieren, sondern auch auf meiner direkten Betrachtung der
Objekte, die ich thematisiere, und die vielen Gespräche, die ich
mit Schmidt und seinen Kunden führen konnte. Ich versuchte,
mich nicht dem bloßen Darlegen seiner Absichten oder Poetik
hinzugeben. Gleichzeitig war ich bemüht, ein zukunftsorien-
tiertes Buch zu verfassen. Nicht nur weil ich von der Art eines
flächendeckenden, definitiv monographischen Stils Abstand
halten wollte, der möglicherweise eher bei verstorbenen
Autoren passend wäre, sondern vor allem weil es mir, der ich
kein Historiker bin, scheint, dass es viel interessanter ist, über
offene Perspektiven und neue Möglichkeiten zu sprechen.
Ich beschloss, das Buch in zwei ineinandergreifende Teile zu
gliedern. Der erste und berechenbarere Teil sind Beschreibun-
gen von einigen seiner Arbeiten, zu denen der Leser ergänzen-
de Informationen auf Schmidts eigener Internetseite findet.
Der zweite Teil besteht aus Themen, die ich als instrumentell
nützlich befand, um die meiner Meinung nach bemerkens-
werteren Charakterzüge seiner Arbeit hervorzuheben. Hier
versuchte ich auch, sein Schaffen in Abhängigkeit eines
breiteren Kontexts zu erörtern, und ich nahm mir die Freiheit,
jedes Kapitel zu charakterisieren, indem ich unterschiedliche

- the solutions which produce excellently performing new buildings are not automatically useful for a much needed improvement of existing buildings. (→§10)

How to read this book.
This book deals with Werner Schmidt's oeuvre, which implies I had to organise and rearrange plenty of documents about past projects, both built and unbuilt. I attempted to report facts based not only on such precious documentation but also on my direct experience of the objects I discussed and on the many talks I had with Schmidt and his clients. I tried not to indulge in relating his intentions or poetics. At the same time, I attempted to compose a future-oriented book. Not only because I wanted to stay away from the kind of all-encompassing, 'definitive' monograph style which is perhaps more appropriate to dead authors, but particularly because it seems to me – not being a historian – much more interesting to talk about open perspectives and new possibilities. I chose to arrange the book in two intertwining ways. The first and more predictable one involves descriptions of some of his works, about which the reader will find supplementary information on Schmidt's own website. The second way concerns themes I found instrumentally useful to highlight the more remarkable – in my opinion – features of his work. Here I also tried to discuss his activity against a wider context, and to do so I took the liberty of employing different visual documentation and making reference to different contemporary and past sources – where I felt the latter best captured a sense of open-minded, wide-angled perspective than certainly better-informed, advanced contemporary books. In a number of chapters, a building has been used as a case study to analyse more concretely the issue in question. Cross-references marked with an arrow direct the reader to other parts of this book and to the bibliography. For instance, (→§05) directs to chapter 05; (→p50-55) to pages 50-55; (→■230-232) to pictures from no. 230 to 232; while (→B036:133+256,070) directs to

Abbildungen einsetzte. Und ich stellte Bezüge zu verschiedenen zeitgenössischen und früheren Quellen her, bei denen ich das Gefühl hatte, dass sie bestmöglich den Sinn einer unvoreingenommenen, breit angelegten Perspektive einfangen, als es zweifelsfrei weiterentwickelte zeitgenössische Bücher ein Stück weit tun. In einer Vielzahl von Kapiteln wurde ein einzelnes Gebäude als Fallstudie verwendet, um die vorliegende Fragestellung konkreter zu analysieren. Quervermerke, die mit einem Pfeil versehen sind, leiten den Leser zu anderen Teilen des Buches und zum Quellenverzeichnis. Zum Beispiel (→§05) verweist auf Kapitel 05; (→p50-55) verweist auf Seite 50-55; (→■230-232) verweist auf die Bilder Nr. 230 bis 232; während (→B036:133+256,070) auf die Seiten 133 und 256 der Quelle Nr. 036, und im Allgemeinen auf die Quelle Nr. 070 verweist, beide sind in der Liste der bibliographischen Referenzen auf Seite 284-286 aufgeführt.

Danksagungen.
Ich möchte mich bedanken bei: Peter Braun, der so nett war, nicht nur einen ganzen Tag aufzuwenden, um mir seine Konzepte zu erklären, sondern sich auch noch Zeit nahm, das Kapitel 9 zu korrigieren. Gernot Minke, der das Vorwort verfasst hat, der mir Ratschläge gegeben und so viel beigebracht hat. Ginevra Puppo für ihre Hilfe, bei der Dokumentation des Ferienbauernhofes Esser und für die Ausführung der ökologischen Wirkungsgradberechnungen des Kapitel 4. Pete Walker für die Vermittlung kostbarer Informationen zu ModCell und zur Strohballenbauweise. Beppe Finessi, ohne dessen Hilfe ich nicht in der Lage gewesen wäre, Schmidts Möbelentwürfe in den richtigen Zusammenhang zu setzen. Anna Rita Bertorello für ihre Hilfe bei der Dokumentation des Ervin Jacomet Hauses und beim Organisieren des Portfolio auf S. 190–195. Maria Jack, die mir half, meinem Englisch ein passenderes Erscheinungsbild zu geben. Marcel Gloor, der mir wertvolle Informationen zum Haus Schmidlin zur Verfügung stellte. Floriana Sabba für die Informationen zu Primärenergie.

pages 133 and 256 of the source no. 036, and in general to the source no. 070, both quoted in the list of bibliographic references at p. 284-286.

Acknowledgements.
I would like to acknowledge: Peter Braun for having been so kind to spend not only a whole day explaining to me his concepts, but also some more time to revise chapter 9. Gernot Minke, for having written the preface, given advice, and having taught me so much. Ginevra Puppo, for her help in documenting Esser holiday farm and for having performed the ecological impact calculations of chapter 4. Pete Walker, for having passed precious information on ModCell and on straw-bale building in general. Beppe Finessi, without whom I would not have been able to put Schmidt's furniture design work in its proper context. Anna Rita Bertorello, for her help in documenting Ervin Jacomet's house and in organising the portfolio at p.190-195. Maria Jack, for helping me give a less unacceptable appearance to my English. Marcel Gloor, for having provided valuable information on house Schmidlin. Floriana Sabba, for information on primary energy. Pat Borer, for insight on BRE Green Guide. I am much indebted to Bellissimo and the Beast – with the providential help of Massimo Pitis – for having been able to give a brilliant form to my intricate book concept. And of course to Werner Schmidt for long days and nights spent discussing both the broad concept of this book and an innumerable quantity of details. I would also like to thank everybody at Atelier Werner Schmidt – particularly Maren Witopil, Felicia Deflorin and Michael Schneider – for having helped put together a whole bunch of visual material and data. I am extremely grateful to the families who have opened the doors of their houses and have been so kind to share their experience. Finally, I would like to thank Momi for her months of patience during which my attention seemed to be more focused on this book than on her.

Pat Borer, für einen Einblick in den BRE Green Guide. Ich stehe Bellissimo and the Beast in tiefer Schuld – mit der glücklichen Hilfe von Massimo Pitis – der in der Lage war, meinem komplizierten Buchkonzept eine glänzende Form zu geben. Und selbstverständlich herzlichen Dank an Werner Schmidt für lange Tage und Nächte, ausgefüllt mit Diskussion, sowohl zum breit angelegten Konzept dieses Buches, als auch der unzähligen Menge an Details. Ich möchte mich auch beim gesamten Atelier Werner Schmidt bedanken – besonders Maren Witopil, Felicia Deflorin und Michael Schneider – für ihre Hilfe, ein ganzes Bündel an Sichtmaterial und Daten zusammenzustellen. Ich bin den Familien äußerst dankbar, die die Türen zu ihren Häusern für mich geöffnet haben und so nett waren, mir von ihren Erfahrungen zu berichten. Und schließlich möchte ich Momi für ihre monatelange Geduld danken, während denen meine Aufmerksamkeit vielmehr auf dieses Buch als auf sie gerichtet schien.

EGGS ⌣ EIER

"Every entity looks like being round."
Karl Jaspers (→B059:50)

"The perfectly crystalline squares and
rectangles of ultra-modern architecture
make no special sense in human or
structural terms. They only express (...)
rigid desires and fantasies."
Christopher Alexander (→B009:191)

„Jedes Dasein scheint in sich rund."
Karl Jaspers (→B059:50)

„Die tadellos kristallenen Quadrate
und Rechtecke der ultra-modernen
Architektur ergeben in Bezug auf
Mensch oder Struktur keinen Sinn.
Sie sind lediglich Ausdruck (...) starrer
Wunschvorstellungen und Fantasien."
Christopher Alexander (→B009:191)

To Werner Schmidt, the distinction between 'straight' and 'rounded' forms in is not only important for arranging his projects into categories (as they come in his website).
According to Schmidt, right angles need not be a principle. They must not be shunned, but neither should they be taken for granted. In consonance with Baubiologie theories, he believes that in the long run living only in parallelepiped rooms may negatively affect people's psyche. Curves and other distractions from the straight line and the right angle make the inhabitants happier and more self-confident, therefore more open to the world.
Bernard Rudofsky reported on the neolithic houses found in Köln-Lindenthal – dubbed *Kurvenkomplexbau* (complex curvilinear structures). These dwellings showed irregular plans, uneven floors, 'organic' shapes and, according to Rudofsky, a "calculated voluptuousness," and a "sequence of hollows that invite one to loll, to insinuate oneself into the soil." He then commented: "If we never developed a taste for irregular space configurations like the Lindenthalers' it is because we do not think of our houses in terms of a wrap but of a box. Ours are hard-edge containers (...), and no deep-pile carpets, no water beds will confer sensuousness upon them. Apart [from] some pardonable affectations, curved walls do not occur in the domestic architecture prejudiced in favor of angularity and edginess. [O]ur domesticity is molded in the cast of the right angle." (→B093:102-107)
Unfortunately, rounded forms are still taboo in educated architecture, unless they are tame, as in the case of vonRoll pavilion: (→p50-55) the plan consists of a regular ellipse, en-

Für Werner Schmidt hat die Unterscheidung zwischen ‚geraden' und ‚runden' Formen in der Architektur große Bedeutung, nicht nur in Bezug auf die Einordnung seiner Projekte in Kategorien (wie auf seiner Internetseite ersichtlich).
Gemäß Schmidt müssen rechte Winkel nicht zwangsläufig das Prinzip sein. Sie müssen nicht vermieden werden, aber auch nicht als selbstverständlich betrachtet werden. In Übereinstimmung mit den Baubiologie Theorien glaubt er, dass parallel ausgerichtete Räume langfristig gesehen möglicherweise negative Auswirkungen auf die Psyche der Menschen haben könnten. Kurven und andere Abweichungen von der geraden Linie und von der rechtwinkligen Form machen die Bewohner glücklicher und selbstbewusster, und deshalb auch weltoffener.
Bernard Rudofsky berichtet über die neolithischen Häuser, die in Köln-Lindenthal gefunden wurden – *Kurvenkomplexbau* bedeutet eine komplexe, krummlinige Struktur. Diese Bauten zeigten unregelmäßige Grundrisse, unebene Böden, ‚organische' Formen und, gemäß Rudofsky, eine „gewisse geplante Üppigkeit" sowie eine „Abfolge von Ausbuchtungen, die einen zum Verweilen einladen, einen der Erde unterstellen." Er kommentierte: „Dass wir nie Geschmack für unregelmäßige Raumkonfigurationen wie die Lindenthaler entwickelten liegt daran, dass wir unsere Häuser nicht als Ummantelung betrachten, sondern als eine Box. Unsere Gebäude sind kantige Behälter (...) und keine dicken Teppiche und keine Wasserbetten werden ihnen Sinnlichkeit verleihen können. Abgesehen von einigen verzeihlichen Affektiertheiten, kommen gekrümmte Wände nicht in der Wohnarchitektur vor, die befangen ist von der Präferenz der Rechtwinkligkeit und der Kantigkeit. Unsere

compassing a cubic box. If you design something rounded, you must always give a justification for its shape. Nothing similar is asked for a squared building. To me, it sounds like when they ask you, how did you decide to become homosexual? Of course, nobody ever asks, why did you choose to be straight? Obviously, round forms do have a strong symbolic meaning and can significantly affect the human psyche. Arnheim noticed the greater centrality of round spaces; (→B011:102) this extends in volume to domed rooms whose continuity cocoons those who find themselves inside them. Thiis-Evensen observed that "when we face a concave wall, the feeling is one of being received:" (→B108:149) such form transmits a sense of embracing, safety, belonging.

The circle and the sphere are associated with ideas of perfection, homogeneity, absence of distinction or division; (→B028) for Jung it is the archetypal symbol of Self, and of the psyche's totality, while the square stands for earthly matter and the body. (→B062) Bachelard thinks that grace is an attribute of curves, hardness of straight lines. Angles are cold and masculine, curves warm and feminine. (→B013:169)

Sloterdijk has developed a philosophy of spheres. (→B103) He postulates that mammals fundamentally differ from other animals because of their being born from their mother's womb, which is why human beings forever try to re-create spheres in which to concentrate and (re)produce themselves – ontologically spherical is the material and symbolic environment they create. In particular, "micro-spheres" (or "bubbles") are the spaces where human beings try to re-create intimacy.

In nature, no rectangular shape can be found. According to Rudolf Steiner's theory, a built environment made with only rectangles means the soul's death. (→B036:93) Free curves can intensify vitality, but can also make us indulge in a dreamy condition and therefore help us forget the practical aspects of reality. On the other hand, straight lines express organisation and power, and absorb life instead of giving it. A balanced and healthy human life lays between these two extremes. (→B036:102)

Häuslichkeit wird geprägt durch das Vorstellungsmuster des rechten Winkels". (→B093:102-107)

Leider scheinen runde Formen nach wie vor ein Tabu in der gängigen Architektur zu sein. Im Falle des vonRoll Pavillons besteht der Grundriss aus einer regelmäßigen Ellipse, die einen kubischen Kasten umschließt. (→S.50-55) Wenn man etwas rundes entwirft, muss man seine Form immer rechtfertigen. Ähnliches wird von einem quadratischen Gebäude nicht gefordert. Mir erscheint dies ähnlich wie wenn man gefragt wird, weshalb man sich dazu entschieden hätte, homosexuell zu werden? – natürlich fragt nie jemand, weshalb man sich entschlossen hätte heterosexuell zu sein?

Offensichtlich haben runde Formen eine starke symbolische Bedeutung und können die menschliche Psyche erheblich beeinflussen. Arnheim bemerkt die größere Zentralität von runden Räumen; (→B011:102) diese weitet sich im Volumen von gewölbten Räumen aus, deren Kontinuität jene, die sich in ihnen befinden, wie in einen Kokon einhüllt. Thiis-Evensen beobachtete, dass „wenn wir einer konkaven Wand gegenüberstehen, das Gefühl entsteht geborgen zu sein": (→B108:149) solche Formen vermitteln ein Gefühl des Umarmens, von Sicherheit und Zugehörigkeit.

Der Kreis und die Kugel werden mit der Vorstellung von Perfektion, Homogenität, des Fehlens von Unterscheidung oder Teilung assoziiert; (→B028) für Jung ist es das archetypische Symbol vom Selbst und der Gesamtheit der Psyche, während das Quadrat für irdische Angelegenheit und den Körper steht. (→B062) Bachelard ist der Meinung, dass Anmut ein Merkmal von Kurven, Härte ein Merkmal von Geraden ist. Winkel sind kalt und männlich, Kurven sind warm und weiblich. (→B013:169)

Sloterdijk hat eine Sphären-Philosophie entwickelt. (→B103) Er postuliert, dass Säugetiere sich grundlegend von anderen Tieren durch die Geburt aus dem Mutterleib unterscheiden, dies sei der Grund, weshalb Menschen immer wieder versuchten, Sphären neu zu kreieren, in denen sie sich konzentrieren und fortpflanzen können – ontologisch sphärisch ist die ma-

Unfortunately, the design of space is often intended as the creation of containers for storing people and their activities, intended in a sheer materialistic way. Much wider options are available: just think of the diversity of animal shelters. Were it not for cupboards, the logical form of a room would be radially symmetrical, and particularly round. Interiors can envelope like a womb. (→B011:110) A hollow volume is perceived as an amplification and extension of the human epicentre (...), as if it had acquired his form. (→B011:113)

A den is the result of the physical penetration of its dweller, and has the form of the excavating body. (→B011:168-172) Rooms constructed for a body take its form from inside, as it were, like a shell or an egg which is shaped by "an intimacy which works physically." (→B013:125) According to Bachelard, "the first effort of life consists in creating shells." (→B013:136) "A man, an animal, an almond, all find maximum repose in a shell. (...) To curl up belongs to the phenomenology of the verb to inhabit, and only those who can do so inhabit with intensity." (→B013:148)

As the sphere, the egg symbolises totality, and specifically primordial reality which contains in germ the multiplicity of beings. It also participates of the symbolism of rest, as it is associated with the home, the nest, the shell, the mother's womb. In addition, it represents nature's periodical renovation and therefore, by extension, the place of all transmutations. (→B028)

Bachelard's invitation was to look for "condensation centres" for intimacy and simplicity in homes. Such centres should retain the primitiveness of a refuge. (→B013:56-57) (→§05)

This is, in my opinion, the fundamental reason why Schmidt creates rounded shapes in many of his projects. But his rooms tend to stay away from regular geometric forms; he prefers them organic and termitesque – to coin a word – as in house Mathis in Amden.

Amden is a mountain village overlooking lake Walen, which in recent decades has developed into a tranquil and very traditional resort.

terielle und symbolische Umwelt, die sie erschaffen. Insbesondere „Mikrosphären" (oder „Blasen") sind Orte, an denen Menschen versuchen Intimität zu schaffen.

In der Natur gibt es keine rechtwinklige Form. Entsprechend Rudolf Steiners Theorie, bedeutet eine rechtwinklig errichtete Umwelt den Tod der Seele. (→B036:93) Freie Kurven können die Vitalität verstärken, aber können uns auch in einen träumerischen Zustand versetzen, und können uns dadurch die praktischen Aspekte der Wirklichkeit vergessen lassen. Andererseits drücken gerade Linien Organisiertheit und Stärke aus und absorbieren das Leben, anstatt es zu geben. Ein ausgeglichenes und gesundes Menschenleben liegt zwischen diesen beiden Extremen. (→B036:102)

Leider zielt der Entwurf von Räumen häufig auf die Schaffung von Containern ab, in denen man Leute samt ihrer Tätigkeiten einlagern kann, mit einer rein materialistischen Absicht. Viel weitläufigere Möglichkeiten wären verfügbar: denken Sie nur an die Vielfalt von tierischen Behausungen. Gäbe es keine Schränke, wäre die logische Form des Raumes radial symmetrisch und vorzugsweise gebogen. Innenräume können eine Person umhüllen wie ein Mutterleib. (→B011:110) Ein hohles Volumen wird wie die Erweiterung und Ausdehnung des menschlichen Epizentrums (...) wahrgenommen, als ob es sich seine Form angeeignet hätte. (→B011:113)

Eine Höhle ist das Ergebnis physischer Einwirkung ihres Bewohners und hat die Form eines ausgehöhlten Körpers. (→B011:168-172) Räume, die für einen Körper konstruiert wurden, generieren ihre Gestalt von innen heraus, sozusagen wie eine Schale oder ein Ei, welches durch „eine Intimität, die physikalisch arbeitet" geformt wird. (→B013:125) Gemäß Bachelard „besteht die erste Anstrengung des Lebens darin, Schalen zu erschaffen". (→B013:136) „Ein Mensch, ein Tier, eine Mandel, alle finden die maximale Ruhe in einer Schale. (...) Sich zusammen zu kauern, gehört der Phänomenologie des Verbs ‚zu bewohnen' an, und nur die, die dies tun können, bewohnen mit Intensität." (→B013:148)

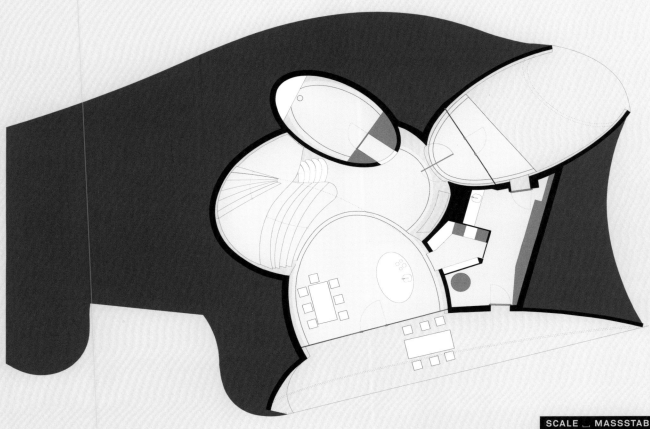

MATHIS HOUSE ⌐ HAUS MATHIS

address ⌐ Adresse: CH-8873 Amden/SG
altitude ⌐ Höhe: 1225 m
degree-days ⌐ Gradtage: 3683
project ⌐ Entwurf: 2011
construction ⌐ Bau: 2012
main building firms ⌐ Wichtigen Baufirmen: Greuter AG, Hochfelden
(sprayed concrete ⌐ Spritzbeton); Hans Alpiger, Alt St. Johann
(mound shaping ⌐ Hügelgestaltung)
plot area ⌐ Grundstückfläche: 1,613 m²
heated floor area ⌐ Geheizte Bodenfläche: 227 m²
main window (SW) area ⌐ Fensterfläche Hauptfassade (SW): 41 m²

Wie die Kugel symbolisiert auch das Ei Gesamtheit und im speziellen eine ursprüngliche Realität, die im Kern die Vielfalt der Lebewesen beinhaltet. Es partizipiert auch vom Symbolcharakter der Ruhestätte, da es mit der Begrifflichkeit von Heim, Nest, Schale oder Mutterleib in Verbindung gebracht wird. Darüber hinaus steht es für die periodische Erneuerung der Natur und deshalb im weiteren Sinne für den Ort aller Umwandlungen. (→028) Bachelard rief dazu auf, nach „Verdichtungszentren" für Intimität und Einfachheit in Häusern zu suchen. Solche Zentren sollten die Primitivität eines Zufluchtortes bewahren. (→B013:56-57) (→§05)

Schmidt's clients are the family of an organ builder, who made the organ in the Sistine Chapel in Rome. They bought a small plot of land with an ordinary building standing on it, next to other buildings and the road to the ski runs. But their ideal holiday house, possibly a place to move to once retired, would

Dies ist meiner Meinung nach der fundamentale Grund, weshalb Schmidt in vielen seiner Projekte runde Formen schafft. Seine Räume tendieren dazu, sich von regelmäßigen, geometrischen Formen zu distanzieren – er bevorzugt sie in organischer Form und ‚termitisch' – um einen passenden

021

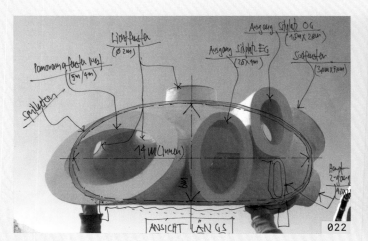

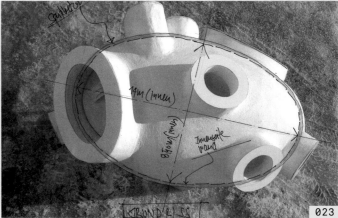

have been round-shaped – however, the local building regulations are very strict and require square-angled plans and conventional roofs.

Werner Schmidt designed different solutions, some larger than others; all of them had in common the demolition of the

Begriff zu generieren –, wie im Haus Mathis in Amden.

Amden ist ein Bergdorf oberhalb des Walensees, das sich in den letzten Jahrzehnten in ein ruhiges und sehr traditionelles Erholungsgebiet verwandelt hat.

Schmidts Kunde ist die Familie eines Orgelbauers, der die Or-

existing building (except one room to keep the house 1.80 m from the property boundary) and an earth covering. In fact, a building somehow embedded in the ground may be seen as lacking a roof, and therefore complies with the regulation even if it has a rounded form. Only a turfed mound appears now. This solution is not a novelty in Switzerland: for decades now Peter Vetsch has been building round-shaped, earth-covered houses; both on aesthetic (to overcome the monotony of squared constructions) and energy-conservation grounds (minimum surface enclosing a maximum volume; high thermal resistance of earth). (→B116)

Perhaps thanks to such a precedent, the municipality of Amden had nothing to object to, and the building is now completed. The large, cave-like volume contains open, flowing spaces on different levels and smaller retreat cocoons. Both the larger and the smaller volumes are ellipsoidal, and stay neatly distinguishable from each other, in spite of their intersection and interpenetration. The master sleeping area is located in a balcony overlooking the living area, while a wellness area is placed in the only room conserved from the pre-existing building. Levels are connected by a grand, open stair.

The interior is linked to the outer space through a number of circular skylights and a huge glazed picture window: while some look only to the sky, others allow for a view – and the picture window visually dominates the slope. Likewise, outdoor spaces have been designed to offer various degrees of intimacy – an over-exposed area next to the indoor living area; a few nest-like places; some introverted nooks.

Schmidt proposed a double-shell, ventilated structure; straw would have been used as insulation in the inner shell. But the clients, not without reason, did not trust the durability of straw placed underground. The structure is therefore a 12 cm thick monocoque shotcrete shell similar to the one used at Cazis (yet in this case falsework was not necessary: once the reinforcing bars were put in place and a mesh was positioned on it, concrete was shot from outside, and then from inside

gel in der Sixtinischen Kapelle in Rom realisierte. Sie kauften eine kleine Parzelle mit einem gewöhnlichen Gebäude darauf, mit benachbarten Gebäuden und entlang der Straße zu den Skipisten. Aber ihr ideales Ferienhaus, welches sie später einmal im Ruhestand beziehen wollten, wäre ein rundes – jedoch sind die lokalen Bauvorschriften sehr streng und schreiben rechteckige Grundrisse und herkömmliche Dachformen vor.

Werner Schmidt entwickelte verschiedene Lösungsansätze, manche größer als andere. Allen Entwürfen lag die Auflösung des Altbaus zu Grunde – mit Ausnahme eines Raumes, um den Grenzabstand des Gebäudes zur Parzellengrenze von 1,80 m einzuhalten – und die anschließende Erdeindeckung des Gebäudes. Tatsächlich könnte ein unterirdisches und mit Gras bewachsenes Gebäude, welches im Boden eingebettet ist, so erscheinen als würde ihm das Dach fehlen. Und es könnte aus diesem Grund regelkonform sein, selbst wenn es eine runde Form hat. So ist jetzt lediglich ein Erdhügel wahrnehmbar.

Diese Lösung ist keine Neuheit in der Schweiz: vor nunmehr einigen Jahrzehnten baute Peter Vetsch erdbedeckte Häuser, sowohl aus ästhetischen Gründen – um die Monotonie von quadratischen Bauten zu überwinden - als auch aus Energiespargründen – minimale Oberfläche, die ein maximales Volumen umschließt; hohe Wärmebeständigkeit durch das Erdreich. (→B116)

Die Gemeinde Amden hatte möglicherweise dank dieses Präzedenzfalls keine Einwände vorzubringen, und das Gebäude wird nun realisiert. Das große, höhlenähnliche Volumen enthält offene, fließende Räume auf verschiedenen Niveaus und kleine Rückzugsmöglichkeiten. Sowohl die größeren als auch die kleineren Volumen sind elliptisch angelegt, und bleiben trotz ihrer Überschneidungen und ihres Ineinandergreifens gut voneinander unterscheidbar. Der Schlafbereich der Bauherrschaft befindet sich auf einer balkonähnlichen Galerie mit Blick auf den Wohnbereich, während ein Wellnessbereich, in dem einzigen, erhaltenen Raum des Bestandsgebäudes platziert wurde. Die Geschosse werden durch eine großzügige, offene Treppe verbunden.

too). The external face was covered with 15-20 cm sprayed PUR foam, sheathing, and about 40 cm earth, and the internal one with a soft-looking layer of cotton flakes to enhance the acoustic performance – the master will enjoy playing a spinet. Door frames and fireplace are of oxidised Cor-Ten steel. Most floors are wood, some anhydrite. They are separated from walls by floor lamps which are intended to give airiness to the space.

Both cocoons for the isolation of the individual or the couple, and family-size (or even larger) rounded rooms can be found in Schmidt's work. The profiles in the following pages describe buildings where different kinds of eggs can be found. Small, individual eggs were used in house Gartmann-Sgier, to accommodate the visitors' restroom and wardrobe; (→■027-028) in the atelier Simon Jacomet, to harbour the sleeping room; (→■026,408) in Werner Schmidt's own residence – where the southern portion of the plan stages a translucent big object which, during the day, makes use of the natural light coming from outdoor and at night glows in the dark like a luminous sculpture. (→■025;§03) This oddly-shaped bubble contains the 10 m² bathroom and is entirely made of 4 mm fibreglass-reinforced polyester. Floor, walls and ceiling are formed by a single, complex overall shape which bends to contain the shower tray, pops out to create a recess for the toilet bowl, becomes props and shelves, etc. – and in Disentis abbey, (→■031-032) where Schmidt refurbished the boarding school (built in 1937-40 according to Walther Sulser's project) to contemporary living requirements. The existing dormitories were transformed into single or double rooms. The 12-to-14-year old boys would thus get private rooms with bed, wardrobe, desk and a small bathroom. The rooms are lined along the perimeter walls of the T-shaped wing – one room for each existing window – while a corridor runs at the centre of the plan. Every two doors there is a large blue egg protruding into the corridor which contains two small bathrooms equipped with shower, sink and toilet. Eggs are made of fibreglass-reinforced polyester and consist

Der Innenraum wird mit dem Außenraum durch eine diverse Anzahl von kreisrunden Oberlichtern und durch ein großes Panoramafenster verbunden. Während einige Öffnungen gen Himmel gerichtet sind, erlauben andere einen Ausblick ins Tal – das Panoramafenster dominiert optisch den Hang. Entsprechend sind die Außenräume derart gestaltet worden, dass sie in unterschiedlichem Grad Intimität gewährleisten – ein sehr exponierter Bereich vor dem Wohnbereich; einige nestartige Plätze; einige introvertierte Alkoven. Schmidt schlug eine zweischalige, hinterlüftete Hülle vor; Stroh wäre als Isolierung auf der inneren Schale verwendet worden. Aber seine Kunden trauten der Haltbarkeit des Strohs unter der Erdoberfläche nicht. Die Konstruktion besteht daher aus einer 12 cm starken Spritzbetonschale, die der Außenhülle von Cazis ähnelt (jedoch war in diesem Fall kein Hilfsgerüst notwendig: sobald die Armierungsstähle platziert waren und ein Gewebe darüber angebracht war, wurde der Beton von außen und dann von innen aufgespritzt). Auf der Außenseite des Spritzbetons wurden 15–20 cm PUR-Schaum aufgesprüht, darüber ein Geotextil und schließlich ungefähr 40 cm Erde aufgebracht, während auf der Innenseite eine weiche Schicht Baumwollflocken aufgebracht wurde, um die Akustik zu verbessern – der Bauherr wird es genießen, darin auf dem Spinett zu spielen. Einschnitte im Volumen, wie Türrahmen oder die Kaminstelle sind hingegen aus Cortenstahl gefertigt. Die meisten Böden haben einen Belag aus Holz, manche sind in Anhydrit gegossen. Die Böden werden zu den Wänden hin mittels Bodenleuchten abgesetzt, die dem Raum eine gewisse Leichtigkeit geben sollen.

In Schmidts Arbeiten findet man sowohl Kokons zur Isolierung von Einzelpersonen oder Paaren, als auch familientaugliche oder sogar größere runde Räume. Die Projektbeschreibungen auf den nächsten Seiten gehen auf Gebäude ein, in denen verschiedene Arten von Eiern zu finden sind. Kleine, individuelle Eier wurden im Haus Gartmann-Sgier er-

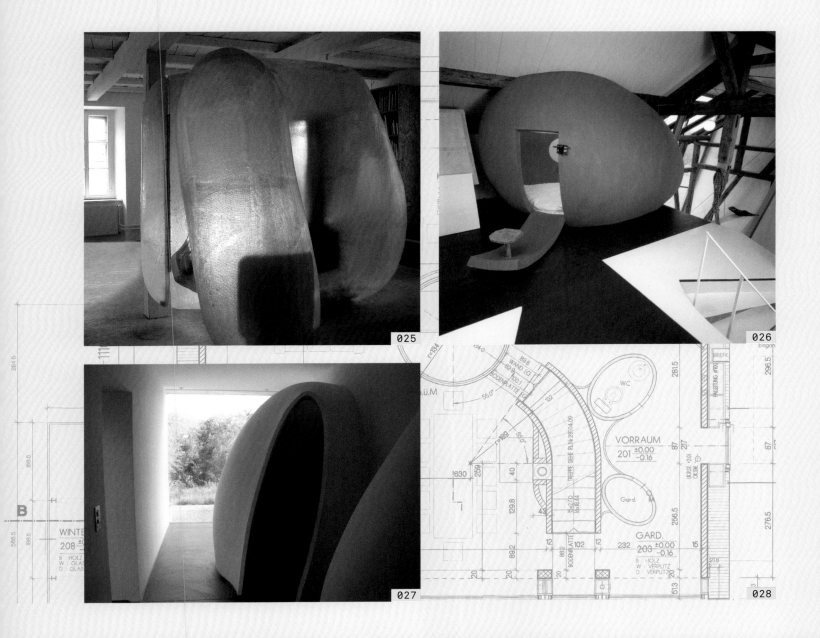

025

026

027

028

of a double-skin, insulated shell. Eggs create a completely new sense of space, their generous curves standing out from the straight lines of the building.

In all these projects, the rounded forms of the eggs contrast successfully with the straight lines of the rest of the buildings inside which they are placed. The same would have happened in Bühler-Seiz house where several egg-shaped sleeping rooms and bathrooms would have to be built inside the existing volume. (→■416-417) Those to be placed in the former barn would have been accessed via a spiral staircase and gangways. The Esserhof holiday rooms also have a curved plan, both to open them towards the southern sun minimising the perimeter wall area, and to physically express their capacity to protect the sleeping guests. (→■160,163-164)

Larger rounded rooms can be found in other projects where they serve as family gathering places – as in Maissen, (→■034-036) Mathis, (→■016,021) Brand houses (→■029) –, or community spaces – first and foremost in Cazis church, (→■041,044) but also in vonRoll training pavilion (→■048) and in the 'Zero carbon village' information centre. In community buildings, circular or rounded spaces are appropriate for meditation and to express a sense of equality.

At the Meranflora – a recurring garden and nursery garden exhibition which took place in Meran from 1990 to 2007 – Schmidt designed and built some bamboo objects with his students at the Chur University of Applied Sciences (HTW). These were placed along the Summer promenade on the south bank of the Passer river. The most impressive was the entrance egg, (→■030) placed close to a Gothic church and a Fascist building, at one of the main entrances to the city centre. The egg contained the ticket and information desks and was the only gateway to the exhibition. It was made of diagonally-crossing bamboo culms coupled where necessary to attain significant lengths (different connection details were tested at the HTW Chur laboratories), and bent and tied together to obtain an ellipsoid. The lattice was actually

richtet, um die Gäste-Toilette und die Garderobe unterzubringen; (→■027-028) im Atelier Simon Jacomet, beherbergt das Ei den Schlafraum. (→■026,408) Ebenso in Werner Schmidts eigenem Wohnsitz – wo der südliche Teil des Grundrisses einem lichtdurchlässigen, großen Objekt Raum gewährt, welches tagsüber das natürliche Licht von außen nutzt und nachts in der Dunkelheit wie eine leuchtende Skulptur erscheint. (→■025;§3) Diese sonderbar geformte Blase enthält das 10 m² große Badezimmer und ist ganzheitlich aus 4 mm dickem, Glasfaser-verstärkten Polyester gefertigt. Boden, Wände und Decke wurden in einer einzigen, komplexen Form ausgebildet, die sich im Bodenbereich nach außen wölbt, um die Duschwanne auszubilden; und die sich im Bereich von Toilette und Waschtisch nach innen wölbt, um eine Ablage für Handtücher und kleine Utensilien zu schaffen. Und im Kloster Disentis finden sich Eiformen, (→■031-032) wo Schmidt das Internat an die zeitgemäßen Anforderungen an Wohnraum anpasste. Das Internat wurde in den Jahren 1937–40 gemäß den Entwürfen von Walther Sulser errichtet. Die vorhandenen Schlafsäle wurden in Einzel- oder Doppelzimmer umgewandelt. Die 12- bis 14-jährigen Jungen erhielten somit ein Privatzimmer mit Bett, Garderobe, Schreibtisch und einem kleinen Badezimmer. Die Räume wurden entlang der Umfassungsmauern des L-förmigen Flügels platziert – ein Raum für jedes vorhandene Fenster – während ein Korridor in der Mitte des Grundrisses verläuft. An jeder zweiten Türe befindet sich ein großes, blaues Ei, das in den Korridor hinausragt, und welches zwei kleine Badezimmer enthält, die mit Dusche, Waschtisch und Toilette ausgestattet wurden. Die Eier sind aus Glasfaser-verstärktem Polyester gefertigt und bestehen aus einer zweifachen, isolierten Schale. Die Eier schaffen ein vollständig neues Raumgefühl, ihre großzügigen Kurven heben sich von den geraden Linien des Gebäudes ab.

In all diesen Projekten kontrastieren die runden Formen der Eier erfolgreich die geraden Linien des restlichen Gebäudeinneren, in dem sie platziert wurden. Dasselbe war beim Projekt

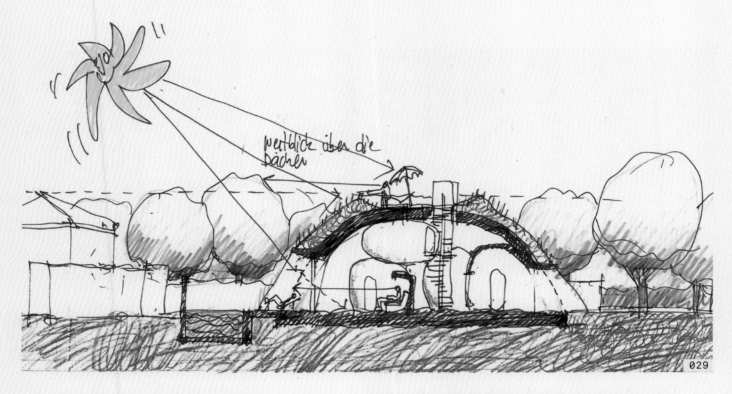

weitblick über die Dächer

029

constituted by four grid systems superimposed one on top of the other, so that the network was very close at the bottom and much more airy at the top, 13.6 m above ground. This lattice structure was surrounded by horizontal rings to secure the egg against bulge. Culms were fastened with coconut rope and metal ties. The egg was built at the City Parks Department court and spectacularly flown by helicopter to the site. The provisional building gained great popularity, and was consequently kept in place for one year after the end of the exhibition.

Bühler-Seiz beabsichtigt, wo einige eiförmige Schlafräume und Badezimmer innerhalb des vorhandenen Volumens errichtet worden wären. (→■416-417) Jene Eier, die in der ehemaligen Scheune geplant waren, hätte man über eine Wendeltreppe und Stege erreicht.
Auch die Esserhof-Ferienanlage hat einen gekrümmten Grundriss, um sie zum einen in Richtung der Südsonne zu öffnen, und den Anteil der Umfassungswände zu minimieren, und zum anderen physisch gesehen, um eine Schutzfunktion für die schlafenden Gästen zu vermitteln. (→■160,163-164) Größere, runde Räume finden sich in anderen Projekten, in denen sie als Familientreffpunkte dienen – wie in den Häusern Maissen-Petschen, (→■034-036) Mathis (→■016,021) und Brand (→■029) – oder als Gemeinschaftsräume, in erster

030

031

Linie in der Cazis-Kirche, (→■041,044) aber auch im vonRoll
Trainingspavillon (→■048) und im Traismauer-, Zero-Carbon-
Village' Informationszentrum. In den Gemeinschaftsbauten
sind kreisförmige oder runde Räume für Meditation geeignet
und drücken eine Form von Gleichheit aus.

Bei der Meranflora – einer Pflanzenschau, die alle vier Jahre
in Meran stattfindet – entwarf und errichtete Schmidt 2004
fünf Bambusobjekte, zusammen mit seinen Studenten der
HTW Chur, dem Bauingenieur Benno Barth und der Architektin
Margareta Schwarz. Diese Objekte wurden entlang der Som-
merpromenade am Südufer der Passer aufgestellt. Das wohl
eindrucksvollste Objekt war das Eingangs-Ei, (→■030) welches
nahe einer gotischen Kirche und einem Gebäude aus der Zeit
des Faschismus errichtet wurde. Das Ei war der Haupteingang

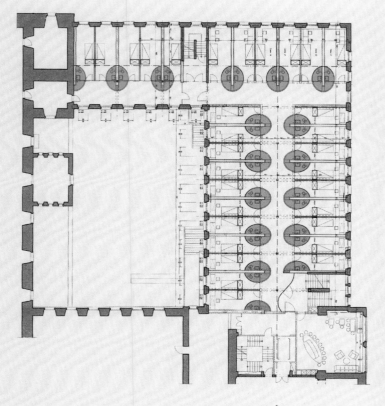

zur Gartenausstellung. Es enthielt den Kartenschalter und diente als Informationszentrum. Die Konstruktion bestand aus mehrlagigen, diagonal gekreuzten Bambusstangen von circa 3 cm Durchmesser und einer Länge von bis zu 4,5 m. Teilweise wurden bis zu vier Stangen miteinander verbunden, um eine optimale Länge zu erreichen. Verschiedene Verbindungstechniken wurden in den Werkstätten der HTW Chur statisch geprüft. Das Gitter wurde in vier übereinander lappende Netzstrukturen zerlegt, so dass in Bodennähe ein sehr dichtes Gefüge entstand, das sich wiederum an der Spitze lichtete – 13,6 m über dem Boden. Diese Gitterstruktur wurde von horizontalen Ringen umschlossen, um das Ei zusammen zu halten, vergleichbar mit Fassringen von Weinfässern. Die Bambusstangen wurden mit Armierungsbindern verbunden und teilweise mit Metalldraht und Kokosnussseilen noch verstärkt. Das Ei wurde in der Stadtgärtnerei errichtet und mittels Hubschrauber auf spektakuläre Weise zum definitiven Standort im Stadtzentrum geflogen. Das temporäre Objekt gewann an großer Popularität, und wurde auf Grund dessen noch ein Jahr lang nach Ende der Ausstellung an derselben Stelle belassen.

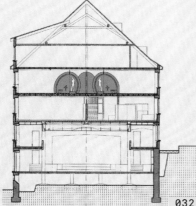

SCALE ⌐ MASSSTAB 1:500

032

MAISSEN EXTENSION ⌐ ERWEITERUNG HAUS MAISSEN-PETSCHEN

ADDRESS ⌐ ADRESSE:
Casa Plaunca, Sum il vitg,
CH-7166 Trun/GR

ALTITUDE ⌐ HÖHE:
850 m

DEGREE-DAYS ⌐ GRADTAGE:
3704

PROJECT ⌐ ENTWURF:
1996

CONSTRUCTION ⌐ BAU:
1996-97

BUILDING FIRMS ⌐ BAUFIRMEN:
Lauber, Biasca (wood construction ⌐
Holzbau); Maissen,
Trun (interior decoration ⌐ Innenausbau)

**PROJECT MANAGER ⌐
PROJEKTLEITUNG:**
Werner Schmidt + Vic Cajacob

PLOT AREA ⌐ GRUNDSTÜCKFLÄCHE:
1,122 m²

**HEATED FLOOR AREA ⌐
GEHEIZTE BODENFLÄCHE:**
55 m²

**MAIN WINDOW (SW) AREA ⌐
FENSTERFLÄCHE
HAUPTFASSADE (SW):**
24 m²

BUILDING COST ⌐ BAUKOSTEN (BKP2):
280,000 CHF (skeleton construction
work only ⌐ nur Schale) [5,000 CHF/m²]

A traditional *Strickbau* (log house), dating from 1933, was the home to the family Maissen; it also accommodated the master's medical practice. The family wanted to expand the shared living space, building an extension. This lean-to should not match the common building technique of the area, on the contrary it was the clients' will that it be clearly distinguishable from the existing building both in construction and form. Werner Schmidt designed a rounded volume containing a single room with the flavour of a winter garden, where all desired functions are merged – cooking, eating and sitting by the fireplace. The Municipality issued the permit, but the Canton fire police required that sprinklers be installed because of the shingle cladding. The new space was a large, hospitable cave, much higher than the *Strickbau* building rooms – giving the family the sensation of "going on holiday" when they moved into it, and soon became the most used room in the entire house.

The frame of the shell-like extension is made of curved glulam beams. The form was certainly an artistic gesture, but was above all motivated by the intention of minimising the area/volume ratio. The building envelope contains 60 cm cellulose insulation, which means the roof is more than 70 cm thick. However, the overhang protecting from summer irradiation is tapered to avoid appearing too bulky.

The add-on is level with the main floor, and nestled on the north side of the old building where it meets the foyer containing stairs to the upper floor. The new volume deliberately intersects the roof and windows of the existing

Ein traditioneller Strickbau aus dem Jahre 1933 ist das Zuhause der Familie Maissen-Petschen; es beherbergt auch die medizinische Praxis des Bauherrn. Die Familie wollte durch einen Erweiterungsbau den gemeinsamen Wohnraum vergrößern. Dieser Anbau sollte sich von der herkömmlichen Bauweise der Gegend unterscheiden. Es war sogar der Wunsch der Bauherren, dass er sich sowohl in seiner Konstruktion als auch Form deutlich vom Altbau unterscheiden sollte.

Werner Schmidt entwarf ein aus einem einzigen Raum bestehendes rundes Volumen, in dem alle gewünschten Funktionen realisiert wurden – Kochen, Essen und eine Sitzmöglichkeit am Kamin sowie das Gefühl von einem Wintergarten. Das Bewilligungsverfahren war ziemlich heikel: die Gemeinde genehmigte zwar das Projekt, aber die kantonale Feuerpolizei forderte die Installation von Sprinkleranlagen wegen der Schindeleindeckung. Der neue Raum wirkt wie eine große, freundliche Höhle, viel höher als die Räume des bestehenden Strickbaus, und bescherte der Familie beim Einzug ein wahres „Urlaubsgefühl", und schon bald wurde der Anbau zum meist genutzten Raum im gesamten Haus.

Der Rahmen der Schalenkonstruktion besteht aus gebogenen Leimträgern. Die Form ist zweifellos eine künstlerische Geste, aber vor allem durch die Absicht eines optimierten Oberflächen-Volumen-Verhältnisses motiviert. Die Gebäudehülle enthält 60 cm Zelluloseisolierung, was bedeutet, dass die Wandstärke über 70 cm beträgt. Daher wurde der horizontale Überstand, der vor

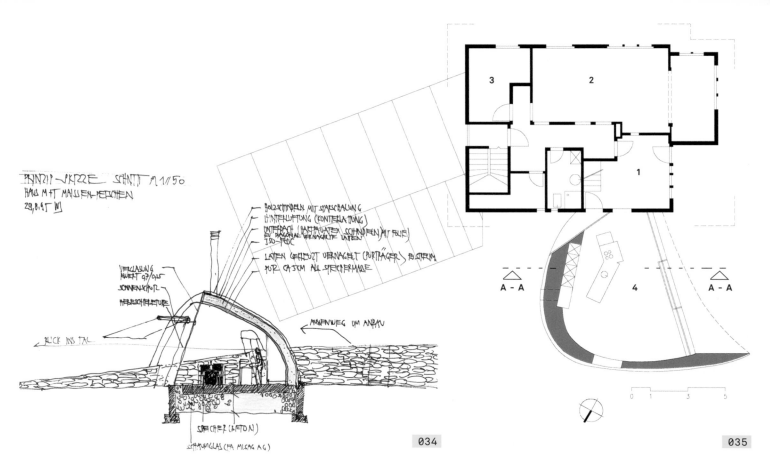

1 Entrance ⌣ Foyer
2 Living room ⌣ Wohnen
3 Room ⌣ Zimmer
4 Kitchen/Eating room ⌣ Kochen/Essen

**SCALE ⌣ MASSSTAB
1:200**

building, so as to partially stand on the log wall.

The room opens to the southwest via a generous glass façade, which gives it the appearance of a winter garden, and is inclined 17 degrees backwards. A large section of the façade is a sliding door which gives way to the terrace. This virtuoso choice of Schmidt's called for very skilled craftsmen, capable of accomplishing unusual and expensive results: to avoid permanent unsightly hardware, a removable suction handle and a neoprene compressed-air-operated gasket were developed. This system later became a standard product of Air-Lux.

Round windows in the wooden shell are

der sommerlichen Sonneneinstrahlung schützen soll, spitz zulaufend ausgeführt, um nicht zu voluminös zu wirken.

Der Anbau liegt auf demselben Niveau wie das Bestandsgebäude und schmiegt sich auf dessen Nordseite im Bereich des Foyers und seiner Verbindungstreppe in die oberen Stockwerke an. Das neue Volumen kreuzt absichtlich Dach und Fenster des Altbaus, und knüpft so an die Strickwand an.

Der Raum öffnet sich nach Südwesten durch eine großzügige Glasfassade, die ihm den Schein eines Wintergartens verleiht, und ist 17 Grad nach hinten geneigt. Ein großer Teil dieser Glasfassade besteht aus einer Schiebetür, die den Weg auf die Terrasse

036

037

placed so that one offers a view towards the village of the mistress, the other overlooks an apple tree in the garden.

The wood-burning soapstone stove was made rotatable about its own axis, because the clients could not decide where it should face. The extension also incorporates a partly passive, partly active heating system – the incident solar radiation directly heats the black soapstone floor; but at the same time rising warm air is collected at ceiling height, and a pump recirculates it in tubes inserted in the floor, to which it cedes its thermal energy.

freigibt. Dieser virtuose Entwurf von Schmidt forderte sehr erfahrene Handwerker, die in der Lage waren, ungewöhnliche und hochwertige Ergebnisse zu erzielen: um unhandliche Gerätschaften zu vermeiden, wurden ein entfernbarer Sauggriff und eine mit Druckluft unterstützte Türdichtung entwickelt. Dieses System wurde später ein Standardprodukt der Firma Air-Lux.

Zwei runde Fenster wurden so in der hölzernen Schale platziert, dass beim einen Fenster eine Sichtachse in Richtung des Geburtsortes der Bauherrin entsteht, und beim zweiten der Blick auf den Apfelbaum im Garten fällt.

Der Stückholzofen aus Speckstein ist um seine eigene Achse drehbar, weil die Bauherren sich nicht einigen konnten, in welche Richtung er sich öffnen sollte. Der Erweiterungsbau enthält ein teils passives und teils aktives Heizsystem – die direkte Sonneneinstrahlung erhitzt den schwarzen, einheimischen Specksteinboden; gleichzeitig wird die aufsteigende, warme Luft auf Deckenhöhe gesammelt, und eine Pumpe bringt sie über Wandkanäle wieder in den Boden ein, an den sie ihre Wärme abgibt.

CAZIS REFORMED CHURCH ⌐ EVANGELISCHE KIRCHE CAZIS

ADDRESS ⌐ ADRESSE:
Pitgongas, CH-7408 Cazis/GR

ALTITUDE ⌐ HÖHE:
700 m

DEGREE-DAYS ⌐ GRADTAGE:
3248

PROJECT ⌐ ENTWURF:
1994

CONSTRUCTION ⌐ BAU:
1996-2002

BUILDING FIRM ⌐ BAUFIRMA:
Bösiger, Langenthal

**PROJECT MANAGER ⌐
PROJEKTLEITUNG:**
Werner Schmidt + Vic Cajacob

PLOT AREA ⌐ GRUNDSTÜCKFLÄCHE:
3,000 m²

**HEATED FLOOR AREA ⌐
GEHEIZTE BODENFLÄCHE:**
320 m²

BUILDING COST ⌐ BAUKOSTEN (BKP2):
3,900,000 CHF [12,200 CHF/m²]

The Cazis Protestant parish was founded in 1968. On the occasion, a parsonage with a small integrated meeting room was built. At the same time a plot of land on the town outskirts was purchased from the Dominican convent, where one day a church was to be realised. In 1994 a competition was announced, to which some architects from the region were invited. The program included a liturgical space – that might contain up to 240 people or be subdivided into separate rooms – and annexes, including a bell tower. Werner Schmidt's unconventional project was selected out of seven entries and won the competition; in 1996 the project was approved by the parish assembly. The building's cost was financed equally by the cantonal church fund and by the sale of land belonging to the parish.

The architect's concept was founded on honesty and transparency. Three rounded bodies – which may be reminiscent of boulders, stones rounded by the flow of a stream, or dinosaur eggs – blend together creating a highly sculptural landmark in a meadow along the Posterior Rhine valley national road. The 80+42+65 m² spaces can be interconnected or separated from each other by the use of retractable partitions. In each of these bodies is a slit-shaped window: "The east window is directed towards the sky, the middle one to the horizon, and the west one to the road. The view from the windows moves in a line from the sky to the human realm." (→B122) These slits produce a very bright interior with smooth transitions, and – depending on the time of day – different intensities in the natural lighting and "de-

Die evangelische Gemeinde Cazis wurde im Jahre 1968 gegründet. Anlässlich der Gründung des dominikanischen Klosters in Cazis erstand die Gemeinde ein Grundstück am Dorfeingang. Als ersten Schritt wurde darauf ein Pfarrhaus mit einem Mehrzwecksaal errichtet. Das Kirchengebäude sollte in einem zweiten Schritt realisiert werden. Im Jahre 1994 wurde ein Wettbewerb ausgeschrieben, zu dem einige Architekten aus der Region eingeladen wurden. Das Programm umfasste einen liturgischen Raum, der bis zu 240 Menschen fassen und in mehrere Räume unterteilt werden können sollte, und einen Verbindungstrakt einschließlich Glockenturm. Werner Schmidts unkonventioneller Entwurf wurde aus sieben eingereichten Entwürfen ausgewählt und gewann den Wettbewerb. Im Jahre 1996 wurde das Projekt durch die Gemeindeversammlung genehmigt. Die Baukosten wurden zu ungefähr gleichen Teilen von der Landeskirche Graubünden und der Kirchengemeinde Cazis finanziert.

Das Konzept des Architekten gründete auf Ehrlichkeit und Transparenz. Drei runde Körper, die an Flusskiesel erinnern, Steine, die durch den Strom des Flusses gerundet wurden – oder aber auch ‚Dinosauriereier' – schmiegen sich aneinander und bilden einen in hohem Grade bildhauerischen Markstein inmitten einer Wiese entlang der hinteren Rheintal Nationalstraße. Die drei 80, 42 und 65 m² großen Räume können miteinander verbunden oder unter Anwendung von hochfahrbaren Zwischenwänden voneinander getrennt werden. Die Räume können sich die entsprechenden Beleuchtungsverhältnisse je nach Anlass zu Nutze machen.

039

lightful patterns to stimulate quiet contemplation throughout the day." (→B030:182)
Rooms can exploit the appropriate lighting conditions according to the occasion.
The interior of the church is "a warm and protective cave-like space," (→B030:181) where – as outside – "there is deliberately no explicit 'front' or 'rear.'" (→B122) The space is free-flowing, so that visitors can feel free to arrange themselves – literally and metaphorically – according to their own point of view on God and other people.
The structural project was developed with Heinz Isler, a specialist in skin structures and the Swiss father of shotcrete shells. It was not common for him to be involved as a consultant on pre-determined form – usually he participated in designing it. Werner Schmidt recalls that "Isler was initially wary of the lack of structural optimisation of the forms, but with time came to accept and appreciate them." (→B030:178)
Construction work started in April 1996, and shells were completed one year later. Transferring the forms that had been designed making use of hand-made models and sketches into concrete reality was a particular challenge, and involved 3D computer modelling able to generate a large number of polar coordinates and contour lines. In practice, the shape was created using 96 different custom-made, timber-frame, radial elements; one every 11°15'. They were subsequently coated with thin perforated metal sheets and a felt separating membrane. Shuttering was then externally covered with armature nets and several layers of shotcrete until a thickness of about 15 cm was reached. "Concrete was applied in layers of approximately 30 to 40 mm, as the timber falsework was not strong enough to receive the weight of the full shell thickness of wet concrete. Subsequent layers were, therefore,

Der Innenraum der Kirche ist „ein warmer, schützender und höhlenartiger Raum", (→B030:181) wo – von außen betrachtet – „es absichtlich keine ausdrückliche ‚Vorder-' oder ‚Rückseite' gibt." (→B122) Der Raum ist frei fließend, wodurch sich die Besucher frei bewegen können – im buchstäblichen und metaphorischen Sinn – gemäß ihrem eigenen Standpunkt zu Gott und gegenüber ihren Mitmenschen.
Die Konstruktion wurde mit Heinz Isler entwickelt, einem Spezialisten in Sachen Schalenkonstruktion und der schweizerische Vater von Spritzbetonschalen. Für ihn war es ungewöhnlich, als Berater einer bereits bestehenden Form zu fungieren – normalerweise nahm er direkt am Entwurfsprozess teil. Werner Schmidt erinnert sich, „Isler war zuerst wegen des Mangels an struktureller Optimierung der Formen nicht sehr glücklich, aber mit der Zeit nahm er die Formen an und schätzte sie." (→B030:178)
Die Bauarbeiten begannen im April 1996 und die Schalen waren ein Jahr später errichtet. Die Umsetzung der mittels handgemachter Modelle und Skizzen entstandenen Formen, war eine besondere Herausforderung und beinhaltete eine 3D Computermodellierung, durch die eine Vielzahl polarer Koordinaten und Höhenlinien erfasst werden konnten. In der Praxis wurde die Form unter Verwendung von 96 unterschiedlichen, maßgefertigten Bauholzrahmen und Radialelementen geschaffen – je eines alle 11°15' positioniert –, welche Schicht um Schicht mit dünnen, perforierten Lochblechen und einer Trennschicht aus Filz beschichtet wurden. Die Holzschale wurde dann schließlich von außen mit Stabarmierung und vier Schichten Spritzbeton bedeckt, bis eine Stärke von ungefähr 15 cm erreicht war. „Der Beton wurde nach und nach in Schichten von circa 3 bis 4 cm aufgetragen,

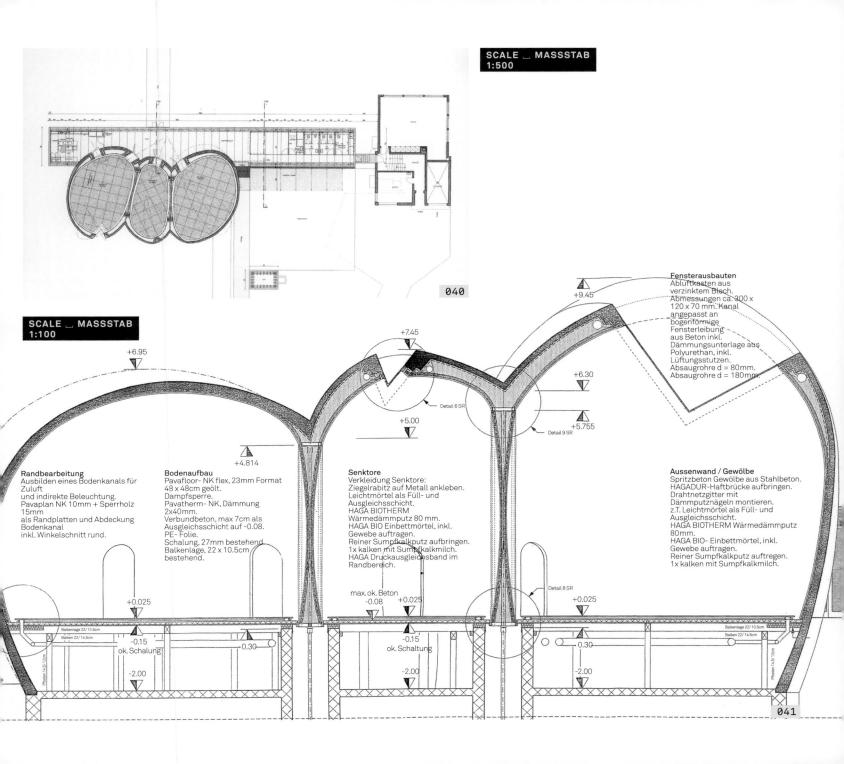

040

+6.95

+9.45

+7.45

Fensterausbauten
Abluftkasten aus
verzinktem Blech.
Abmessungen ca. 300 x
120 x 70 mm. Kanal
angepasst an
bogenförmige
Fensterleibung
aus Beton inkl.
Dämmungsunterlage aus
Polyurethan, inkl.
Lüftungsstutzen.
Absaugrohre d = 80mm.
Absaugrohre d = 180mm.

+6.30

+5.00

Detail 6 SR

+5.755

Detail 9 SR

+4.814

Randbearbeitung
Ausbilden eines Bodenkanals für
Zuluft
und indirekte Beleuchtung.
Pavaplan NK 10mm + Sperrholz
15mm
als Randplatten und Abdeckung
Bodenkanal
inkl. Winkelschnitt rund.

Bodenaufbau
Pavafloor- NK flex, 23mm Format
48 x 48cm geölt.
Dampfsperre.
Pavatherm- NK, Dämmung
2x40mm.
Verbundbeton, max 7cm als
Ausgleichsschicht auf -0.08.
PE- Folie.
Schalung, 27mm bestehend
Balkenlage, 22 x 10.5cm
bestehend.

Senktore
Verkleidung Senktore:
Ziegelrabitz auf Metall ankleben.
Leichtmörtel als Füll- und
Ausgleichsschicht.
HAGA BIOTHERM
Wärmedämmputz 80 mm.
HAGA BIO Einbettmörtel, inkl.
Gewebe auftragen.
Reiner Sumpfkalkputz aufbringen.
1x kalken mit Sumpfkalkmilch.
HAGA Druckausgleichsband im
Randbereich.

Aussenwand / Gewölbe
Spritzbeton Gewölbe aus Stahlbeton.
HAGADUR-Haftbrücke aufbringen.
Drahtnetzgitter mit
Dämmputznägeln montieren.
z.T. Leichtmörtel als Füll- und
Ausgleichsschicht.
HAGA BIOTHERM Wärmedämmputz
80mm.
HAGA BIO- Einbettmörtel, inkl.
Gewebe auftragen.
Reiner Sumpfkalkputz auftregen.
1x kalken mit Sumpfkalkmilch.

max.ok. Beton
-0.08

+0.025

Detail 8 SR

+0.025

+0.025

Balkenlage 22/ 10.5cm

Balken 22/ 14.5cm

Balkenlage 22/ 10.5cm

Balken 22/ 14.5cm

-0.15
ok.Schalung

-0.30

-0.15
ok.Schalung

-0.30

-2.00

-2.00

-2.00

Pfosten 14,5/ 12cm

Pfosten 14,5/ 12cm

041

042

043

supported by the partially cured previous layers. Heavier supporting ribs were required at the intersection of the individual ovoid shells and substantial box-outs to form the openings." (→B030:180-181)

The interior face was layered with 80 mm insulating plaster and then lime-plastered, while the outer face was not further sheathed and appears in smooth, fair-faced concrete which was left to weather naturally. Schmidt and Isler "intended that the forms would mature over time, acquiring a patina of mosses and lichens." (→B030:181)

The windows are geometrically defined by triangular prisms which intersect the 'eggs' – obtaining them was particularly tricky and requested a lot of analogical as well as digital modelling. "To transfer forces across the openings in the shells, the sides of the cut were to be linked by steel bars, whilst the glazing was installed in the plane of the cut surfaces. In order to clarify the forces in the bars, Isler made (…) thin latex rubber shells complete with the cut-out openings and with flexible cords linking the two sides. These rods were disposed in a diagonal 'zig-zag' configuration similar to that of (…) shoe-laces. When the rubber surface was loaded it was easy to see (…) that the rods would mainly be subject to compression near the top of the ovoids and in tension towards the base. In the final scheme the forces are carried by high-tensile Macalloy bars, some of which are left exposed whilst others – carrying high compression forces – are enclosed in steel tubes. The anchorage detail required a thickening of the shell edge around the openings." (→B030:179) Their steel frames were hand-concreted, and not sprayed. Schmidt's original design also included a free-standing tower and an elongated low wing on the back side of the church. Both would have been square-based prisms –

zumal das Bauholzgerüst nicht stark genug gewesen wäre, um das Gewicht der vollen Schalendicke aus Frischbeton zu tragen. Nachfolgende Schichten wurden durch die bereits gehärteten vorhergehenden Schichten gestützt. Stärkere Stützrippen wurden im Überschneidungsbereich der einzelnen eiförmigen Schalen sowie den Fensterschlitzen benötigt." (→B030:180-181)

Die Innenseite wurde mit 8 cm Isolierputz und dann mit Kalkputz überzogen, während die Außenseite keine weitere Deckschicht erhielt, sondern als Sichtbeton belassen und der natürlichen Bewitterung überlassen wurde. Schmidt und Isler „beabsichtigten, dass die Formen im Laufe der Zeit reifen würden und eine Patina von Moosen und von Flechten erhalten würden." (→B030:181)

Die Fenster sind geometrisch als dreieckige Prismen definiert, die sich in die ‚Eier' einschneiden – diese so umzusetzen war besonders heikel und erforderte viel analoges sowie digitales Modellieren. „Um die Kräfte über den Öffnungen der Schalen zu abzutragen, wurden die Seiten der Schlitze mittels diagonalen Stahlstangen verbunden, während die Verglasung in den Ebenen der Schnittflächen installiert war. Um die Kraftwirkung in den Stahlstangen zu überprüfen, fertigte Isler (…) dünne Latexschalen inklusive der Öffnungsschlitze an, die beidseitig mit Schnüren verbunden waren. Diese Schnüre wurden diagonal, im ‚Zickzack' angeordnet, ähnlich wie bei Schnürsenkeln (…). Wurde nun die Latexoberfläche belastet, war einfach zu erkennen, (…) dass an den Schnüren hauptsächlich nahe der Spitze des eiförmigen Körpers, und in Form von Zugkraft in Richtung Boden Spannungen auftraten. Im umgesetzten Entwurf werden diese Kräfte durch zugfeste Macalloy-Stangen aufgefangen, von denen einige in ihrem Äußeren so belassen sind und andere,

overhangs. This very simple, effective concept nonetheless allows an articulation of
spaces: outside, the covered area is larger on
the west side to obtain a place for training
exercises with pipes and hydrants (serviced
through an easily accessible underground
air space); inside, a cube in black, matt
waxed MDF panels divides the substantially
unobstructed volume into a lobby and a
multipurpose room, and at the same time
contains all the ancillary spaces – toilets,
wardrobe, kitchenette, and storage. The walls
of these spaces are painted warm orange.
The building stands on an in-site cast
concrete platform which performs as flooring as well – outside with just an anti-slip
broom finish, inside with a polished and
waxed anthracite powder coat. Twenty-four

schen Ballungsraumes. Der Grundriss ist
ellipsenförmig, mit Türen in allen vier Him-
melsrichtungen, bedeckt mit einer Kuppel,
deren visuelle Wirkungskraft durch eine weit
darüber gespannte Membran noch verstärkt
wird. Dieses sehr einfache aber effektive
Konzept erlaubt eine Definierung der Räume:
im Außenraum auf der Westseite ist der
überdachte Bereich größer, um Schulungen
an den Schläuchen und Hydranten durchfüh-
ren zu können (ausgestattet mit einem Zugang zu einem unterirdischen Luftraum); im
Innenraum teilt eine schwarze Box aus matt
gewachsten MDF Platten das ansonsten
offene Volumen in einen Eingangs- und einen
Allzweckbereich, und beherbergt gleichzeitig
alle notwendigen Räume – Toiletten, Garderobe, Miniküche und Lager. Die Wände dieser

Räume sind orange hinterleuchtet.
Das Gebäude steht auf einer vor Ort gegosse-
nen Betonplatte, die gleichzeitig als Bodenbelag dient – im Außenbereich mit einem rutsch-
hemmenden Besenstrich, im Innenbereich mit
einer polierten und gewachsten anthrazitfar-
benen Beschichtung. 24 Leimbinder tragen das
Gewicht der Kuppel, die im unteren Bereich
zum Innenraum hin frei vor der dreifach verglasten Außenhülle stehen (U = 0,71 W/m²K). Diese
Verglasung bildet ein 2.5 m hohes transparen-
tes, umlaufendes Band und erlaubt einen 360
Grad Rundumblick, einschließlich dem Schloss
auf der gegenüberliegenden Hangseite. Die
Verglasung kommt ohne zusätzliche Verschattung aus, da sie von der Fiberglas verstärkten
Teflon-Membran überdeckt wird. Diese ist
mittels Stahlseilen über zehn verzinkte Stahl-

oberlicht:

acrylglaskuppel, 4-schalig
u = 1.34 W/m2K
g = 62 %
durchmesser licht = 2,5 m

tragwerk:

bsh-spinne mit cnc-abbund

membrane:

polyesterfieberglass membran,
teflonbeschichtet,
gespannt

wandaufbau:

kalk-schlämme
kalk-leichtputz   3.0 cm
kraftpapier
sparschalung
seitenbretter   2.5 cm
strohdämmung   50 cm
dampfbremse
sparschalung
seitenbretter   2.5 cm
mineralwolle   6.0 cm
baumwollputz

fenster:

isolierverglasung
u = 0.71 W/m2K
g = 52 %
fensterkasten 3 Schichtplatten

bodenaufbau innen:

betonplatte
abtalouchiert,
versiegelt   28 cm
bauteilaktivierung
luftwärmepumpe
xps   12 cm
erdreich

bodenaufbau aussen:

betonplatte
besenstrich radial   20cm
kofferung kies

SCALE ⌐ MASSSTAB
1:40

049

glulam posts bear the load of the pavilion. Their lower portion stands visible against the inner side of the triple-glazed perimeter wall (U = 0.71 W/m²K). This constitutes a continuous transparent strip, 2.5 m high, that allows a 360° vista including the castle on the facing hill. The glass walls lack any screening, being shaded by the exterior canopy made with a polyester-teflon, fibreglass-reinforced membrane, which is tended by steel wires anchored to the ground and on ten galvanised steel poles.

Above the glazed walls, a cornice contains the lighting, which is not directly visible to minimise glare.

The dome is made of 50 cm thick straw bales between the rafters, lined with lime plaster on a wooden board on the exterior side; and 5 cm mineral wool panels, 30 min fire-resistant, fastened by metal plates to the above boarding, on which white, cotton cellulose flakes have been sprayed, on the inside. Both such internal layers are meant to increase acoustic performance. The total U value of the building envelope is 0.10 W/m²K.

A 2.5 m diameter oculus tops the vault; a rotating screen can shade it from the inside, and a hydropneumatic hoist can raise the four-glass-panes skylight by 50 cm to ventilate the pavilion.

Thanks to the high thermal insulation values and passive gains from glazed walls, lighting, and occupants, the building can almost do without heating, which is operated in extremely cold days only.

stangen gespannt und im Boden verankert. Auf dem umlaufenden Holzkranz oberhalb der Verglasung ist die indirekte Beleuchtung platziert.

Die Kuppel besteht aus 50 cm dicken Strohballen, die zwischen den Leimholzträgern eingebracht und von außen mit einer Lattung abgedeckt sind, und von innen mit 5 cm starken Mineralwolle-Platten, die mittels Metallplatten befestigt sind, beplankt ist und auf denen schließlich ein Baumwollputz angebracht wurde. Diese beiden inneren Schichten sind aus akustischen und brandschutztechnischen Gründen angebracht worden. Der U-Wert der gesamten Gebäudehülle beträgt 0,10 W/m²K.

Ein im Durchmesser 2,5 m breites Oberlicht schließt das Gewölbe ab; eine rotierende Blende kann den Raum von innen her verschatten, und eine Hydraulikanlage kann die Vierfachverglasung bei Bedarf um 30 cm anheben, um dem Pavillon Frischluft zuzuführen. Dank der guten thermischen Isolationswerte und der passiven Energiegewinnung durch die Verglasung, die Beleuchtung und die Benutzer, kommt das Gebäude beinahe ohne zusätzliche Heizung aus. Diese wird nur während weniger kalter Tage aktiviert.

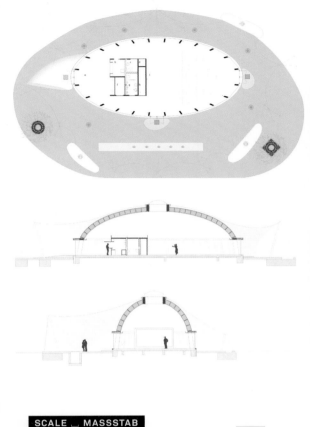

SCALE ⌐ MASSSTAB
1:200

050

FOLDABLES _ FALTMÖBEL

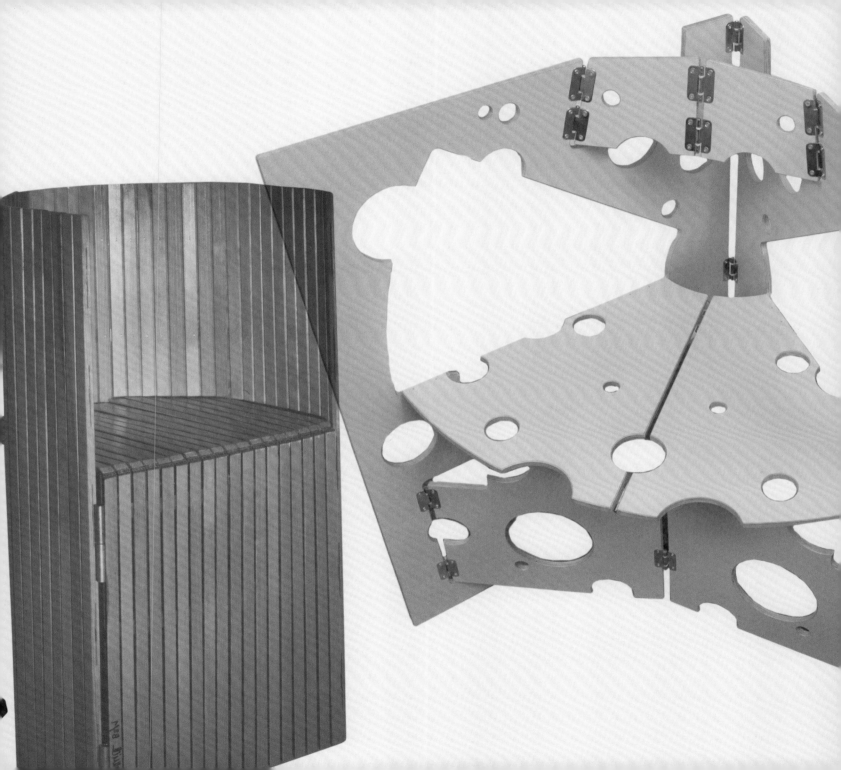

051

052

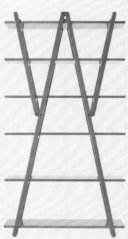

053

Folding furniture is a witty demonstration of Werner Schmidt's early creativity and was showed in a number of art and design exhibitions between the late 1980s and early 1990s. Enrichetta Ritter defined a foldable object as "a single body, that comes already assembled, and can be unfolded in one or a few moves to be ready for use." (→B089:5) The book she edited in the Design fundamentals series directed by Bruno Munari is a visual catalogue of examples, both anonymous and by renowned industrial designers of the time. It includes traditional fans, bridges, spatial probes, umbrellas. Among the most convincing models are two designs by De Pas, D'Urbino, Lomazzi (a fold-up wardrobe for BBB Bonacina (→■051) and a folding coat stand for Zanotta), (→■052) two by Vico Magistretti (the diverse series *Broomstick* for Alias Distribuzione and the bookshelf *Nuvola rossa* manufactured by Cassina), (→■053) the celebrated Bremshey trolley, as well as everyday objects like an ironing board, (→■054) an easel with paintbox, a portable music rest, a clothes-horse, (→■055) and an archetypal deckchair. (→■056)

Die Faltmöbel sind eine witzige Demonstration aus Werner Schmidts frühem kreativen Schaffen und sie wurden in einigen Kunst- und Designausstellungen zwischen den späten 80er Jahren und Anfang der 90er gezeigt. Enrichetta Ritter beschreibt einen faltbaren Gegenstand als „einzelner Körper, der bereits fertig montiert geliefert wird, und der in einen oder mehreren Handgriffen auseinandergefaltet werden kann und gebrauchsfertig ist." (→B089:5) Das Buch, welches sie in der Entwurfsgrundlagen-Reihe von Bruno Munari verfasste, ist ein visueller Katalog an Beispielen, sowohl anonymer als auch bekannter Industriedesigner unserer Zeit. Er umfasst traditionelle Ventilatoren, Brücken, Regenschirme und Raumstudien. Unter den überzeugendsten Modellen sind zwei Entwürfe von De Pas, D'Urbino, Lomazzi – eine Falt-Garderobe für BBB Bonacina (→■051) und ein faltbarer Kleiderständer für Zanotta –, (→■052) zwei von Vico Magistretti – die unterschiedliche *Broomstick* Reihe für Alias Distribuzione und das Bücherregal *Nuvola rossa* hergestellt

054

055

056

However, many objects in the rich collection are chairs, stools, and sitting furniture in general. Seats and backs are made of fabric or other flexible products, while their frame is made of wood, metal or also plastic, and is of course collapsible. An exception is *Plia* chair by Giancarlo Pinetti for Castelli. Garden chairs are much more clumsy than their indoor cousins and have wooden slat seat and backrest.

Folding furniture has not been the field of much dedication and innovation in the decades following Ritter's book – of course with some brilliant exceptions, such as Thomas Heatherwick's *Plank* manufactured by Benchmark Furniture. Today, as in the past, folding objects are designed to reduce the space they take to facilitate transportation and storage, and possibly to cut their costs. The core of the issue is joints (as obviously these items are better dry-assembled) and, in most cases, hinges. Geometric precision is called for both in design and manufacture. Werner Schmidt has dedicated a considerable part of his creativity to envisage furniture which

von Cassina –, (→■053) der gefeierte Bremshey Servierwagen sowie Alltagsgegenstände wie ein Bügelbrett, (→■054) eine Staffelei mit Farbenkasten, eine tragbare Notenablage, ein Wäscheständer, (→■055) ein archetypischer Liegestuhl. (→■056) Jedoch sind viele Gegenstände dieser reichen Sammlung Stühle, Schemel und Sitzmöbel im Allgemeinen. Die Sitzflächen und Rücklehnen sind aus Geweben oder anderen flexiblen Materialien hergestellt, während ihr Gestell aus Holz, Metall oder auch aus Plastik gefertigt ist, und sie sind selbstverständlich zusammenklappbar. Eine Ausnahme stellt der *Plia* Stuhl von Giancarlo Pinetti für Castelli dar. Gartenstühle wirken viel klobiger als ihre Verwandten im Innenraum und besitzen hölzerne Lattensitze und -rückenlehnen.

Gemäß Ritters Buch waren Faltmöbel in den letzten Jahrzehnten nicht gerade im Fokus von Innovation und Hingabe–selbstverständlich mit ein paar wenigen herausragenden Ausnahmen, wie Thomas Heatherwicks Sitzhocker *Plank* hergestellt von Benchmark Furniture zeigt.

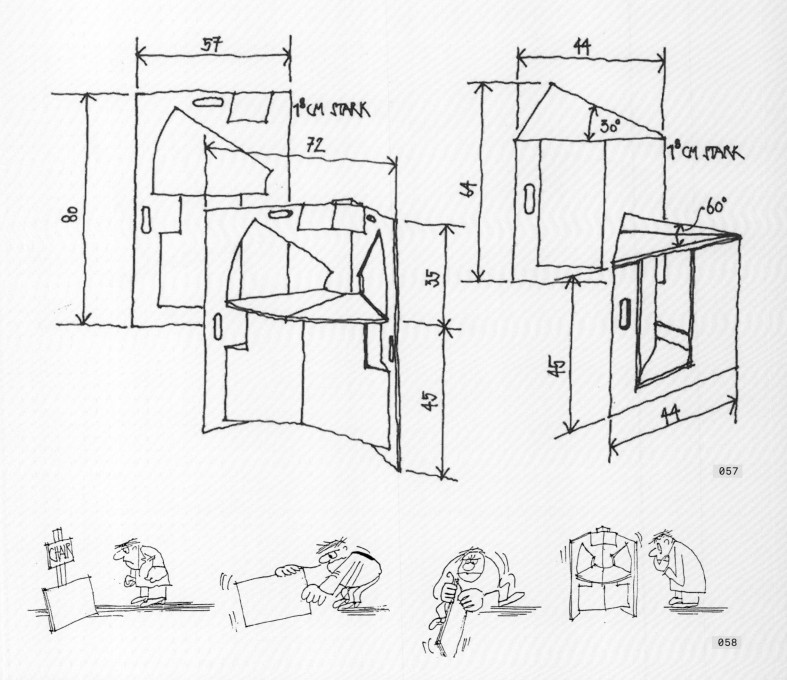

057

058

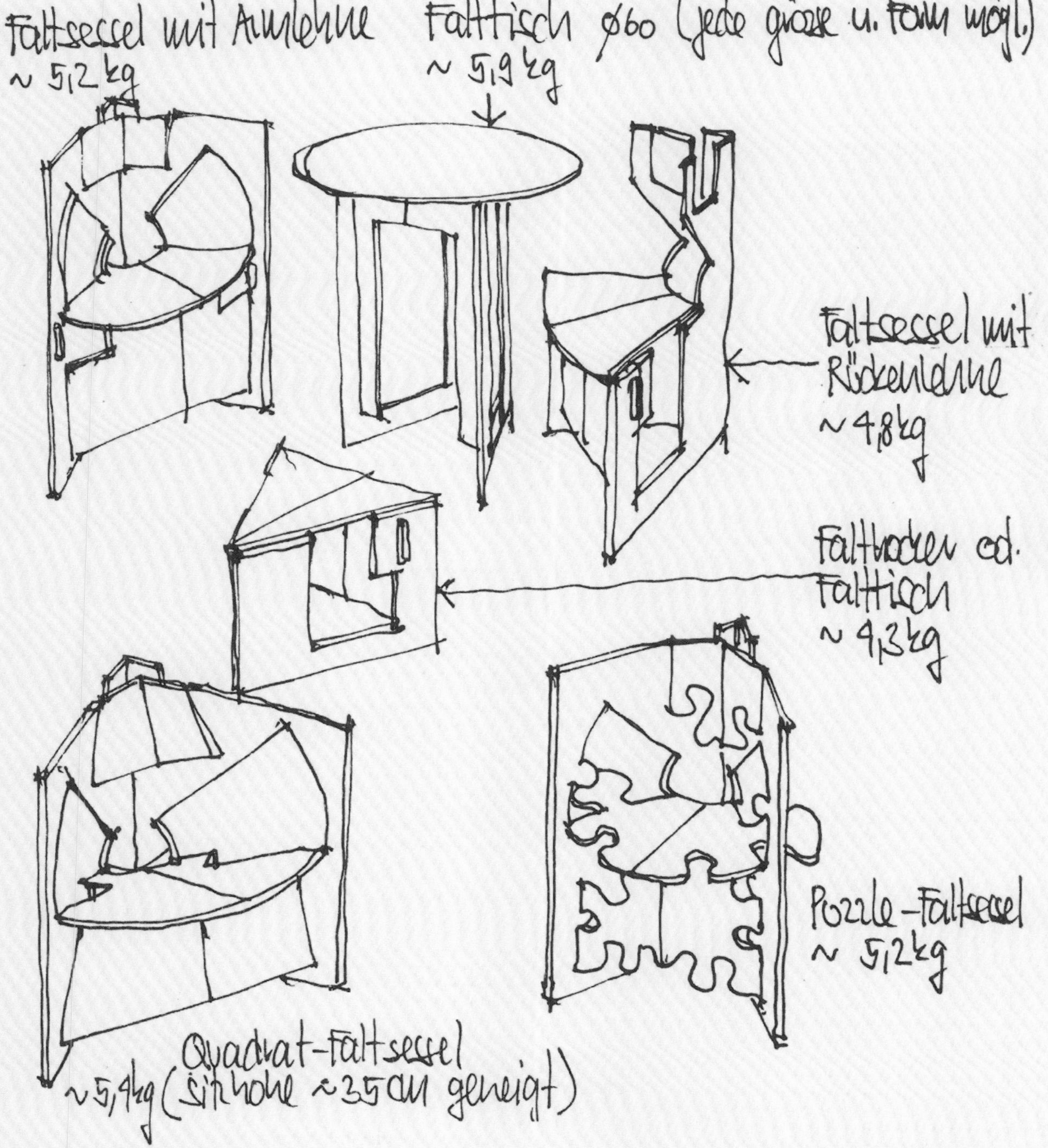

Faltsessel mit Armlehne
~ 5,2 kg

Falttisch ⌀60 (jede grösse u. Form mögl.)
~ 5,9 kg

Faltsessel mit
Rückenlehne
~ 4,8 kg

Falthocker od.
Falttisch
~ 4,3 kg

Puzzle-Faltsessel
~ 5,2 kg

Quadrat-Faltsessel
~ 5,4 kg (Sitzhöhe ~35 cm geneigt)

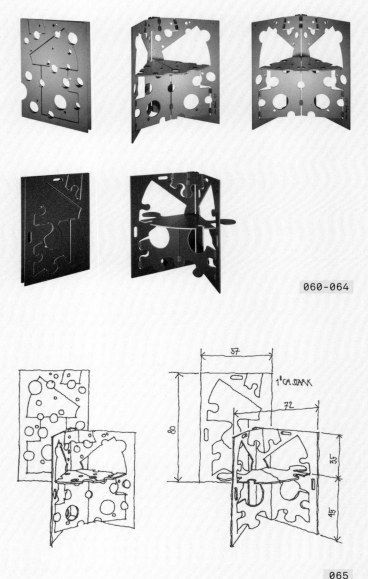

060-064

065

Heute wie auch in der Vergangenheit, werden gefaltete Gegenstände entworfen, um den Raum, den sie einnehmen zu verringern, um Transport und Lagerung zu erleichtern, und auch möglicherweise ihre Kosten zu reduzieren. Der Kern der Aufgabenstellung sind die Gelenke – offensichtlich sind diese Bestandteile besser vor Ort zusammen zu bauen – und bestehen in den meisten Fällen aus Scharnieren. Geometrische Präzision wird sowohl vom Design als auch von Hersteller gefordert. Werner Schmidt hat einen beträchtlichen Teil seiner Kreativität der Umsetzung von Möbeln gewidmet, die beinahe zweidimensional sein können – eine eindrucksvolle Reihe an Übungen angewandter Geometrie. (→§07) Nicht nur die Geometrie in der Erscheinung dieser statischen Objekte und ihren Linien, die sie umschreiben, wenn sie zusammengefaltet werden, ist reizvoll, sondern auch ihr klar lesbarer Aufbau, wie es auch in einigen seiner Architekturprojekte der Fall ist. Die Stühle, die Schmidt entworfen hat, funktionieren und sind in der Tat bequem – und gleichzeitig gibt es ein offensichtliches Interesse für den Prozess des Faltens, das mechanische Wunder eines Objektes, das durch eine simple Geste in ein anderes umgewandelt wird. Es sei erwähnt, dass eine solche Leichtigkeit der Manipulation Schmidts Objekte nicht nur praktisch macht, sondern „auch emotional zufriedenstellend wirkt, indem sie den Benutzer einladen, an den Entwurfslösungen teilzunehmen." (→B129:57-58)
Die meisten seiner faltbaren Möbel sind aus Melamin beschichteten Sperrholzplatten hergestellt, deren Schnittkanten sichtbar belassen wurden. Die Prototypen wurden von Hand entwickelt, aber der Entwurf wurde schließlich für die CNC gesteuerte Produktion optimiert. Die Klappstühle wurden von der Firma Lorenz Gasser in Haldenstein in begrenzter Auflage hergestellt.
Die ersten Projekte waren der einfache *Faltsessel* und der *Faltstuhl*. (→■057-058) Alle Modelle wurden aus 9 mm Birkensperrholz gefertigt. Der Stuhl entstand im Rahmen des Vitra Studentenwettbewerbs von 1985. Schmidt gewann den ersten Preis.

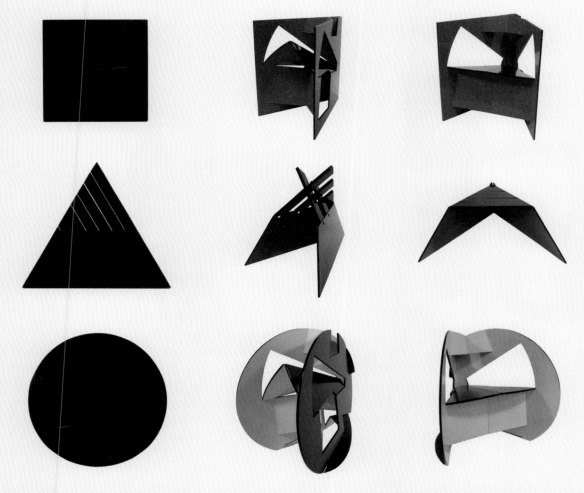

066-074

can became almost bi-dimensional – an impressive series of exercises of applied geometry. (→§07) Not only is geometry neat both in the appearance of the static objects and in the curves described by their parts when they fold – but also their construction is clearly legible, as in some of his architectural projects.

The chairs Schmidt designed do work, and are comfortable indeed – but at the same time there is a patent interest for the process of folding, the mechanical wonder of a thing that be-

Im selben Jahr entstanden der witzige *Käsefaltsessel* und der *Puzzlefaltsessel*. (→■060-065) Material und Technik sind dieselben wie oben; nur die Farben sind anders – entsprechend passend ist der *Käsefaltsessel* gelb und erinnert an eine Emmentaler Käsescheibe. Die Stühle sind derart gestaltet, dass sie zusammengefaltet als dekorative Gegenstände an die Wand gehangen werden können; ihr konstruktivistisches Erscheinungsbild wird durch den Einsatz von klaren, Grundfarben verstärkt. Das gleiche Prinzip und die gleichen Eigen-

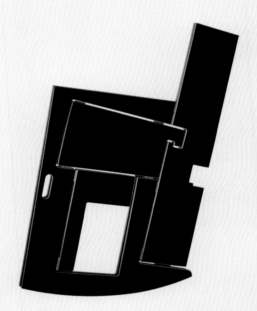

075-076

comes another in a single gesture. It has been remarked that such ease of manipulation makes Schmidt's objects not only practical but also "emotionally satisfying in that they invite the user to participate in the design solutions." (→B129:57-58) Most of his foldable and knock-down furniture is made of plastic-laminated plywood whose plies are left exposed at the edge. Prototypes were hand-developed, but the design was optimised for CAM-operated production. Folding chairs were manufactured in limited edition by the Lorenz Gasser company in Haldenstein.

The first projects were the *Simple folding chair* and the *Folding stool*. (→■057-058) Both were made of 9 mm birch plywood, coated with dark brown phenolicrisin. The chair was designed on the occasion of the Vitra student competition of 1985. Schmidt won first prize.

In the same year came the witty *Cheese* and *Jigsaw folding*

schaften treffen auf den neueren *Mathematiker* zu (eine Serie von zwei Stühlen und einem Schemel in den grundlegenden geometrischen Formen: Kreis, Quadrat, Dreieck) (→■066-074) und den *Faltschaukelstuhl*. (→■075-076)

Der *Schuhputzstuhl* aus dem Jahre 1987 wurde ebenfalls in einer handsignierten, limitierten Auflage von 10 Stück produziert. Der *Schuhputzstuhl* von Schmidt bietet eine Sitzfläche zum Telefonieren sowie eine Arbeitsfläche zum Schuhe putzen und Stauraum für die Reinigungswerkzeuge. Der *Schuhputzstuhl* ist ein verhältnismäßig seltenes Exemplar eines transformierbaren Einzelobjektes, das zwei verschiedene Funktionen so praktisch in sich vereint – häufig scheitern solche Objekte beim Versuch, beides zu sein und sind zum Schluss weder das eine noch das andere.

Der *Rolladenstuhl* von 1988 ist wahrscheinlich von allen faltbaren Möbelstücken, die Werner Schmidt entwickelte,

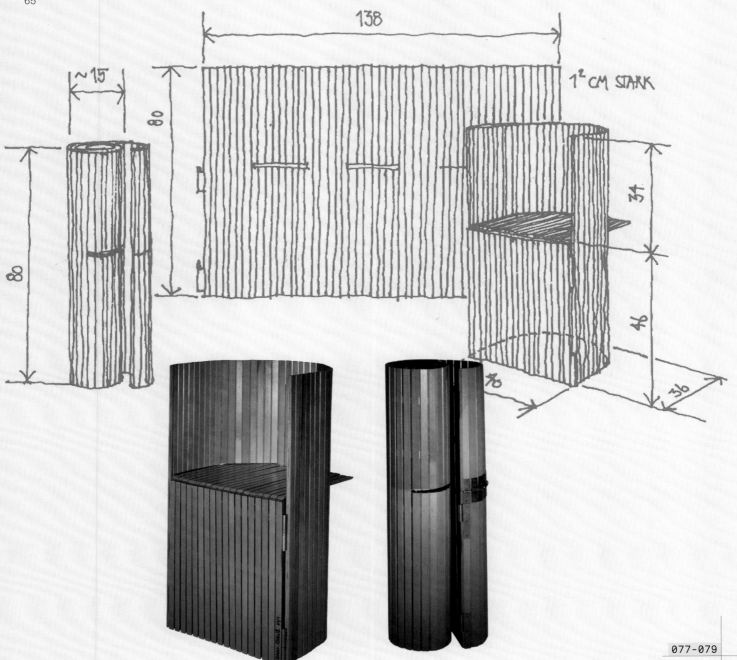

138

~15

80

80

1² CM STARK

31

46

46

36

080-081

chairs. (→■060-065) Material and technique are the same as above; only the colours are different – appropriately, the *Cheese folding chair* is yellow to evoke an Emmental cheese slice. The chairs are also designed to be used as decorative objects, when folded up and hung on the wall; their constructivist appearance is reinforced by the use of solid, basic colours. The same principle and characteristics apply to the later *Mathematiker* (a series of two chairs and a stool in basic geometrical forms: circle, square, triangle), (→■066-074) *Folding swinging chair*, (→■075-076) and *Swiss flag folding chair*. The *Shoeshine chair*, 1987, was also produced in 10 hand-signed pieces. As traditional stools used by street shoe-shin-ers, the piece of furniture designed by Schmidt comes with a space to put your shod foot on and a cabinet to store cleaning tools; once folded, it doubles as a phone chair. The *Shoeshine chair* is a relatively rare case of transformable item which succeeds in performing two different functions – often, in the attempt of being two things, a design fails to be any. The *Shutter chair* of 1988 is perhaps the most surprising of all foldable pieces of furniture by Schmidt. (→■077-079) In this case, a single roll of 12 mm larch roller blind was used instead of plywood cut-outs. Here, he demonstrates his excellence in finding unexpected construction principles: the right combi-

das überraschendste. (→■077-079) In diesem Fall wurde eine einzelne Bahn eines 12 mm starken Lärchenrolladens anstelle von Sperrholzlatten verwendet. Hier demonstriert Schmidt seine hervorragende Fähigkeit, unerwartete Konstruktions-prinzipien zu finden: die richtige Kombination von Schnitten, Faltungen und Drehbewegungen macht den Stuhl aufrollbar und leicht tragbar – sowie bequem und stabil bei der Benut-zung. Als Schmidts Möbelentwurf bei einer Ausstellung des Art Institute of Chicago ausgestellt war, wurde anerkennend erwähnt, „sowohl die Vielzahl an Formen, als auch der über-raschende Gebrauch von vertrautem Material (sic), machen diesen Stuhl sehr ansprechend." (→B129:58) Er wurde in einer limitierten Auflage von sieben Stück produziert.
Aber Schmidt beschränkte sich nicht nur auf das Entwerfen von Stühlen. Der *Aluminiumfalttisch* und der *faltbare Alumi-niumschemel* aus dem Jahre 1987 (→■080-081) überzeugen durch ihre Synthese aus Einfachheit in der Form und ihrer Funktionalität, welche mit Hilfe von 2 mm starkem, eloxierten Aluminiumblech erreicht wird. Zukowsky und Wardropper konstatierten, dass der Tisch „die elegante Wirtschaftlichkeit einer mathematischen Gleichung besitzt. Acht Kreissegmente sind mittels Scharnieren miteinander und mit den rechtecki-gen faltbaren Stützelementen verbunden. (...) das Material ist leicht genug, um einfach gefaltet werden zu können wie ein Fächer und besitzt[, dennoch] große Zugfestigkeit. Die Genia-lität des Entwurfs und die grenzenlosen (sic) Einstellmöglich-keiten vom geschlossenen bis zum ausgedehnten Zustand, machen diesen Tisch intellektuell zufriedenstellend und vi-suell reizvoll. (...) Optisch wird die reine Geometrie des Tisches durch den matten Glanz des Aluminiums beschwichtigt und durch die Beschaffenheit der BOB Nieten, die seine Oberflä-che schmücken, belebt." Nur ein paar Dutzend Tische wurden produziert, und dennoch – wie Zukowsky und Wardropper passend beobachteten – der *Aluminiumfalttisch* ist „eindeutig für die Massenproduktion geeignet und könnte eine weite Verbreitung erfahren." (→B129:57-58)

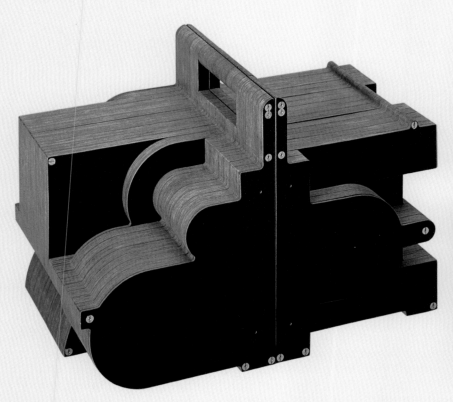

082-085

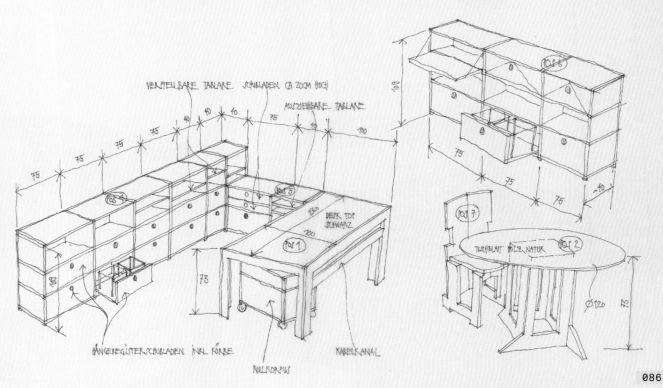

VERSTELLBARE TABLARE   SCHUBLADEN CA 20CM HOCH
AUSZIEHBARE TABLARE
VENSTELLBARE TABLARE
75 75 75 75 40 40 40 75
POS 4
POS 5
POS 6
DESK TOP SCHWARZ
POS 1
POS 7
POS 2
TISCHBLATT HOLZ NATUR
100
73
75 75 75 ~40
100
73
Ø 120
Ø 120
HÄNGEREGISTER/SCHUBLADEN INKL. KÖRRE
ROLLKORPUS
KABELKANAL

086

nation of cuts, folds, and rotations makes the chair rollable and easily portable – as well as comfortable and stable when in use. Presenting Schmidt's furniture design at an exhibition at the Art Institute of Chicago, it was remarked that "[b]oth the variety of shapes and the surprising use of a familiar material (sic) make this chair appealing." (→B129:58) It was produced in a limited edition of seven pieces.

But Schmidt did not restrict himself to designing chairs. The *Aluminium folding table* and *Aluminium folding stool* of 1987 (→■080-081) are convincing in their synthesis of simplicity of form and functionality, and are obtained from 2 mm, elox aluminium sheet. Zukowsky and Wardropper stated the table possesses "the elegant economy of a mathematical equation. Eight sections of a circle hinge to each other and to rectan-

Das *Toylight* war ein Entwurf für einen Lampenwettbewerb, ausgeschrieben im Jahre 1987 durch Woka-Lampen in Wien und in Partnerschaft mit der Universität der Angewandten Künste Wien. Schmidts Idee war, einen leuchtenden Gegenstand zu kreieren, dessen Form je nach Wunsch des Benutzers umgewandelt werden könnte, und der auch unverkabelt funktionieren würde. Er entwarf ein sehr helles, kleines Objekt, welches man in der Hand halten kann – eine Art modifiziertes Kinderspielzeug, das aus acht faltbaren Quadraten besteht. Es gewann den 2. Preis, 10 Stück wurden davon produziert. Schließlich entstand das tragbare *Picknick Set*, welches das komplette Geschirr für vier Personen enthält, und das sich beim Ausklappen zum niedrigen Tischlein mit Schemeln verwandelt. (→■082-085) Das Hauptmerkmal dieses ‚Picknickkor-

087-092

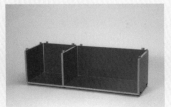

gular supports. (…) the material is light enough to fold easily as a fan [, yet] has great tensile strength. The ingenuity of the design and the limitless (sic) conformations from closed to extended make this table intellectually satisfying and visually provocative. (…) Visually, the absolute geometry of the table is softened by the dull shine of aluminium and enlivened by the spiky texture of the rivets adorning its surface." Only several dozen tables were produced, yet – as Zukowsky and Wardropper aptly observed – the *Aluminium folding table* was "clearly designed for mass-production and could sustain wider distribution." (→B129:57-58)

The *Toy light* was designed as an entry for a lamp competition, launched in 1987 by Woka lamps, Vienna, in partnership with the Vienna University of Applied Arts. Schmidt's idea was to create a luminous object, whose form could be transformed at the user's will, and which could operate unplugged. He came up with a very light, small thing you can hold in your hand – a modified child's toy consisting of eight foldable squares, which won 2nd prize. Only ten pieces were produced.

Finally, the portable *Picnic set*, containing complete tableware for four, which once unfolded becomes a low table-cum-stools. (→■082-085) The main feature of this hamper is to be "designed from the inside out instead of outside in." (→B129:58) The *Picnic set* exists in two prototypes only.

In 1992-93, Werner Schmidt put his mind to furniture design again. This time, the goal was to find innovative, appropriate uses for local fir wood, (→p168-169) and in fact it was first used to furnish the Canton Graubünden Forest Inspectorate. Schmidt designed the *AWS panel system*, a modular, knock-down furniture system made of coated plywood, three-ply panels or OSB. (→■086-092) The supporting structure consists of horizontal and vertical (side) rectangular boards – elements are interlocked together during assembly, thanks to a very simple and ingenious slot joint, without any ironmongery or any further finishing. Front and back can be left open to form

bes' ist „sein Design von innen heraus anstatt von außen nach innen." (→B129:58) Von dem *Picknick Set* existieren zwei Prototypen.

In den Jahren 1992–93 widmete sich Werner Schmidt erneut dem Möbeldesign. Diesmal war das Ziel, eine innovative und angemessene Nutzung von heimischem Fichtenholz zu finden, (→S.168-169) und tatsächlich wurden verschiedene Büros des Bündnerischen Forstinspektorats mit diesen Entwurfsergebnissen ausgestattet. Schmidt entwarf das *AWS-Plattensystem*, ein modulares Möbelsystem, das aus beschichteten Sperrholz-, 3Schicht- oder OSB Platten hergestellt ist. (→■086-092) Die Tragkonstruktion besteht aus horizontalen und vertikalen rechteckigen Platten – die Elemente werden dank einer sehr einfachen und klugen Zapfenverbindung, ohne irgendwelche weiteren Beschläge oder Zusatzteile, zusammengesteckt. Vorder- und Rückseite können offen gelassen und als Regale genutzt werden oder mit weiteren Brettern ausgestattet werden, um Fächer, Schränke und Kabinette herzustellen. Die Zusammensetzung kann an die individuellen Anforderungen angepasst werden.

Das *AWS-Plattensystem* erinnert ein wenig an Angelo Mangiarottis *Junior System* (→■097) (1966, hergestellt von Casaluci), ebenfalls für den einfachen Auf- und Abbau von Sperrholzplatten entworfen, dessen Kombinationsmöglichkeiten dank einer größeren Anzahl an Komponenten sogar noch breiter angelegt war, und dessen Konzept Beppe Finessi „exemplarisch" nannte. (→B044:196-199)

Neuere Beispiele der praktisch endlosen Erweiterung, die durch ein einzelnes, grundlegendes Element erreicht wird, sind erfolgreich von Werner Aisslinger entworfen worden: Ich beziehe mich auf das *Endless shelf* (1994, produziert von Porro) (→■095) – wo horizontale und vertikale Platten durch kreuzförmige Aluminiumdruckgussgelenke zusammengehalten werden – und auf die *Plus Unit* (2001, für Magis): ein lasttragendes, modulares Schubkastensystem, dessen Elemente

093

094

095

096

097

shelves, or filled in with further boards to create drawers, cupboards, and cabinets. The composition can be expanded according to individual needs.

The *AWS panel system* somewhat recalls Angelo Mangiarotti's *Junior system* (→■097) (1966, produced by Casaluci), also made for easy assembly and disassembly of plywood boards, whose combination possibilities were even wider thanks to a larger range of components, and whose concept was dubbed "exemplary" by Beppe Finessi. (→B044:196-199)

More recent examples of virtually endless extension obtained from a very basic element were successfully designed by Werner Aisslinger: I refer to the *Endless shelf* (1994, produced by Porro) (→■095) – where horizontal and vertical panels are held together by cross-shaped die-cast aluminium joints – and the *Plus unit* (2001, for Magis): a self-load-bearing modular drawer system, whose elements are connected with aluminium extrusions. (→■096)

It seems to me that Werner Schmidt exploited in other fields the principles he applied in furniture design. For instance, in his study of aerial linkage walkways to connect the Ferrari plants, Schmidt devised a modular spatial structure – similar to a spine – from a standard joint. (→■098) An accessible supply channel – including the lighting – would have hung from the ceiling. Different variations were developed for the supporting steel frame, and also the shading was considered.

In projects like the *AWS bus*, and the museum of Disentis abbey, (→■093-094) one can recognise the same careful search for spatial exactness as in the *Picnic set*, so as to create a place (or a box) for each thing. The AWS 'bus' is actually an old VW T4 van Schmidt has converted to run on burnt vegetable oil. The diminutive interior has been ingenuously refurbished so that it is possible to cook, eat and sleep in.

The room chosen to accommodate the museum's entrance and cash desk was small, and had six doors as well as countless installations. Schmidt superimposed a unifying grid

durch Strangpressformstücke aus Aluminium zusammengefügt werden. (→■096)

Mir scheint Werner Schmidt machte sich auf anderen Gebieten die Prinzipien, die er im Möbeldesign anwendete, zu nutzen. So zum Beispiel plante Schmidt in einer Studie für in der Luft hängende Verbindungsstege, die die Firmenanlagen von Ferrari miteinander verknüpfen sollten, eine modulare, räumliche Struktur – vergleichbar mit der Wirbelsäule – abgeleitet von einem Standardgelenk. (→■098) Ein zugänglicher Versorgungskanal – einschließlich Beleuchtung – wäre unter der Decke hängend montiert worden. Verschiedene Varianten wurden für dieses Stahlskelett unter Berücksichtigung der Verschattung entwickelt.

In Projekten wie dem *AWS-Bus*, und dem Museum im Kloster Disentis, (→■093-094) kann man dieselbe sorgfältige Suche nach räumlicher Ordnung wie im *Picknick Set* erkennen, um für jedes Ding einen eigenen Platz (oder eine Box) zu schaffen. Der *AWS-Bus* ist ein alter VW Bus T4, den Schmidt für den Betrieb mit Altspeiseöl umbauen ließ. Der winzige Innenraum wurde mühevoll so ausgestattet, dass es für zwei Personen möglich ist, zu kochen, zu essen und zu schlafen.

Der Museumsraum, der für den Eingangs- und Kassenbereich gewählt wurde, war klein, hatte sechs Türen und wies unzählige Installationen auf. Schmidt legte den Wänden und der Decke ein vereinheitlichendes Schachbrettmuster aus grau lackierten MDF Platten und Glasscheiben zugrunde. Sämtliche Zusätze, Schränke, Entlüftungen und Installationen wurden somit versteckt, während relevante Türen und Vitrinen durch helle Strahler in Szene gesetzt wurden.

Ich denke auch, dass unter den antreibenden Kräften für Schmidts Entwürfe – von den Faltsesseln hin zu seinen Architekturprojekten – dieselbe geometrische und räumliche Präzision steht. Der vonRoll Pavillon (→S.50-55) ist nichts anderes als ein enormes, skulpturales Möbelstück, mit der Genauigkeit, die ein in diesem Maßstab vorfabriziertes Einzelteil erfordert. (→§07)

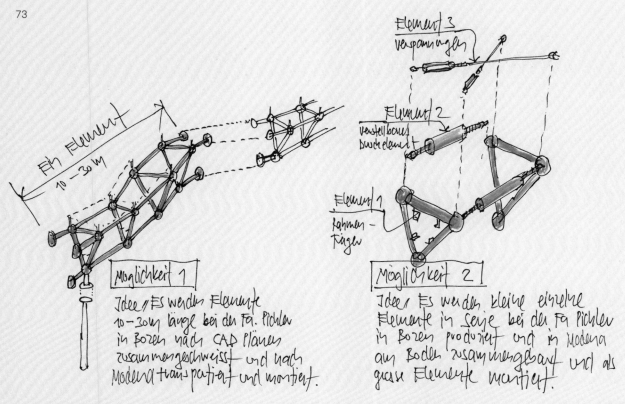

Eh Element
10 – 30 m

Element 3
verspannungen

Element 2
verstellbaus
Druckelemut

Element 1
Rahmen-
Träger

Möglichkeit 1

Idee // Es werden Elemente
10 – 30 m Länge bei den Fa. Pichler
in Bozen nach CAD Plänen
zusammengeschweisst und nach
Modena transportiert und montiert.

Möglichkeit 2

Idee: Es werden kleine einzelne
Elemente in Serie bei den Fa. Pichler
in Bozen produziert und in Modena
am Boden zusammengebaut und als
ganze Elemente montiert.

098

pattern to walls and ceiling, formed by blue-grey lacquered MDF panels and glass panes. Add-ons, cabinets, vents and installations were thus concealed, while relevant doors and display cases were emphasised by glowing lights.
I also think that among the drivers of Schmidt's designs – from folding chairs to architectural projects – lays the same geometric and spatial precision. vonRoll pavilion (→p50-55) is nothing but a huge, sculptural piece of furniture, with all the exactness requested by a largely prefabricated item. (→§07) Finally, it seems to me that legibility of construction may also be recognised as a recurring principle in Schmidt's work. Not in all of his projects, though: in Caplazi stair tower everything is almost didactically discernible; (→p74-77) in Maissen extension, construction is not apparent. (→p40-43) Both options are available, provided that once one chooses one of them, the subsequent design steps are consistent with such choice.

Letztlich scheint mir, dass auch die Lesbarkeit der Konstruktion als wiederkehrendes Prinzip in Schmidts Arbeiten erkennbar wird. Nicht in all seinen Projekten vielleicht: im Caplazi-Treppenturm ist fast alles didaktisch erkennbar; (→S.74-77) bei der Maissen-Erweiterung ist die Konstruktion nicht offensichtlich. (→S.40-43) Beide Möglichkeiten sind vorhanden, in jedem Fall werden sie konsequent ausgeführt.

STAIR TOWER CAPLAZI ⌷ TREPPENTURM CAPLAZI

ADDRESS ⌷ ADRESSE:
CH-7172 Rabius

ALTITUDE ⌷ HÖHE:
960 m

PROJECT ⌷ ENTWURF:
1990

CONSTRUCTION ⌷ BAU:
1991

BUILDING FIRM ⌷ BAUFIRMA:
Bearth, Rabius

**PROJECT MANAGER ⌷
PROJEKTLEITUNG:**
Werner Schmidt

FLOOR AREA ⌷ BODENFLÄCHE:
18 m²

**BUILDING COST ⌷ BAUKOSTEN
(BKP2):**
100,000 CHF

A turn of the 20th century house had to be subdivided in four independent residential units, one for each storey. The creation of an interior staircase would have meant demolishing a part of the house to comply with the building regulations. It was therefore decided to build a 12 m high exterior stair tower, to give the flats additional living space and comply with acoustical requirements. In formal terms, the addition clearly stands out of the existing building – nevertheless, the tower respectfully keeps itself lower than the house. Initially, a cylindrical volume was planned, but this was changed to an elliptical one because of the property boundaries. One enters the stair tower though a metal-plate box. The stair tower itself is made of a filigree structure consisting of larch glulam posts and galvanized-steel, solid rectangular sections forming nine horizontal rings like the hoops of a barrel. Outside these are vertical, thin larch lintels that form a see-through sheath around the staircase. The structure can therefore be perceived from the inside only, and the larch cladding allows natural light to diffuse in. Five series of St. Andrew's-cross metal braces prevent the construction from twisting.
Supports were positioned after dimensioning the steps, a masterly exercise of applied geometry which originates from a Viennese traditional model. The steps are made of cross-laminated larch wood, and are hung to the roof plate by way of metal rods. Apart from the central plate, the roof is glazed: from indoor, the composition looks like the hub of an elliptical wheel. Everything is built in such a way that it cannot be damaged by rain.

Ein Haus aus der Wende des 19. Jahrhunderts, sollte in vier eigenständige Einheiten, pro Geschoss eine, unterteilt werden. Das Platzieren eines innen liegenden Treppenhauses hätte eine Zerstörung des Raumgefüges im Zuge der Anpassung an die Bedürfnisse und Vorschriften zur Folge gehabt. Daher wurde entschieden einen 12 m hohen Treppenturm im Außenbereich zu errichten, um den einzelnen Wohnungen mehr Raum zu geben, und um die akustischen Vorgaben einzuhalten.
Formell betrachtet, hebt sich der Anbau deutlich vom Bestandsgebäude ab und dennoch ordnet sich der Turm dem Haus respektvoll unter. Ursprünglich war ein zylindrisches Volumen geplant, aber auf Grund der Grundstücksgrenzen, kam es schließlich zu einer Anpassung an einen elliptischen Grundriss.
Man begeht den Treppenturm über eine Metallplattenbox. Der Treppenturm selbst ist aus einer filigranen Struktur aus Lärchenholz Leimbinderstützen, Querstreben und verzinkten Stahlbändern gefertigt, neun horizontale Bänder, die den Stahlbänder eines Weinfasses ähneln. Von außen sind in der Vertikalen schmale Lärchenholzlatten angeordnet, die den Blick nach draußen freigeben. Daher kann das Traggerüst nur von innen her betrachtet wahrgenommen werden und die Lärchenholzlattung erlaubt dem Tageslicht einzudringen. Fünf Metallkreuz wirken den Torsionskräften entgegen.
Die Stützen wurden gemäß der Dimensionierung der Stufen gesetzt, eine Meisterarbeit angewandter Geometrie, die einem Wiener Modell von elliptischen Treppenhäusern

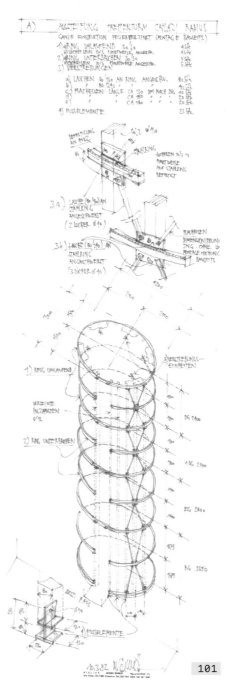

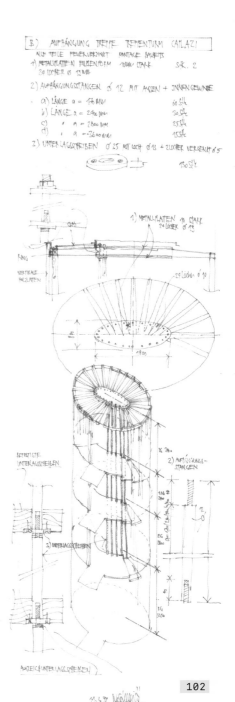

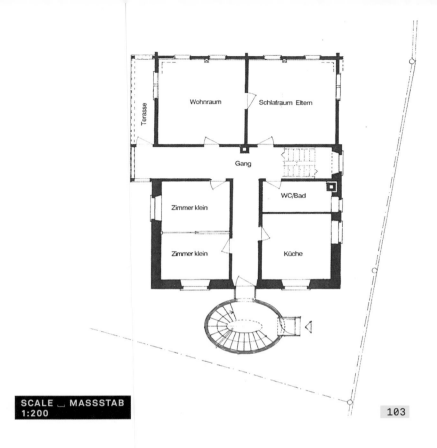

Terasse

Wohnraum

Schlafraum Eltern

Gang

Zimmer klein

WC/Bad

Zimmer klein

Küche

The connection to the house is as unobtrusive as possible – a barely noticeable glazed volume, whose only opaque parts are thin steel plates for the roof and catwalks to the storeys.

entstammt. Die Stufen sind aus kreuzverleimtem Lärchenholz hergestellt und sind an der metallenen Deckenplatte aufgehängt. Abgesehen von dieser zentralen Scheibe, ist das Treppenturmdach verglast: von innen betrachtet wirkt es wie die Nabe eines elliptischen Rades. Alles wurde so errichtet, dass es durch den Regen nicht beschädigt werden kann.

Die Verbindung zum Bestandsgebäude ist so dezent wie möglich gehalten – ein kaum wahrnehmbares, gläsernes Volumen, dessen einzige blickdichten Teile die dünnen Platten des Daches und der Verbindungsstege zum Haus sind.

DESIGN FOR AUTARCHY
DESIGN FÜR AUTARKIE

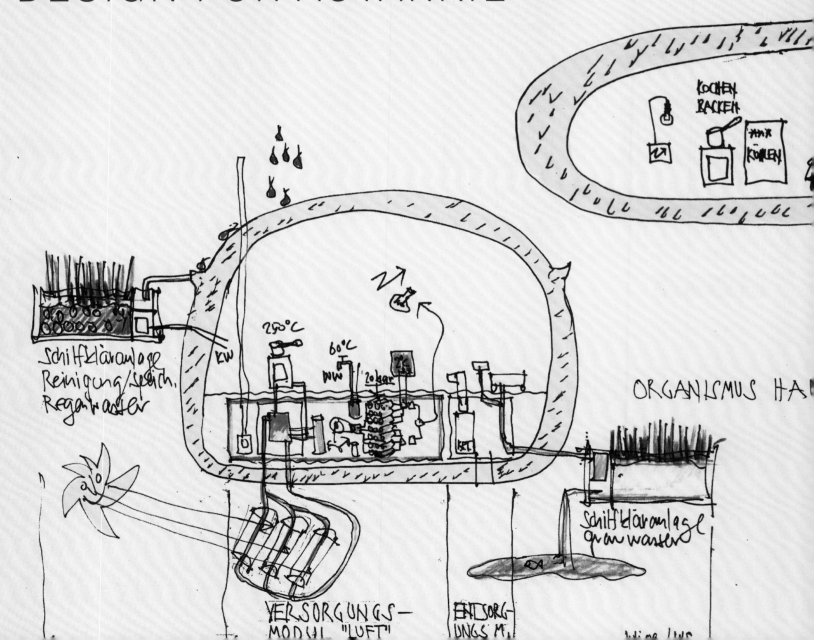

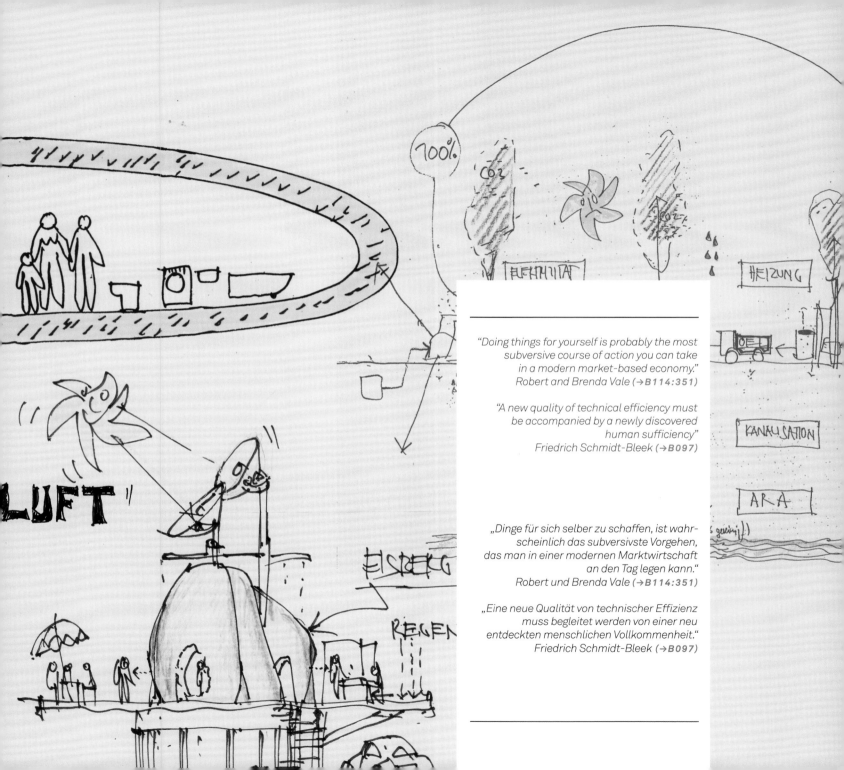

"Doing things for yourself is probably the most subversive course of action you can take in a modern market-based economy."
Robert and Brenda Vale (→B114:351)

"A new quality of technical efficiency must be accompanied by a newly discovered human sufficiency"
Friedrich Schmidt-Bleek (→B097)

„Dinge für sich selber zu schaffen, ist wahrscheinlich das subversivste Vorgehen, das man in einer modernen Marktwirtschaft an den Tag legen kann."
Robert und Brenda Vale (→B114:351)

„Eine neue Qualität von technischer Effizienz muss begleitet werden von einer neu entdeckten menschlichen Vollkommenheit."
Friedrich Schmidt-Bleek (→B097)

Werner Schmidt's design goal is much more the in-depen-dence of the house from external supplies, than 'sustainabil-ity,' as the latter remains an abstract, elusive concept. In his opinion, there exists a direct correlation between the autonomy and the sustainability of a building. Schmidt wants to "create buildings that do not need connections anymore, either for heating, water, waste water, or electricity." He refers to energy supply and public servicing in general, but also to high technol-ogy products which only conglomerates can obtain: his political goal is to oppose "the increasing dependence of people on institutions, corporations and energy suppliers." (→B064)
Were this the appropriate place, one could write a history of the tendency towards self-sufficiency or autonomy during recent decades. Such a tendency is a recurring product of the desire to escape a crowded, noisy society to look for a life more authentic, since it puts one in touch with the funda-mental cycles of nature and it makes one take responsibility for one's own actions. In this view, ecological motivations for autonomy have merged quite recently with a human urge, as old as urban life.
This said, it is more than clear that a tradition of pleas and practical solutions has established itself during the previous decades, finding in Fuller's self-sufficient or 'autonomous' design of the Dymaxion house, (→B075) in the New Alchemy Institute's 'Bioshelters,' (→B109) in Mike Reynolds's 'Earth-ships,' (→B088) and in the Vales's 'Autonomous House' (→B112) some of its most renowned and influential prototypes. Obviously, the prospective 'self-sufficient' house would be just a tessera in a much larger mosaic encompassing lifestyle

Werner Schmidts gestalterisches Ziel ist das Realisieren von autarken Häusern, die unabhängig von Energielieferanten und anderen Versorgern sind. Schmidt sieht einen direkten Zusammenhang zwischen der Unabhängigkeit und Nachhal-tigkeit eines Gebäudes – je unabhängiger desto nachhal-tiger. Schmidt möchte „Gebäude realisieren zu können, die keinerlei Anschlüsse mehr benötigen, weder für Wasser noch für Abwasser, und auch keine für Elektrizität." Er bezieht sich auf die Energielieferanten und den öffentlichen Service im Allgemeinen, aber auch auf high-tech Produkte, die nur den Großkonzernen dienen: sein politisches Ziel ist, „die immer größere Abhängigkeit von uns Menschen von irgendwelchen Institutionen, Konzernen und Energielieferanten" (→B064) abzulehnen und dieser Abhängigkeit entgegenzuwirken.
Wäre dies der passende Ort, könnte man eine Geschichte über die Tendenz der vergangenen Jahrzehnte in Richtung Unabhängigkeit schreiben. Diese Tendenz ist ein immer wiederkehrendes Resultat aus dem Wunsch heraus, sich von der überfüllten, lauten Gesellschaft abzukehren und sich einem authentischeren Leben zuzuwenden, da einen dies mit den grundlegenden Zyklen der Natur in Verbindung bringt und dazu führt, für die eigenen Taten Verantwortung zu übernehmen. Von diesem Standpunkt aus betrachtet, hat sich wirtschaftliches Streben nach Autonomie erst vor kurzem aus einem menschlichen Verlangen heraus entwickelt, das so alt ist wie das städtische Leben selbst.
Dies bedeutet, es ist offensichtlich, dass sich eine Tradition aus Appellen und praktischen Lösungen während der letzten Jahrzehnte verfestigt hat, welche sich in einigen der bekann-

and societal structures, as was clear to thinkers such as Illich and Schumacher. The current tendency is for 'smart' and/or 'sustainable' solutions, possibly sophisticated and proprietary, to be installed in an unchanged context. Long before ecological footprint calculations and the first report on *The Limits to Growth*, Schumacher already called for "alternative methods of production and patterns of living" (→B098:4) and "a lifestyle designed for permanence." (→B098:9) It was clear to him that "every increase of needs tends to increase one's dependence on outside forces over which one cannot have control, and therefore increases existential fear." (→B098:20)

Local, cheap, and small-scale solutions seemed therefore the most rational way – firstly from an economic point of view – of managing human problems. Resource accessibility and control of actions and deliberations were the key matters of their discourse. A path of research was thus drawn: "the direction should be towards the noiseless, low-energy, elegant, and economical solutions normally applied in nature," (→B098:117) striving for straightforwardness.

Such path was epitomised by Godfrey Boyle and Peter Harper's book *Radical Technology*, where techniques were strongly put in a wider social and political context, and much emphasis was accorded to human fulfilment and communal life. Autonomy was intended basically as group autonomy; it implied a preference for "simplicity and frugality in life and technology," (→B022:8) and for direct gratification of one's own needs and expectations, rather than through commodities.

In 1970s experimental projects, autonomy was – and still largely is for the few who cultivate it – a rural dream: the appropriate setting where "real positive health" (→B101:299) might be found in hard manual work, fresh air, sunshine, and unadulterated food.

As intended by the counter-culture, the 'autonomous' house was to be a paradigmatic response to global problems, (→B113:55) and became one of the most conspicuous symbols of 'alternative technology.' (→B022:135) It was defined

testen und einflussreichsten Prototypen wiederfindet, wie in Fullers autarkem oder ‚autonomen' Entwurf, dem ‚Dymaxion House', (→B075) im ‚Bioshelters' des New Alchemy Institute, (→B109) in ‚Earthships' von Mike Reynolds (→B088) und im ‚Autonomous House' (→B112) von den Vales.

Offensichtlich wäre das potenzielle ‚autarke' Haus wie ein Mosaiksteinchen in einem wesentlich größeren Gefüge zu sehen, welches einen bestimmten Lebensstil und gesellschaftliche Strukturen enthält, wie es bereits Denkern wie Illich und Schumacher klar war. Der gegenwärtige Trend geht in Richtung ‚smarte' und ‚nachhaltige' Lösungen, vielleicht anspruchsvoll und urheberrechtlich geschützt, um in einem unveränderten Kontext platziert zu werden. Lange vor den ökologischen Fußabdruck-Berechnungen und vor dem ersten Bericht über *Die Grenzen des Wachstums*, forderte Schumacher bereits „alternative Produktionsverfahren und Lebensmuster" (→B098:4) und „einen Lebensstil, entwickelt mit Blick auf Beständigkeit." (→B098:9) Ihm war klar, dass „jede Zunahme an Bedürfnissen dazu führen kann, jemandens Abhängigkeit gegenüber Kräften von außen, auf die man keinen Einfluss (über die man keine Kontrolle) hat, zu erhöhen, wodurch die Existenzängste größer werden." (→B098:20)

Lokale, günstige und kleine Lösungen scheinen daher die rationalste Herangehensweise, um mit menschlichen Problemen umzugehen – in erster Linie vom wirtschaftlichen Gesichtspunkt aus betrachtet. Zugänglichkeit zu Ressourcen, Steuerung von Handlungen und Entscheidungen waren die Schlüsselpunkte dieses Diskurses. Ein Forschungsansatz war folglich: „es sollte in Richtung geräuschlose, niederenergetische, elegante und wirtschaftliche Lösungen gehen, die normalerweise in der Natur zum Einsatz kommen", (→B098:117) das Streben nach Einfachheit.

Eine solche Herangehensweise findet sich in Godfrey Boyle und Peter Harpers Buch *Radical Technology,* in dem Technologie in einen weit größeren sozialen und politischen Kontext gestellt wird, und in dem der menschlichen Erfüllung und dem

by the Vales in 1975 as "a house operating independently of any inputs except those of its immediate environment." (→B113:9) Such complete self-sufficiency was more evident in the phrase "autarkic house." (→B113:10) After more than thirty years, the Vales's stance has changed little. They now recognise the theoretical and political advantage of being grid-linked, but are still persuaded that "the alternative-technology approach to the design of an autonomous house is the appropriate one. (…) An autonomous house has to depend on the resources that can be collected on its site, and the technology that it uses to harvest these resources needs to be simple, robust and controllable by the occupants." (→B113:41) In other words, the advantage should be as measurable in terms of lessened burden on the environment as it is in terms existential sense of awareness and ownership of one's own destiny.

Werner Schmidt obviously agrees with the Vales when they say that "one of the logical implications of the concept of sustainable development is that buildings should be designed so as to eliminate the need for non-renewable fuels;" (→B113:13) actually his houses hardly need any fuels, at least as long as thermal comfort is concerned.

Energy availability basically depends on how much incident solar radiation each site receives: although other renewable energy sources could be used, this is the more widely available where Schmidt happened to work. (→■105) Whatever the insolation and efficiency of the systems used, first of all it is imperative to reduce consumption in tune with the principles of passive solar architecture, as defined by authors such as Edward Mazria (→B076) and David Wright, (→B127) to name but a few. Schmidt continues such a long-established tradition. Of course, comfort temperature is also a cultural product, and varies widely in history and geography: were it not possible to attain Schmidt's spectacular performances, it is debatable whether the most reasonable solution would not be to encourage the residents to adapt to lower temperatures instead.

Leben in der Gemeinschaft viel Geltung beigemessen wird. Autonomie wird im Grunde genommen als Gruppenautonomie betrachtet; sie beinhaltet eine Vorliebe für „Einfachheit und Sparsamkeit im Leben und in der Technik," (→B022:8) und der direkten Erfüllung von Bedürfnissen und Erwartungen vielmehr als Waren.

Autonomie galt in den experimentellen Projekten der 1970er Jahre als ländlicher Traum – und ist es noch immer für die wenigen, die diesen Traum weiterhin pflegen: das passende Szenario, bei der „wirklich positive Gesundheit" (→B101:299) erlangt werden kann, ist harte Arbeit mit den Händen, frische Luft, Sonnenschein und saubere Nahrung.

Wie in der Gegenkultur angedacht, war das ‚autonome' Haus als eine paradigmatische Antwort auf die globalen Probleme zu sehen (→B113:55) und wurde eines der auffälligsten Symbole der ‚alternative technology.' (→B022:135) Es wurde 1975 von den Vales als „Haus, das unabhängig von irgendwelchen Einflüssen funktioniert, ausgenommen derer aus seiner unmittelbaren Umgebung" definiert. (→B113:9) Eine solche komplette Unabhängigkeit war in der Begrifflichkeit „autarkes Haus" offensichtlicher. (→B113:10) Nach mehr als dreißig Jahren, hat sich an der Haltung der Vales wenig geändert. Sie erkennen jetzt den theoretischen und politischen Vorteil des Vernetztseins, aber sie sind noch immer davon überzeugt, dass „der Ansatz alternativer Technologien für das Design eines autonomen Hauses der passende ist. (…) Ein autonomes Haus muss von den Ressourcen abhängen, die an seinem Standort vorhanden sind, und die Technologie, die es braucht, um diese Ressourcen zu nutzen, muss einfach, robust und kontrollierbar für seinen Benutzer sein." (→B113:41) In anderen Worten gesagt bedeutet dies, der Vorteil wäre genauso messbar im Hinblick auf die verminderte Belastung der Umwelt, wie auch im Hinblick eines existenziellen Bewusstseins und der Kontrolle über das eigene Schicksal.

Werner Schmidt stimmt offensichtlich mit den Vales überein, wenn sie sagen, dass „eine der logischen Folgerungen des

PHOTOVOLTAIC SOLAR ELECTRICITY POTENTIAL IN EUROPEAN COUNTRIES
PHOTOVOLTAIK SOLARSTROM POTENTIAL IN EUROPÄISCHEN LÄNDERN

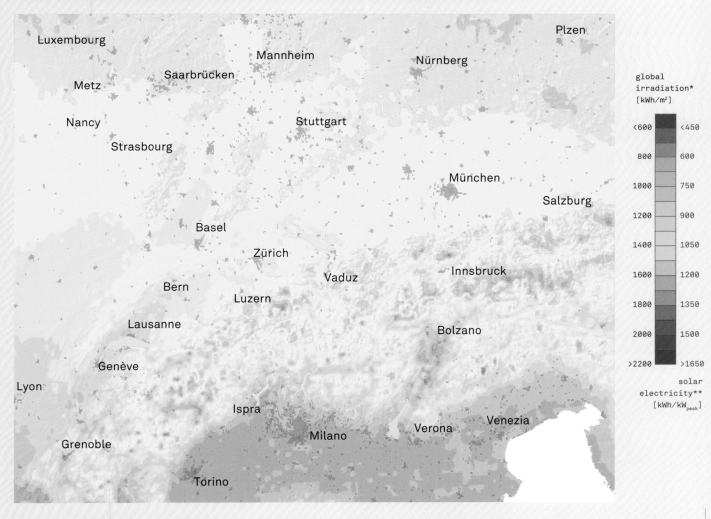

* yearly sum of global irradiation incident on optimally-inclined south-oriented photovoltaic modules
** yearly sum of solar electricity generated by optimally-inclined 1kW$_p$ system with a performance ratio of 0.75

The 'efficient' plant-engineering solutions tend to have high proprietary costs and high embodied energy; they have a relatively low durability and require high maintenance. Committed designers and clients should instead look for solutions which stay simple and inexpensive during their long service life. This should be even more true nowadays, when we enjoy the use of much more advanced solar technology than in the 1970s. According to Treberspurg, the first choice in applying the 'solar strategy' is between maximising solar gains and minimising thermal losses. (→B110) Schmidt's houses succeed in doing both these things at the same time, inasmuch as one can find in them "a combination of southerly glazing, superinsulation, and internal mass." (→B069:8-9) If one were completely reassured about the durability of straw-bale construction, such houses would turn out excellent from the point of view of autonomy and sustainability. (→§04)

The general principle of what used to be called 'solar' architecture is; why use enormous amounts of solar energy stored in fossils when we could make direct use of it? Solar radiation can be used in three main ways, matching "the available resources as closely as possible to the jobs they have to do, both qualitatively and quantitatively:" (→B022:144)

1) to produce the appropriate indoor climate. The building itself, or some of its elements, is the system and is used to collect and transport heat without mechanical equipment. For this reason, it is dubbed 'passive.' The building exploits 'autonomously' the energy available in its immediate surroundings thanks to its siting and exposure, its geometry, and the performance of its components. (→B053) The two fundamental elements of passive heating systems are a solar collector (a glazed wall facing south) and a thermal mass for absorbing, storing and distributing heat. (→B076:39) To these one must add a high-thermal resistance envelope to entrap the heat. In Schmidt's houses, one finds an almost textbook application of many of Mazria's principles, with the difference that jumbo straw bales and triple glazing allow Schmidt to attain

Konzeptes nachhaltiger Entwicklung ist, dass Gebäude derart gestaltet sein sollten, dass sie den Bedarf an nicht erneuerbaren Brennstoffen überflüssig machen" (→B113:13) – tatsächlich benötigen seine Häuser kaum Brennstoffe, zumindest was den thermischen Komfort betrifft.

Energieverfügbarkeit hängt grundlegend davon ab, wie viel Sonneneinstrahlung ein jeder Standort vorweist: obgleich andere erneuerbare Energiequellen verwendet werden könnten, ist die Sonnenenergie die am meisten verfügbare, wo Schmidt zum Einsatz kam. (→■105) Egal welche Isolierungen oder welche effizienten Systeme auch verwendet werden, ausschlaggebend ist eine Verminderung des Verbrauchs, gemäß den Prinzipien von passiver Solararchitektur, wie es von Autoren wie Edward Mazria (→B076) und David Wright (→B127) definiert wird, um nur ein paar Namen zu nennen. Schmidt setzt jene alteingesessene, bewehrte Tradition fort.

Selbstverständlich ist der Grad an Komfort auch von kulturellem Belang, und schwankt weit im Hinblick auf Geschichte und Geografie: wäre es nicht möglich, Schmidts großartige Leistungen zu erzielen, dann könnte man natürlich auch argumentieren, ob es nicht die angemessenste Lösung wäre, die Bewohner anzuregen, sich stattdessen an niedrigere Temperaturen zu gewöhnen.

Die ‚effizienten' anlagentechnischen Lösungen tendieren zu hohen Eigenkapitalkosten und einem hohen Anteil an Grauer Energie; sie haben eine relativ geringe Lebensdauer und erfordern hohen Instandhaltungsaufwand. Engagierte Designer und Verbraucher sollten stattdessen nach Lösungen Ausschau halten, die einfach und günstig sind bei gleichzeitig langer Nutzungsdauer. Dies sollte immer wichtiger werden, zumal wir heute viel fortgeschrittenere Solartechnologie besitzen als in den 1970er Jahren.

Gemäß Treberspurg liegt die erste Wahl bei der Anwendung der ‚Solarstrategie' zwischen solarer Gewinnmaximierung und thermischer Verlustminimierung. (→B110) Schmidts Häuser können beides zur selben Zeit, da man in ihnen „eine Kombi-

an extremely high thermal insulation performance and drop the most intricate 1970s solutions: (→§08) but the plan of his houses is still elongated on the east-west axis; the south façade is completely glazed and duly shaded; masonry partition walls and dark, massive floors store heat; etc.

2) applying solar energy directly as heat – for cooking, and for operating devices which can be heat-driven. The 'low-tech' solution is to collect heat at low temperatures by allowing solar radiation to heat up objects directly exposed to it. "Solar cookers which will boil water, bake bread, etc., by focusing the solar radiation onto a small area by the use of reflectors" (→B022:65) are in operation in several southern countries, and Schmidt has enjoyed constructing cooking mirrors (→■107) which do work, but only in favourable and uncontrollable weather conditions. Today, the more viable solution to this approach is to collect heat at high temperatures, e.g. by curved reflectors (parabolic collectors, Fresnel lenses) which concentrate the radiation at a linear focus. Obviously, you will need to adjust the tilt – a solar tracker will make the whole apparatus more expensive and perhaps delicate, but performance will be higher. In a number of self-sufficient home schemes, Schmidt incorporated such linear collectors which can heat a heat transfer oil up to 300°C. (Some heat transfer fluids can reach higher temperatures without boiling but can be toxic, and need to be substituted every few years because they tend to lump). This could then operate an oven, a stove, or (through a reversed Stirling engine) an absorption refrigerator or a heat pump, thus eliminating the largest electricity consumption in homes.

3) to generate electricity from photovoltaic cells but also, indirectly and less conventionally, with heat collected from the sun. The sun can produce steam to heat the hot side of a Peltier-Seebeck thermocouple, (→■108) or activate a low-temperature Stirling engine operating an alternator which can be adjusted in momentum by temperature differences. In order to be as powerful as is needed, these engines must be large, but according to Schmidt this does not matter in

nation von Südverglasung, Superisolation und innerer Masse" (→B069:8-9) vorfindet. Wenn man von der Haltbarkeit der Strohballenkonstruktion gänzlich überzeugt ist, erscheinen diese Häuser unter dem Gesichtspunkt der Autonomie und der Nachhaltigkeit perfekt. (→§04)

Das generelle Prinzip dessen, was einst ,solare' Architektur genannt wurde, ist die Frage warum verbrauchen wir enorme Mengen an solarer Energie, die in fossilen Energieträgern gelagert ist, wenn wir sie stattdessen direkt nutzen können? Sonnenstrahlung kann auf drei Hauptarten genutzt werden, indem man „die am nächst besten verfügbaren Ressourcen mit ihrem jeweiligen Aufgabenbereich, sowohl in qualitativer als auch in quantitativer Hinsicht, aufeinander abstimmt:" (→B022:144)

1) das notwendige Innenraumklima erzeugen. Das Gebäude selbst, oder einige seiner Elemente, ist das System selbst und wird dazu genutzt, Wärme ohne mechanische Ausstattung zu sammeln und zu transportieren. Aus diesem Grund wird es ,passiv' genannt. Das Gebäude nutzt dank seines Standorts und seiner Ausrichtung, seiner Geometrie und der Effizienz seiner Bestandteile ,autonom' die verfügbare Energie in seinem unmittelbaren Umfeld. (→B053) Die beiden fundamentalen Elemente von passiven Heizsystemen sind Sonnenkollektoren, die nach Süden gerichtet sind, und eine dick isolierte, thermische Masse, um Wärme zu speichern und zu verteilen. (→B076:39) In Schmidts Häusern finden sich beinahe schon schulbuchartige Anwendungen von Mazrias Prinzipien, mit der Ausnahme, dass Schmidt durch die Jumboballen und Dreifachverglasungen bereits eine sehr gute Wärmedämmleistung erhält, und einige der komplizierten Lösungen aus den 70er Jahren vernachlässigen kann: (→§08) aber der Grundriss seiner Häuser ist meist entlang der Ost-Westachse ausgerichtet, die Südfassaden sind komplett verglast und entsprechend verschattet; Steinwände trennen Räume und massive Böden speichern die Wärme, etc.

2) Die direkte Verwendung von Sonnenenergie zum Kochen

106

und für andere Funktionen, die wärmegesteuert sind. Die ‚low-tech' Variante besteht darin, Hitze bei niedrigen Temperaturen zu sammeln, dadurch dass man Objekte mittels der Sonneneinstrahlung erwärmt. „Solarkocher, die Wasser zum Kochen bringen, Brot backen, etc., indem man die Strahlung auf einen Punkt bündelt und indem man Reflektoren einsetzt" (→B022:65) werden in unterschiedlichen südlichen Ländern eingesetzt. Und Schmidt hat Freude daran gefunden, Parabolspiegel ähnliche Kochgeräte zu entwickeln, die jedoch leider nur bei günstigen Wetterbedingungen funktionieren. (→■107) Die Hitze bei hohen Temperaturen einzufangen, zum Beispiel mit Hilfe von gebogenen Reflektoren (Parabolrinnenkollektoren, Fresnel-Linsen), die die Strahlung auf einen Brennpunkt konzentriert, ist eine praktikable Lösung. Hierbei muss man die Neigung entsprechend anpassen. Ein Solartracker macht die Ausrüstung zwar teurer und vielleicht etwas heikler, aber der Ertrag wird höher. Schmidt hat solche Kollektoren in einigen Schemen des energieautarken Hauses eingeplant, die ein Wärmeträgeröl auf bis zu 300 Grad erhitzen würden. (Manche Wärmeträgeröle können sogar noch höhere Temperaturen erreichen ohne zu verdampfen, diese sind allerdings toxisch und müssen alle paar Jahre ausgewechselt werden, da sie verklumpen.) Diese Wärmeträgeröle könnten einen Ofen, einen Herd oder (mittels eines Stirlingmotors mit umgekehrter Drehrichtung) einen Absorptionskühlschrank oder eine Wärmepumpe versorgen. Auf diese Weise wäre der größte Energieverbrauch im Haushalt eliminiert.
3) Elektrizität mittels Photovoltaikzellen, aber auch mittels thermischer Energie, indirekt und weniger konventionell erzeugen. Die Sonne erzeugt Dampf, um die heiße Seite eines Thermoelementes mit Hilfe des Peltier-Seebeck Effektes (→■108) oder eine Niedrigtemperatur Stirlingmaschine zu aktivieren, die einen Generator antreibt. Damit diese Maschinen die nötige Leistung erbringen können, müssen sie relativ groß sein, aber Schmidt ist der Meinung, dass dies bei einem Haus nichts ausmacht. Anstelle des konventionellen Technikraumes

a house. Instead of a boiler room, there would be a room to accommodate two engines – to produce enough electricity to meet the optimised domestic demand, as well as to charge the battery of an electric vehicle. Schmidt thinks the powerful like photovoltaics because the construction of 'solar farms' is generously subsidised, and such proprietary technology makes people dependent on capital-intensive industries which can afford huge R&D investments. (→B090) The reduction of electricity consumption and its generation from heat allow for the avoidance of such dependency and can have no negative effects on comfort. True, this method is not highly efficient – but neither is a PV array. To overcome uneven availability of solar energy, Schmidt prefers storing it in the form of heated oil or pressurised air, instead of batteries.

An extremely well insulated, passive house like the ones he has been designing since 1994 can do without any heating, but other energy uses still need to be fuelled. In the last decade, Schmidt has been elaborating partial or complete schemes of autarkic houses, also re-interpreting some 'low-tech' solar-powered, well-established and reliable machinery. This would allow the substantial reduction, if not the complete eradication, of imports of fossil fuels for running houses. In the last 120 years, the technologies he favours have been almost effaced by more modern machines. However, at present Stirling engines are regaining popularity thanks to the ease with which they can use almost any external heat source, their quiet operation, their versatility, their safety, and their low maintenance requirements. (→B066,124) Machines of this kind are indeed quite primitive and sometimes large and heavy, but their operation is easily comprehensible, and they can be built and fixed virtually by any ironsmith – in fact Schmidt has conceived and built several of them. (→■106,109-110)

Schmidt's concept of an autarkic house is clearly expressed in a series of drawings. (→■111-112) The well-insulated building envelope (made, of course, of load-bearing straw bales) allows the house do to without space heating. It is equipped with

107

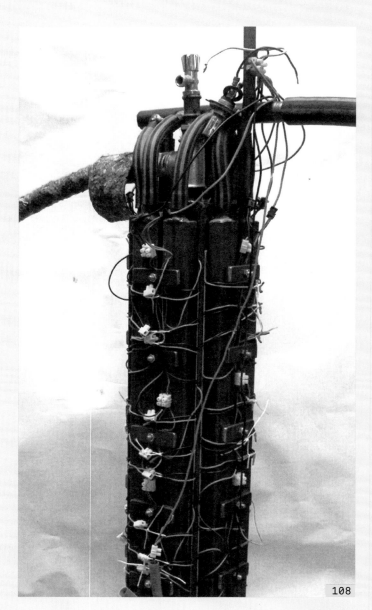

108

gibt es einen Raum, in dem zwei Maschinen stehen, die genug Elektrizität produzieren, um den häuslichen Bedarf zu decken und die Batterie eines elektrisch betriebenen Fahrzeuges zu laden. Schmidt ist der Meinung, dass die großen Photovoltaikanlagen nur entstehen, weil die Errichtung von PV-Anlagen weitläufig subventioniert wird. Solche urheberrechtlich geschützten Technologien machen die Menschen abhängig von Kapital intensiven Industriezweigen, die sich große Investitionen leisten können. (→B090) Elektrizitätserzeugung mittels Wärme und die Reduktion des Elektrizitätsverbrauches ohne Komforteinbuße ermöglichen eine Befreiung von dieser Abhängigkeit. Es ist wahr, dass diese Methode nicht hocheffizient ist, aber genauso wenig ist es eine Photovoltaikanlage. Um die unregelmäßige Verfügbarkeit der Sonnenenergie auszugleichen, zieht Schmidt es vor als Batterieersatz Hochtemperaturspeicher und/oder komprimierte Luft einzusetzen.

Ein solch extrem gut isoliertes Haus, wie es Werner Schmidt seit 1994 entwirft, kann ohne Heizung (Notheizung) auskommen, allerdings müssen die weiteren Energiebedürfnisse nach wie vor bedient werden. In den vergangenen zehn Jahren hat Schmidt Konzepte zu gänzlich oder teilweise autarken Häusern ausgearbeitet, und hat außerdem auch einige bekannte, mit Sonnenenergie betriebene und zuverlässige low-tech Maschinen neu entwickelt. Ein solches Haus würde einem erlauben, den Bedarf an fossilen Brennstoffen für das gesamte Haus zu einem guten Teil zu verringern, wenn nicht sogar gänzlich zu eliminieren. Die Technologien, die er bevorzugt, wurden in den letzten 120 Jahren komplett durch moderne Maschinen ersetzt. Jedoch gewinnen Stirling Maschinen derzeit wieder an Popularität, dank der banalen Tatsache, dass sie fast jede äußere Wärmequelle nutzen können, sehr geräuscharm sind, und dank ihrer Vielseitigkeit, Sicherheit und ihrer geringen Instandhaltungsansprüche. (→B066,124) Maschinen dieser Art sind tatsächlich recht primitiv und manchmal auch groß und schwer, aber ihr Betrieb ist einfach zu verstehen und sie können quasi von jedem örtlichen Hand-

109

110

werker hergestellt und repariert werden – und in der Tat hat Schmidt selbst einige entworfen und gebaut. (→■106,109-110) Schmidts Konzept vom autarken Haus kommt in einer Vielzahl von Skizzen und Zeichnungen zum Ausdruck. (→■111-112) Die gut isolierende Gebäudehülle (natürlich aus lasttragenden Strohballen) erlaubt dem Haus ohne Heizung auszukommen. Es ist ausgestattet mit konzentrierenden Sonnenkollektoren, mit deren Hilfe Wärmeträgeröl auf bis zu 300 Grad erhitzt und in einem Hochtemperaturspeicher einlagert wird; dies erlaubt zu kochen, zu backen, einen Absorptionskühlschrank zu betreiben, Brauchwasser zu erwärmen und Elektrizität zu erzeugen (mittels Stirling Motoren). Eis wird in der Winterzeit produziert und in einem Eisspeicher aufbewahrt. Frischwasser wird aus Regenwasser gewonnen, gefiltert, in einer Zisterne gespeichert und für den häuslichen Gebrauch verwendet. Eine Komposttoilette und eine Schilfkläranlage zur Reinigung des Grauwassers kommen zum Einsatz. Die Kühlung des Gebäudes im Sommer wird durch einen 5–8 m hohen, schwarz gestrichenen Kamin erzeugt, der die Raumluft bei Erwärmung des Kamins durch die Sonneneinstrahlung nach oben zieht und über ein Erdregister konstant gekühlte Luft nachzieht. In solch extremer und idealer Konfiguration wäre das autarke Haus in keinster Weise an irgendein öffentliches Netzwerk angeschlossen. An der HTW Chur wurde berechnet, dass ein derartiges Haus nach 15 Jahren mehr Energie erzeugt hätte, als es zu seiner Erstellung benötigt. Sein eigener Wasserverbrauch wäre (theoretisch) nur die Wassermenge, die es für die Herstellung des Hauses braucht. (→B056)
Andere Skizzen variieren in den Details etwas vom oben beschriebenen Schema; eine Skizze beinhaltet einen Notofen, der über Gasflaschen betrieben werden kann, oder Elektrizität, die aus verschiedenen Quellen gewonnen (Solarzellen, Windräder, Wasserräder) und in Akkus gespeichert wird. Im Jahre 2004 erstellte Schmidt eine Reihe von Energiekonzepten für ein autarkes Haus, das er *Dampfhaus*, (→■113) *Schwerkrafthaus* (→■114) und *Lufthaus* nannte. (→■115) Die

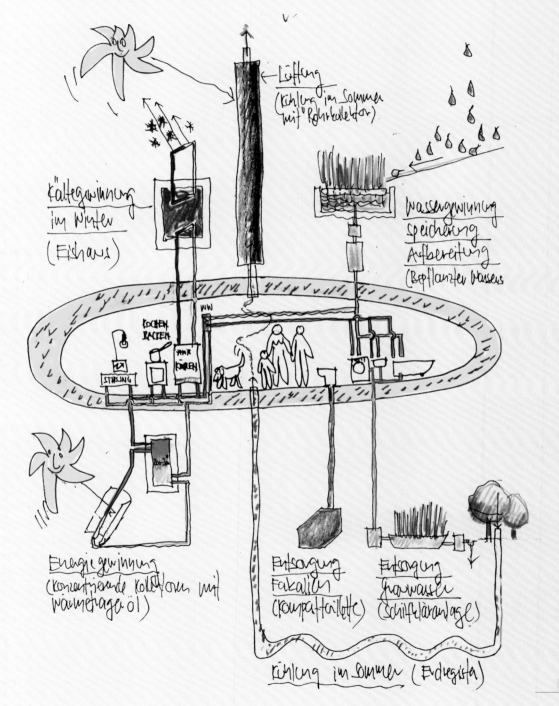

Lüftung
(Kühlung im Sommer
mit Rohrkollektor)

Kältegewinnung
im Winter
(Eishaus)

Wassergewinnung
Speicherung
Aufbereitung
(Bepflanzter Wassers

KOCHEN
BACKEN

STIRLING

WW

KÜHLEN

Energiegewinnung
(konzentrierende Kollektoren mit
Wärmeträgeröl)

Entsorgung
Fäkalien
(Kompattoilette)

Entsorgung
Grauwasser
(Schilfkläranlage)

Kühlung im Sommer (Erdregister)

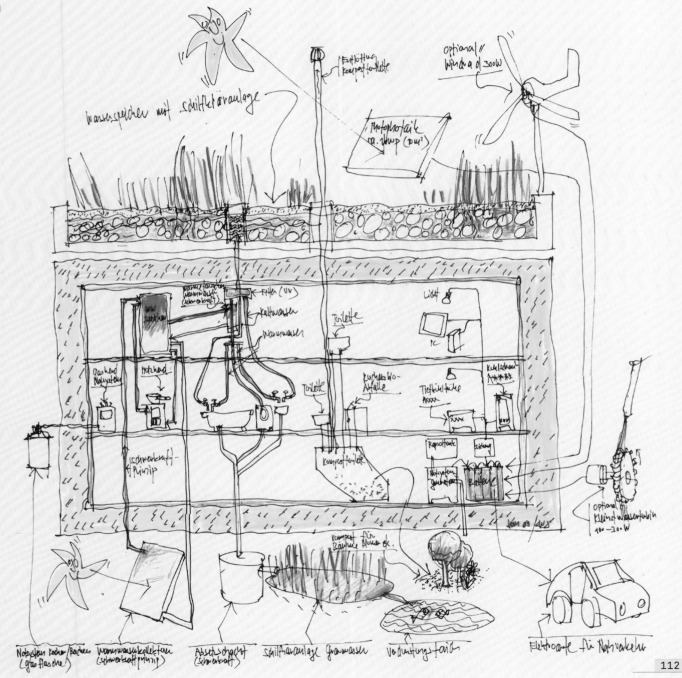

Wasserspeicher mit Schilfkläranlage

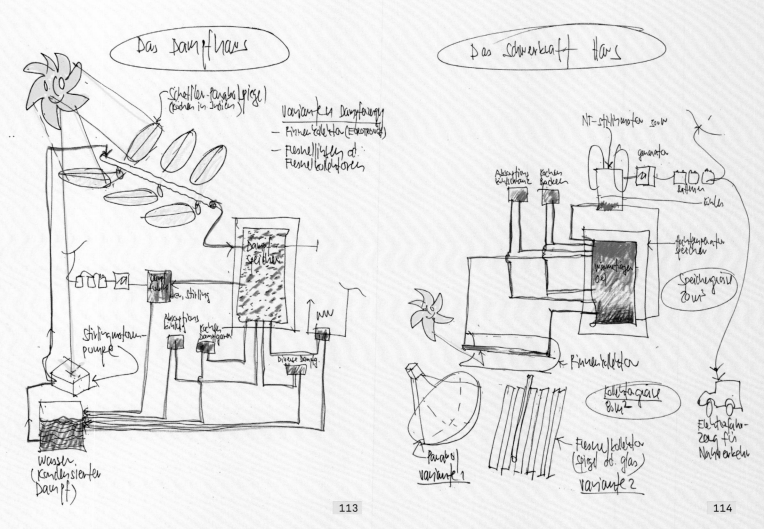

solar collectors which heat a heat transfer oil that is stored in a tank; this allows one to cook, bake, operate an absorption refrigerator, heat sanitary water, and produce electrical power (by way of a Stirling engine). Ice is produced in winter operation and stored in a freezer. Fresh water is collected from rain, filtered, stored in a cistern, and employed for all domestic uses. A dry toilet and a constructed wetland for greywater treatment deal with waste. Ventilation is provided by a 5–8 m high, black-painted stack which sucks stale air away, and an

Sonne ist immer die zentrale Energiequelle und die Konzepte unterscheiden sich in der Art und Weise, wie sie die Energie umwandeln, transportieren und speichern. Beziehungsweise beinhalten sie Dampf, Wärmeträgeröl (beides würde in Tanks gespeichert) und Druckluft (gelagert in 5–10 m³ Tanks mit 30 MPa). Auch hier würde ein Teil der Energie direkt verwendet (Dampf würde den Steamer und andere Apparate steuern und Apparate zum Kochen erhitzen oder den Absorptions-kühlschrank steuern; heißes Öl würde den Ofen und Herd

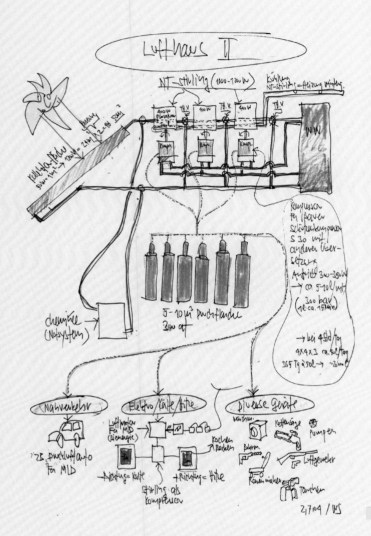

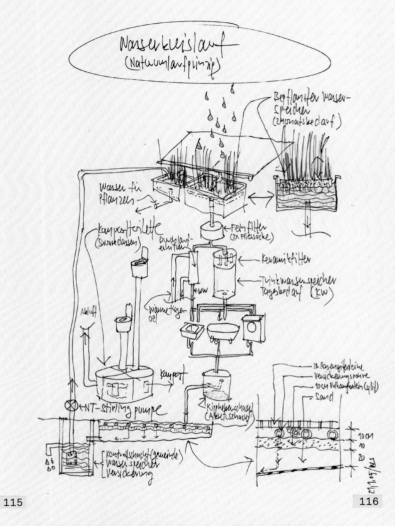

earth tube which provides fresh air at a stabilised temperature – moreover, the pipe which takes fresh air to the stove can be used in summer to cool it down and transform it into some sort of 'coolness storage.' In such extreme and ideal configuration, the 'autarkic house' would not be connected to any public utility network. At the HTW Chur, it has been calculated that after 15 years such a house would have produced more energy than was necessary for its construction, while its only (theoretical) water consumption at any time would be the amount

erhitzen; Druckluft würde Pumpen, Sägen, Waschmaschine, Spülmaschine, Rasenmäher, etc. antreiben oder auch ein Auto). Währenddessen bleiben einige andere Dinge elektrisch angetrieben wie bisher, mit dem einzigen Unterschied, dass sie über eine Dampf- oder Stirlingmaschine oder einen Kompressor betrieben wären.

Das *Lufthaus* ist das weiter entwickelte Konzept mit verschiedenen Variationen. In der einfachsten Variante wäre ein Stirling Motor im Fokus eines Parabolspiegels platziert;

needed to build it. (→B056)

Other sketches differ in a few details from the above-described scheme; one would include an emergency stove fuelled with bottled gas, and electricity generated from various sources (solar cells, wind turbine, water turbine) would charge accumulators.

In 2004 Schmidt drew a number of energy concepts for autarkic houses, which he dubbed *Dampfhaus* ('steam house'), (→■113) *Schwerkraft Haus* ('gravity house'), (→■114) and *Lufthaus* ('air house'). (→■115) The sun is always the energy source, whereas they differ in the way they transfer and store energy, respectively: steam, heat transfer oil (both would be stored in insulated tanks) and compressed air (stored in 5–10 m³ tanks at 30 MPa). Here too, there would be some direct uses of the energy vehicle (steam would operate a steamer and other appliances, as well as heating other cooking appliances and powering an absorption refrigerator, etc.; hot oil would heat the cooker and oven, etc.; pressurized air would operate machinery such as pump, saw, washing machine, dishwasher, lawn-mower, etc., as well as a car), while the remainder would be electricity-propelled as usual, with the only difference being that this would be generated by a steam engine, a Stirling engine, or a compressed air engine.

The *Lufthaus* is the more developed scheme, with a number of different versions. In the most basic one, a single Stirling engine would be placed at the focus of a parabolic mirror; in a more advanced one, a 50 m² array of solar collectors would produce enough heat to operate a set of three 400 W Stirling engines: in both cases, their scope would be the compression of air.

Finally, some sketches from 2009 concentrate in a single 'organism' the different cycles intervening in the operation of the autarkic house (water, waste, air, energy) and depict the 'energy supply module.' This would combine the heat transfer oil concept (such oil would be used directly for applications which require heat, and to produce steam to compress air) and

in einer fortgeschrittenen Variante erzeugt ein 50 m² großes Solarkollektorenfeld genügend Energie, um drei 400 W Stirling Motoren anzutreiben. In beiden Fällen wäre das Ziel Druckluft. Einige Skizzen von 2009 beschreiben einen einzigen Organismus, bei dem verschiedene Kreisläufe für den Betrieb des autarken Hauses ineinander greifen (Wasser, Abfall, Luft und Energie). Sie führen das Energieliefermodul zusammen, welches aus der Kombination des Wärmeträgeröls (ein solches Öl würde für Geräte zum Einsatz kommen, die die direkte Hitze benötigen, und um Dampf für die Druckluft zu erzeugen) und dem Druckluftkonzept (Druckluft würde bei 2 MPa gespeichert und für die Produktion von Elektrizität genutzt werden) besteht. Es gibt einige Skizzen aus den Jahren 2004 und 2005, die Details wie das Energiemanagement des ganzen Systems beschreiben (→■117) (so zum Beispiel indem sie ein 24 V Gleichstrom beinhalten), und Wassermanagement. (→■116) Eine der jüngeren Skizzen beinhaltet unter anderem eine Erläuterung zum Mehrfachfiltersystem, welches unterschiedliche Frischwasserqualitäten liefern könnte, und das die Reinigung mittels eines Setztanks und die anschließende Filtration des Schmutzwassers ermöglicht.

Das fortschrittlichste Energiekonzept aus dem Jahre 2009 zeigt einen Kreislauf aus konzentrierenden Sonnenkollektoren (und ein Notfallsystem mit Stückholzofen und Speicher) verbunden mit einem Hochtemperaturspeicher, in dem das Wärmeträgeröl gespeichert werden könnte. Von hier aus würde es mittels Schwerkraft bei sinkender Temperatur an die Kocheinheiten, einen Steamer und einen Absorptionskühlschrank (dessen Gefrierfach im Winter über einen Kälte-Kollektor versorgt würde) geführt. Dieses Konzept beinhaltet einen Dampfgenerator, der zwei Dampfmaschinen betreiben würde, die wiederum elektrische Energie erzeugten, die in Batterien gespeichert werden könnte. Diese Batterien würden über eine Windkraftanlage und/oder eine 5 m² große Solaranlage und/oder ein Wasserrad und/oder ein Kohlenwasserstoff-Elektrogenerator gespeist. Und zu guter Letzt könnten Abgase

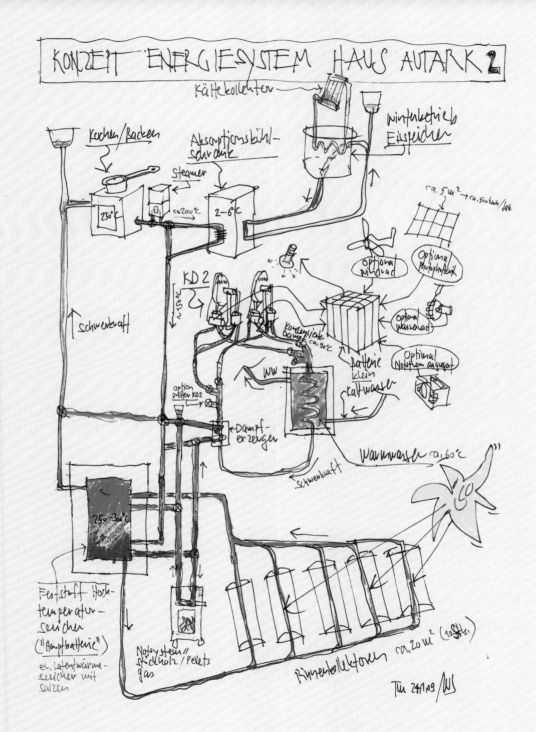

KONZEPT ENERGIESYSTEM HAUS AUTARK 2

the pressurized air concept (compressed air would be stored at 2 MPa and used to produce electricity as needed). There are also some sketches from 2004 and 2005 which detail some parts of the whole system, such as energy management (→■117) (for instance, including a 24 V, direct current net) and water management. (→■116) One of the latter sketches contains, among other things, an explanation of the multi-step filtering arrangement, which would allow varying qualities of fresh water to be obtained, and also purification via a settling tank and the subsequent percolation of greywater.

The most advanced energy concept, from 2009, shows an integrated circuit from linear, concentrating solar collectors (and, occasionally, from an emergency wood-burning boiler) to a superinsulated tank, where the heat transfer fluid would be stored. From here, it would be delivered by gravity at progressively lower temperatures to the cooking unit, a steamer, an absorption refrigerator (whose freezer unit would be fed by a 'coolness collector' in winter), and a steam generator which would operate two steam engines generating electric power to be stored in a set of batteries. These might be charged by an optional wind turbine and/or 5 m² photovoltaic cells and/or water turbine and/or a hydrocarbon-fuelled electricity generator as well. Finally, condensed exhaust steam would exchange heat with sanitary water.

Such concept studies can be traced back to the 'Self-sufficient [actually, minimal energy consumption] dormitory for girls' Schmidt proposed in 2000 to his then most important client, Disentis abbey. Unfortunately, the proposal was not accepted; instead the abbey decided to launch a competition to substitute the dilapidated 'Unterhaus' outside the monastery precinct, on the town's main street. The project of his fellow Graubünden architect, Gion Caminada, was chosen. His building is attractive and provides its young residents with dignified and comfortable spaces, but it is reported to be quite expensive as far as running costs are concerned.

After the Disentis dormitory concept, Schmidt had a few

ihre Wärme an das Brauchwasser abgeben.

Diese Konzeptstudien können bis zum Entwurf für ein autarkes Mädchenpensionat zurückverfolgt werden, den Schmidt im Jahre 2000 seinem damals wichtigsten Kunden, dem Kloster Disentis, vorstellte. Leider wurde dieser Vorschlag nicht angenommen; stattdessen beschloss das Kloster einen Wettbewerb für einen Ersatzbau für das marode ‚Unterhaus' Gebäude außerhalb der Klosteranlage entlang der Hauptstraße des Dorfes auszuschreiben. Gewählt wurde der Entwurf des Bündner Architektenkollegen Gion A. Caminada. Sein Entwurf ist sehr ansprechend und bietet seinen jungen Bewohnern schöne und bequeme Räumlichkeiten, allerdings sollen die Energiekosten für Heizung und Elektrizität recht hoch sein.

Nach dem Konzeptvorschlag für das Mädchenpensionat hatte Schmidt einige Gelegenheiten, bei denen er Teile seiner Idee vom autarken Haus entwickeln und realisieren konnte. So im Jahre 2002 als Schmidt als Gastprofessor an der Freien Universität Bozen dozierte und wo er seinen Studenten die Aufgabe gab, solarbetriebene Haushaltsapparate zu entwerfen und umzusetzen. Diese wurden der Öffentlichkeit präsentiert und auf einer Messe vorgeführt. Einer der Entwürfe war Kylmä, (→■118) ein Kühlschrank, der mit Hilfe von verdunstendem Wasser an der Außenwand des Kühlschranks, und eines Luftzirkulationssystems um seine Hülle herum, welches durch die Druckdifferenz eines Erdregisters und eines hohen Kamins erzeugt wird, den erwünschten Kühleffekt liefert.

Der Kühlschrank war mit verschiedenen Fächern ausgestattet und einer durchsichtigen Klappe verschlossen, so dass der Benutzer immer nur einen Teil öffnen musste. Der Prototyp jedoch enthält nur eine große Front. Außerdem gab drei Kochgeräte, die Sonnenenergie von Röhrenkollektoren mittels Wärmeträgeröl nutzten:

- Huluma2: (→■119) eine Kochplatte, die aus drei horizontalen, rotierenden Elementen bestand, das mittlere Element diente zum Kochen, die beiden anderen konnten hinzugeschalten werden (die Temperatur wurde über ein Ventil reguliert). Der

118

119

120

occasions to develop some parts of his idea of a self-sufficient house. The first notable case was in 2002, when he was invited as a guest professor to the Free University of Bozen, and gave his students the assignment of designing and building solar domestic appliances. These were shown to the public and tested on the occasion of a commercial fair. They included *Kylmä* (→■118) (a refrigerator operating thanks to the cooling effect of the evaporation of water on the external wall, and air circulation around the casing created by the pressure difference between an underground pipe and a high chimney. The fridge was designed to include several compartments with a glazed door each, so that the user would only need to open one at a time, but the prototype actually had a single door) and three cooking appliances operated by heat transfer oil obtained from high-performance solar collectors:

- *Huluma 2*, (→■119) a hotplate made of three rotating, horizontal elements: the middle one for cooking (temperature was regulated by a valve), while the lower and upper lid could be closed and used as supports. The prototype showed that the design was not satisfactory, because it dispersed too much energy.
- *Solarofen*. (→■120) Superinsulation and the combination of hot oil storage and baking in a single device made this oven highly efficient. It required no pre-heating, as energy was immediately available.
- *Sonnengrill*. The oil tank under the gridiron acted as a heat store and thus could bridge short sun outages.

In the following year, Schmidt was one of the designers invited to La Habana by Hansgrohe, to envisage new forms of dealing with the issue of water in the residential environment. He elaborated two sensual concepts:
- *Self-sufficient icehouse*: (→■123-124) a cave-like room made of ice for hot climates, in which to refresh oneself or to use as 'coolness storage' for the rest of the house. Ice would be produced by a high-tech parabolic mirror, a reversed Stirling-engine pump and an absorption refrigerator, and would con

Prototyp zeigte, dass das Design nicht zufriedenstellend war, da die Platte zu viel Energie benötigte.
- *Solarofen*: (→■120) die Superisolation und die Kombination aus Wärmeträgeröl und Backen in einem Gerät machte diesen Entwurf hoch effizient. Es bedurfte hierbei keines Vorheizens, zumal die Energie direkt verfügbar war.
- *Sonnengrill*: der Öltank unter der Heizplatte funktionierte als Wärmespeicher und sorgte für ausreichend Energie bei kurzfristigen Sonnenausfällen.

Im darauffolgenden Jahr wurde Schmidt von Hansgrohe in La Habana eingeladen, um neue Formen zum Thema Wasser für Wohnhäuser zu entwickeln. Er erarbeitete zwei sensuelle Konzepte:
- *autarkes Eishaus*: (→■123-124) ein höhlenartiger Raum aus Eis, geeignet für heiße Gegenden, in dem man sich erfrischen konnte oder der als Kühllager für das restliche Haus diente. Das Eis würde durch einen high-tech Parabolspiegel, eine umgekehrte Stirlingmaschine und einen Wärmetauscherkühlschrank erzeugt werden, und würde in künstlerisch gestalteten Röhren Eis produzieren. Das System wäre selbstregulierend – je mehr Sonneneinstrahlung, desto mehr Eis würde produziert werden.
- *autarkes Wasserhaus*: (→■122) Eine Einheit, die hauptsächlich wasserverbrauchende Haushaltsgeräte umfasst. Vorfabrizierte Module, die die einzelnen Funktionen (WC, Waschtisch, Dusche, etc.) enthalten, wären gemäß den Bedürfnissen der Verbraucher an ein Zentralanschluss angeschlossen. Badewanne, Dusche, Waschbecken, Regale Toilettenpapierhalter, etc. wären gänzlich aus transluzenten, schalenförmigen Teilen gebaut (zum Beispiel Fiberglas verstärktes Polyester) und mit einem einlaminierten LED Licht beleuchtet. Das Ergebnis wäre eine Art Blase, eine Leuchtskulptur, die frei im Raum platziert werden kann. In der Theorie wären diese ,Wasserhäuser' modifizierbar, aber weder Werner Schmidts eigenes Badezimmer, (→■025) welches dem ,Habana' Konzept sehr ähnelt, noch die nachfolgende ,Wunderbox' (→§07) sind derart gebaut.

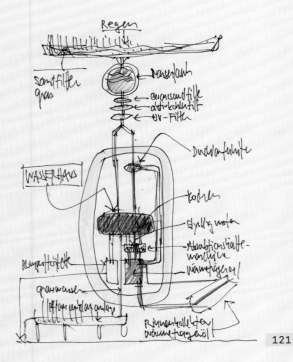

121

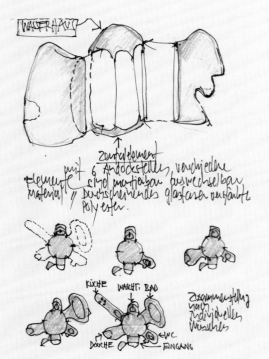

122

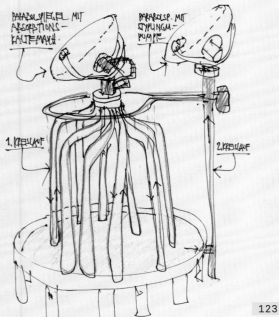

123

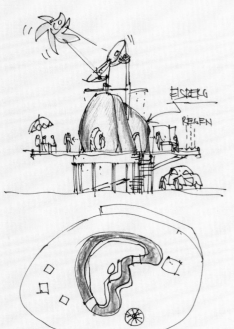

124

densate on artistically-shaped circuits. The system would be self-regulating; the more the sun shines, the more ice is produced.

- *Self-sufficient water house*: (→■122) a unit enclosing most water-using domestic appliances. Prefabricated modules containing the different fixtures would be attached to a core according to the users' preferences. Bathtub, shower, washbasin, shelves, toilet paper holders, etc., would be entirely built into thin shells of translucent material (e.g. glass-fibre reinforced polyester), in which the LED lighting would be laminated. The result would be a kind of bubble, a luminous sculpture to be freely placed in the space of a room. In theory, such a 'waterhouse' would be modifiable; but neither the bathroom of Werner Schmidt's own house, (→■025) which has much in common with the Habana concept, nor the subsequent 'wonder boxes' (→§07) are.

While Schmidt has succeeded in building several houses whose space heating requirements are close to nil and which use abundant, renewable, low-embodied-energy, beautiful materials, the more holistic concepts I have been discussing in this chapter have produced no built result so far. Schmidt is intensifying his efforts to experiment with autarkic houses, and one of his clients will probably soon accord him enough trust to have one built; or he will build one for himself close to his atelier. Only after a few attempts will it be possible to see which solutions are viable and which ones present some practical problems.

Almost 40 years ago, the editors of *Radical Technology* had already observed that "Trying to guarantee high standards of performance in highly autonomous systems is very expensive. Trying to reduce costs at a high level of autonomy leads to lower standards of performance. Trying to reduce costs at a high level of performance leads to lower levels of autonomy." (→B022:159) This state of affairs has not changed. Choices are therefore to be made if 'autonomy' is not to be restricted to an

Während Schmidt bereits einige Häuser realisieren konnte, deren Heizwärmebedarf praktisch gleich null ist, und in denen eine Vielzahl an schönen, ökologischen Materialien mit geringem Anteil an Grauer Energie enthalten sind, konnte er die ganzheitlicheren Konzepte, die im Kapitel oben beschrieben sind, bislang so noch nicht realisieren. Schmidt ist dabei, die Anstrengungen hin zu einem autarken Haus auszubauen, und vielleicht fasst einer seiner Bauherren genug Vertrauen, um ein solches bauen zu lassen – oder Schmidt wird sich selbst eines neben seinem Bürogebäude errichten. Nach einigen Versuchen wird sich herausstellen, welche Lösungen brauchbar sind und welche in der Nutzung Probleme mit sich bringen. Bereits vor 40 Jahren haben die Autoren von *Radical Technology* bereits beobachtet, dass „der Versuch, hohe Leistungsstandards und gleichzeitig autarke Systeme zu garantieren, sehr teuer ist. Der Versuch, die Kosten bei gleichzeitig hohem Anspruch an Autarkie zu senken, führt automatisch zu einer Leistungsverminderung des Gebäudes. Versucht man die Kosten trotz eines hohen Grades an (Energie-)Leistung gering zu halten, führt dies zu einem geringeren Level an Autarkie." (→B022:159) Diese Sachlage hat sich nicht verändert. Entscheidungen müssen getroffen werden, wenn Autarkie nicht nur auf eine kleine Zahl wohlhabender, aufgeklärter Menschen beschränkt sein soll. Und vielmehr muss geklärt werden, unter welchen Umständen es sinnvoller ist, die Bedürfnisse durch öffentliche und wann durch autonome Einrichtungen zu stillen? Sollte eine solche Entscheidung nur auf Basis des Sich-leisten-könnens getroffen werden? Oder auf Basis von Überzeugung? Ist es eine Frage der existenziellen Unabhängigkeit oder des Erkennens der Last, die durch ein bestimmtes Entwicklungsmodell der Zahlungsbilanz und der politischen Abhängigkeit eines Landes entsteht? Sicherlich müssten einige Trends ins Rollen gebracht werden, und dann braucht es ständig Pioniere, die mit neuen Entwürfen und alternativen Lebenskonzepten experimentieren. Schmidts Ziel ist es, ein kostenoptimiertes, autarkes Gebäude realisieren zu können.

élite of certainly rich and perhaps enlightened people. More-over, under what circumstances should one accord preference to public servicing instead of providing autonomously for all needs? Should the decision be taken only on the basis of what one can afford, or on the basis of one's beliefs? Is it a matter of existential independence, or a recognition of the burden caused by a certain development model on a country's balance of payments and political dependency? Certainly, some trends have to be anticipated, and there is a constant need for pioneers who experiment with new designs or alternative life-styles. Schmidt's goal is to realise a cost-optimised, self-sufficient building.

But at the societal level, a general behavioural shift away from consumerism would have a much larger impact than elaborate systems, allowing a few people to live in a completely autonomous way. There is a risk that autonomy be interpreted as "'privatisation,' going now beyond personal transport, personal laundry, personal garden, to personal power plant, water works, sewage farm." (→B022:161) Of course, there are remote places "where network costs from central plants are high, [while] ambient resources are abundant" and diffuse: there, it would not make much sense to collect, concentrate and redistribute them again. However, in cities and highly built-up areas, technological and social efforts should give priority to the strengthening of solidarity, the revitalisation of communal (physical as well as intangible) facilities, and the user-involved rehabilitation of existing buildings. (→§10) In cases of acute resource crisis, the point might not be to live comfortably – it could be instead a matter of survival. (→B046)

Auf dem sozialen Level betrachtet, hätte ein genereller Verhaltenswandel weg vom Konsum wesentlich höhere Auswirkungen, als das Erarbeiten von Systemen, die nur einer kleinen Anzahl von Menschen erlauben, komplett autark zu leben. Es besteht die Gefahr, dass „die Autarkie in Richtung Privatisierung geht – mein persönliches Transportmittel, meine persönliche Waschmaschine, mein persönlicher Garten, mein persönliches Kraftwerk, Wasser- und Abwassersystem", (→B022:161) und dass die essentiellen immateriellen Elemente, die der menschlichen Existenz Bedeutung verleihen, übersehen werden. Natürlich gibt es abgelegene Orte, „wo die Netzwerkkosten für zentrale Werksanlagen sehr hoch sind, während unmittelbare Ressourcen zur Genüge vorhanden und greifbar sind." Dort würde es nicht viel Sinn machen, sie zusammen zu tragen und zu bündeln und sie dann schließlich wieder zu verteilen. Jedoch in Städten und in gut ausgebauten Gebieten sollten technologische und soziale Anstrengungen vorangetrieben werden, die die Solidarität, die Wiederbelebung von gemeinschaftlichen Anlagen und die Nutzer einschließende Wiederbelebung bestehender Gebäude stärken. (→§10) Im Falle einer akuten Ressourcenkrise könnte in solchen Gemeinschaften nicht der Komfort ausschlaggebend sein, sondern eine Frage des Überlebens. (→B046)

ENVIRONMENTAL IMPACT ⌐
ÖKOLOGISCHER FUSSABDRUCK

In many fields the lowest-impact, most-efficient models might be run on a communitarian scale only – and in any case, at the political level preference should be given to changes promising the widest overall impact. It is both a matter of critical mass and of approach, because "autonomy implies also responsibility, solidarity, and belonging." (→B022:136) It is worth remembering that none amongst the most influential autonomy thinkers (Illich, Schumacher, even Seymour) speculated that self-sufficiency was an issue to be dealt with the individual or family level – on the contrary, it is only achievable in a co-operative way.

Social and economic sustainability are very relevant, but the Vales argue that environmental sustainability should be the first priority. Obviously this goal calls for a complete reconsideration of lifestyles, since "making just one change, such as walking to work rather than driving, may not be enough." (→B114:106) A complete picture of autonomy should take into account several facets, including energy, food, means of conveyance, frequency of travel, diet, and waste as well as household goods, clothes, etc. Work patterns should change as much as the place of work. Significant savings might be achieved growing food at home. (→B113:212) Health and the ecological footprint would benefit from people spending more time outdoors. There is a greater need for behavioural changes rather than technological innovations – and incidentally the first cost nothing. For instance, in the Vales's words, "the many words written about rainwater collection in pursuit of the sustainable house would be better spent exhorting people to change their behaviour in ordinary houses." (→B114:157)

In vielen Bereichen könnten Modelle nach dem Prinzip der kleinsten Auswirkung und größten Effizienz nur auf einer gemeinschaftlichen Ebene funktionieren – und in manchen Fällen müsste auf politischer Ebene das Augenmerk auf den Veränderungen liegen, die die umfassendste Wirkungskraft versprechen. Es ist beides eine Frage der kritischen Masse und der Herangehensweise, da „Autonomie Verantwortung, Solidarität und Zugehörigkeit voraussetzt". (→B022:136) Hierzu muss man sich in Erinnerung rufen, dass unter den einflussreichsten Autarkie-Denkern (weder Illich, Schumacher, noch Seymour) keiner die These vertritt, dass Autarkie eine Aufgabe ist, die auf individueller oder familiärer Ebene gelöst werden kann – im Gegenteil: erreichbar ist sie nur durch einen gemeinschaftlichen Weg.

Soziale und ökonomische Nachhaltigkeit sind sehr relevant, aber die Vales sind fest davon überzeugt, dass die Nachhaltigkeit in Bezug auf unsere Umwelt die absolute Priorität besitzt. Offensichtlich fordert dieses Ziel eine komplett neue Betrachtung unseres Lebensstils, zumal „es nicht ausreicht, nur eine Änderung vorzunehmen, wie zum Beispiel anstelle mit dem Auto zu Fuß zur Arbeit zu gehen." (→B114:106) Ein komplettes Bild von Autonomie sollte viele Facetten miteinbeziehen, wie Energie, Essen, Transportmittel, Häufigkeit von Reisen, Ernährung, Abfall, ebenso wie Haushaltsmittel, Kleidung, etc. Arbeitsmuster müssten sich ändern, zum Beispiel in Bezug auf den Standort der Arbeit. Signifikante Einsparungen könnten durch den Eigenanbau von Nahrungsmitteln erzielt werden. (→B113:212) Die Gesundheit und der ökologische Fußabdruck würden sich verbessern,

Unfortunately, sustainability-oriented changes are often limited to just one facet, with grotesque results. Peter van Dresser reported of "wealthy drop outs who have bought an expensive wind generator and set it up on top of a dome while still running enormous four-wheel drive vehicles which use a hundred times more energy every day than the wind generator delivers." (→B022:131) This was forty years ago, but the fashion has merely switched from Fuller domes to straw houses. Buildings with extremely low embodied as well as operating energy cannot justify wastes in other sectors. Ugo Sasso used to tell the story of a South Tyrolean family who, thanks to their 'KlimaHaus A' house, spent so little money on heating that they could now afford a holiday in the Caribbean every winter. It would simply make no sense to live in a brand new *Passivhaus* in an 'unspoilt' place somewhere up in the mountains and then commute by car to a city tens of kilometres away. What counts is the global ecological balance, not only the energy performance of the building.

This said, in the building sector one should aim for the reduction of ecological impact not only in terms of energy consumption during building use. Both designers and residents should adopt a holistic vision, which is sometimes obstructed by an all-too-respectful consideration of calculations and certificates. (→§09) In fact, Minergie and Passivhaus standards do not include aspects such as embodied energy – and consumption is expressed in kWh/m² per annum, not kWh per capita per annum. Moreover, "honest researchers will admit that any of [the five possible theoretical] approaches [to assessing the thermal performance of walls] provides only an estimate." (→B063:187)

'Sustainability' in buildings might be the result of an engagement in several issues: (→B126:181)
- responsibility for all the upstream and downstream impacts of decisions;
- respect for site, minimisation of disruption to the ecosystem;
- simplicity and comprehensibility of design;

wenn Menschen mehr an der frischen Luft wären. Es gibt eine wesentlich größere Notwendigkeit in der Verhaltensänderung, als in der Entwicklung neuer Technologien – und im übrigen kostet ersteres nichts. Oder wie die Vales es formulieren – „die vielen Worte, die bereits gesprochen wurden in Bezug auf die Regenwassergewinnung im Zusammenhang eines nachhaltigen Gebäudes, wären stattdessen besser angebracht in der Ermahnung der Menschen, ihr Verhalten in gewöhnlichen Häusern zu ändern." (→B114:157)

Bedauerlicherweise sind Veränderungen in Richtung Nachhaltigkeit oftmals nur auf eine Sache reduziert, mit grotesken Resultaten. Peter von Dresser berichtete von „reichen Aussteigern, die sich eine teure Windkraftanlage kauften und sie auf einer Kuppel platzierten, während sie gleichzeitig nach wie vor mit riesigen, Vierrad angetriebenen Fahrzeugen fuhren, die jeden Tag hundert Mal mehr Energie verbrauchen, als das Windrad liefern kann." (→B022:131) Das war vor 40 Jahren, aber der Trend hat nur von geodätischen Kuppeln zu Strohballenhäusern gewechselt. Gebäude mit außergewöhnlich geringer Grauer Energie und geringen Betriebskosten rechtfertigen nicht die Müllproduktion in anderen Bereichen. Ugo Sasso erzählte die Geschichte von einer Südtiroler Familie, die nun dank ihres ‚Klimahaus A' nun so wenig Geld für ihr Heizsystem ausgab, dass sie sich fortan jeden Winter einen Urlaub auf den Karibischen Inseln gönnte. Es macht einfach keinen Sinn in einem brandneuen Passivhaus, in einer unberührten Umgebung irgendwo oben in den Bergen zu leben, um dann jeden Tag etliche Kilometer in die nächstgelegene Stadt zu fahren. Was zählt ist die globale ökologische Bilanz, nicht nur die Energiebilanz eines Gebäudes.

Dies bedeutet, dass man im Bauwesen auf die Reduktion der ökologischen Auswirkungen abzielen sollte, nicht nur im Sinne von Energieverbrauch solange das Gebäude in Betrieb ist. Sowohl die Gestalter als auch die Bewohner müssten sich eine ganzheitliche Betrachtungsweise aneignen, die manchmal etwas von einer allzu großen Gewichtung von

- building techniques favouring non-industrial supplies and self-construction work;
- limitation of dimensions: "building a larger house will offset the ecological benefits of using environmentally superior materials." (→B040:220) Moreover, a small house facilitates social relationships. The Vales affirm that "by concentrating on trying to improve design and building technologies and materials, we may have missed a very important point. To reduce our environmental impact in terms of footprint we need (...) living in and using smaller buildings. (...) smaller buildings also cost less, so there will be money left over to invest in the more expensive renewable energy systems;" (→B114:189)
- design for long life expectancy, which implies avoiding fashionable looks, providing good weather protection, (→§08) and preferring durable materials and "trusted ways of doing things over the experimental and the daring" in order to facilitate future repair; (→B114:189)
- passive design, conserving thermal energy and working with climate in order to minimise the total energy consumption during operational life and doing without mechanical systems or reducing them to backup systems. (→§08) Moreover, "a properly designed passive building should inherently be more comfortable than a properly designed mechanical building." (→B040:44-45) Such a purpose may include seeking an optimal surface area / volume ratio, and a simple spatial concept;
- efficiency of systems and provision of energy-transforming systems, without much regard for cost-effectiveness (→B114:352) as long as they make use of renewable sources;
- minimisation of water usage;
- minimisation of waste, in particular during building work, and design for reuse or, if not feasible, for recycling and biodegradation;
- minimisation of embodied energy and resource depletion. According to many, "the supply and specification of materials is at the heart of green building," as "the use of manufactured

Berechnungen und Zertifikaten verblendet ist. (→§09) In der Tat beinhalten Minergie- und Passivhaus-Standards nicht den Aspekt der Grauen Energie – und der Verbrauch wird in kWh/m² pro Jahr berechnet und nicht kWh pro Kopf und Jahr. Vielmehr sogar „geben ehrliche Forscher zu, dass jeder der fünf theoretisch möglichen Annäherungsversuche, um die thermischen Abläufe einer Wand zu simulieren, nur eine Schätzung darstellen." (→B063:187)
Nachhaltigkeit in Gebäuden könnte das Ergebnis aus verschiedenen Bereichen sein: (→B126:181)
- Verantwortlichkeit für sämtliche Auswirkungen von Entscheidungen in Bezug auf Herstellung und Wiederverwertung (cradle-to-cradle Prinzip)
- Respekt vor dem Standort, Minimierung der Störung des Ökosystems
- Einfachheit und Umfänglichkeit des Entwurfs
- Gebäudetechnik, die nicht-industrielle Komponenten und Eigenbau bevorzugt
- Begrenzung der Dimensionen: „ein größeres Haus zu bauen wird den ökologischen Gewinn durch die Verwendung von umweltschonenden Materialien aufheben." (→B040:220) Vielmehr fördert ein kleines Haus die sozialen Beziehungen. Die Vales bestätigen, dass „durch den Fokus auf den Versuch, das Design, die Gebäudetechnologie und die Materialien zu optimieren, ein wichtiger Aspekt verpasst wurde. Um unsere Auswirkungen auf die Umwelt im Sinne des ökologischen Fußabdrucks zu reduzieren, müssen wir in kleineren Gebäuden leben. Kleinere Gebäude kosten auch weniger, so dass Geld übrig bleibt, um es in teurere erneuerbare Energiesysteme zu investieren." (→B114:189)
- Design welches auf Langlebigkeit konzipiert ist und welches kein Augenmerk auf modisches Aussehen richtet, guten Schutz vor Witterung bietet, (→§08) und welches dauerhafte Materialien und „eine zuverlässige Handhabung der experimentellen und waghalsigen Vorgehensweise bevorzugt", um spätere Reparaturen zu vereinfachen. (→B114:189)

125

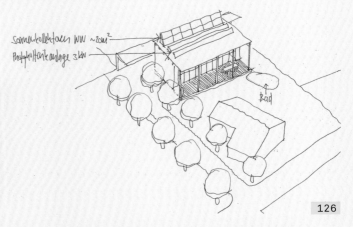

126

and imported materials does have an environmental penalty." (→B126:9) Preference should be accorded to products made from renewable or abundant materials, and those which use raw materials more efficiently, (→B126:16) much more so if one considers that almost everywhere safe, inexpensive and low-energy materials naturally occur which can fit modern building requirements. (→B127:39) Among the variables they manipulate, designers should be more aware of a house's weight and embodied energy. Examples of low-energy design choices include specifying hard floors, concentrating fittings, and avoiding cellars and underground garages;
- avoidance of materials and methods that cause pollution. Buildings should be bio-compatible, i.e. in accord with life and its laws (before, during and after their service life), and should not threaten the health of workers and occupants, as Baubiologie teaches. (→B125) Relevance should be recogn-

- Passives Design, welches die Energie speichert und mit dem Klima arbeitet, um den Gesamtenergieverbrauch während der Laufzeit zu minimieren, und um ohne mechanische Systeme auszukommen oder sie auf ein Backup-System zu reduzieren. (→§08) „Ein angemessener Entwurf eines passiven Gebäudes sollte von Natur aus gemütlicher sein als ein entsprechend gut geplantes mechanisches Haus." (→B040:44-45) Eine solche Absicht könte ein Abwägen des optimalen Oberfläche-Volumen-Verhältnisses und ein einfaches Raumkonzept beinhalten.
- Effizienz von Systemen und die Verfügbarkeit von Energie umwandelnden Systemen ohne großes Augenmerk auf Kosteneffizienz, (→B114:352) solange sie Gebrauch von erneuerbaren Ressourcen machen.
- Minimierung des Wasserverbrauchs.
- Minimierung der Abfälle insbesondere während der Bauphase und ein Konzept für die Wiederverwertung oder falls nicht realisierbar ein Konzept für Recycling und biologische Zersetzung.
- Minimierung der Grauen Energie und des Ressourcenabbaus. „Im Kern des grünen Bauens steht die Versorgung und Spezifizierung von Materialien", da „das Verwenden von

ised to living quality inside the building and post-occupancy evaluation; (→§05)
- inclusion of food production into the design (e.g. greenhouses, vegetable gardens, etc.).

For a long time now, Werner Schmidt has been very concerned with such issues, and he has always tried to move a step further. Around the turn of the 21st century, he built three single-family houses whose thermal energy consumption is negligible in spite of the mountain setting. House Schmid-Cavegn, (→■125) in Camischolas, and house Wolf-Bearth, (→■126) in Untervaz, are both built with prefabricated laminated-wood elements, between which a very thick insulation layer is infilled (mineral wool in the first case, cellulose in the second). They have largely glazed façades to take advantage of the sun's southern rays. House Wolf-Bearth is equipped with solar collectors; its total running costs for electricity, hot water and heating have been ranging from 40 to 60 CHF/month.
These houses, like most of those Schmidt is building today, are two storeys high: this way, the excavated area is smaller, as are the foundations and roof; all of which implies a lower cost.

After these experiences, Schmidt moved on to straw-bale and timber building, which appears to meet a number of the above discussed requirements. (→§08) However, timber is almost always a product of monoculture and is industrially manufactured; moreover, it is often kiln-dried, laminated, glued, treated with preservatives, and imported. Although one can be so aware to specify air-dried, untreated, solid, local wood (and lucky enough to find it!), they will hardly buy real forest-grown timber. Obviously, straw will not be transformed much, all the same it will very likely be "a by-product of an industrial agriculture whose patterns are no less ecologically destructive than those of industry in general." (→B069:23) Moreover, as cereal production has enormously

industriell hergestellten und importierten Materialien eine Umweltsünde darstellt." (→B126:9) Bevorzugt werden sollten Produkte aus nachwachsenden oder reichlich vorkommenden Materialien, und solche, die Rohstoffe effizienter nutzen. (→B126:16) Viel mehr, wenn man bedenkt, dass fast überall sichere, kostengünstige und energiesparende Materialien natürlich vorkommen, die zu den modernen Anforderungen an ein Gebäude passen. (→B127:39) Unter den Variablen, die sie manipulieren, sollten sich Designer vielmehr das Gewicht und die Graue Energie eines Hauses bewusst machen. Beispiele von Niedrigenergie-Entwurfsentscheidungen beinhalten thermische Speichermasse, zentralgelegene Installationen, das Vermeiden von Kellern und Tiefgaragen.
- Vermeidung von Materialien und Methoden, die Verschmutzungen verursachen. Gebäude sollten (vor, während und nach ihrem Betrieb) biokompatibel sein, das heißt in Übereinstimmung mit dem Leben und seinen Gesetzmäßigkeiten stehen, und sollten nicht die Gesundheit von Arbeitern und Bewohnern gefährden, wie es die Baubiologie lehrt. (→B125) Relevanz sollte an die Lebensqualität im Innern des Gebäudes und die POE (post-occupancy evaluation) geknüpft sein. (→§05)
- Einbeziehung von Nahrungsmittelproduktion in den Entwurf (zum Beispiel Gewächshäuser, Gemüsegärten, etc.).

Seit mehr als 30 Jahren beschäftigt sich Werner Schmidt mit solchen Fragen und er hat immer versucht, einen Schritt weiter nach vorne zu machen. Um die Wende zum 21. Jahrhundert herum, baute er Einfamilienhäuser, deren thermischer Energieverbrauch trotz der Berglage vernachlässigbar ist. Haus Schmid-Cavegn (→■125) in Camischolas und Haus Wolf-Bearth (→■126) in Untervaz sind beide aus vorfabrizierten Holzelementen gebaut, die mit einer dicken Isolationsschicht gefüllt sind (Mineralwolle im ersten Fall, Zellulosedämmung im zweiten). Diese Gebäude haben großflächig verglaste Fassaden, um die Vorzüge der Südsonne zu nutzen. Das Haus Wolf-Bearth ist mit Sonnenkollektoren ausgestat-

CEREAL GROWING SURFACE
ANBAUFLÄCHE FÜR BROTGETREIDE

3637 ha
2000 ha
1000 ha
500 ha
100 ha
5 ha

CH: 88419 ha

Source: Survey of farming
structures 2003
© Federal Office of Statistics

Quelle: Landwirtschaftliche
Betriebsstrukturerhebung 2003
© Bundesamt für Statistik

127

decreased in Switzerland (→■127) – and the small output of straw is not enough for cattle breeding (which is on the other hand oversized) often Schmidt has to use imported straw. This is not always the case, however: for instance, in Dora house it was obtained from locally-grown organic spelt. There is no ideal solution; as long as we will go on building, we must be resigned to accept the least of many evils. As long as the structural system is concerned, (→§08,09) there is a certain dispute among authors whether a Nebraska-style house (i.e., with load-bearing straw-bale walls) consumes less timber and whether, more generally, its environmental footprint is smaller than a post-and-beam, straw-bale-infilled house. (→B069:126-127,126:78)

To allow myself an evidence-based idea, I thought it would have made sense to perform thorough calculations of how much timber has been used in three of

tet; seine Gesamtkosten für Elektrizität, heißes Wasser und Heizung betragen zwischen 40–60 CHF/Monat.

Diese Häuser, wie die meisten Häuser, die Schmidt heute baut, sind zweigeschossig: auf diese Weise ist die Aushubfläche kleiner und somit auch das Fundament und das Dach; dies bedeutet im Gesamten weniger Kosten.

Nach diesen Erfahrungen zog Schmidt weiter in Richtung Strohballen- und Holzbauten, die einen großen Teil der oben genannten Anforderungen erfüllen. (→§08) Jedoch ist Holz fast immer ein Produkt aus Monokulturen und wird industriell verarbeitet. Es ist oftmals technisch getrocknet, beschichtet, verleimt, imprägniert oder importiert. Auch wenn jemand sich bewusst für natürlich getrocknetes, unbehandeltes, lokales Holz entscheidet (und sich glücklich schätzen kann, wenn er es findet!), wird er kaum wahrhaftig

128

129

130

Schmidt's straw-bale buildings (house and guesthouse Maya, (→■128-130;p177-183) in Nax, and house Wegmann (→p113-119) in Glarus), and compare the results.

At Nax, the ratio of envelope area/volume is relatively high, both in the guesthouse and in the owners' house – 1.25 and 1.12 respectively. These values are due to the assumptions of our calculations and the particular design of these buildings. In fact, we considered only the inhabitable, interior space as 'volume,' therefore that which was inside the 80 cm-thick straw insulation; while the building envelope area was measured at the exterior face. The same calculation performed for the house at Glarus gives the ratio 1.10.

What is more interesting, the building technique – largely prefabricated in the guesthouse with cross-laminated

im heimischen Wald gewachsenes Holz kaufen können. Das Stroh wird nicht umgeformt oder behandelt, es ist „ein Nebenprodukt aus der Landwirtschaft, deren Strukturen nicht weniger ökologisch zerstörerisch sind als der Industrie im Allgemeinen." (→B069:23) Außerdem muss Schmidt das Stroh häufig importieren, da die Getreideproduktion in der Schweiz stark zurückgegangen ist (→■127) – und der geringe Gewinn an Stroh ist nicht ausreichend für die Verwendung in der Viehzucht, die im Vergleich dazu überdimensioniert ist. Beim Haus Dora jedoch stammt das Dinkelstroh aus lokalem, biologischen Anbau.

Es gibt nicht die eine wahrhaftige oder unantastbare Lösung; so lange wie wir weiter bauen, müssen wir versuchen, das kleinstmögliche Übel von allen anzustreben. Im Hinblick auf

WOOD AND STRAW USE IN THREE BUILDINGS
HOLZ UND STROH NUTZUNG IN DREI GEBÄUDEN

WOOD STRAW
HOLZ STROH

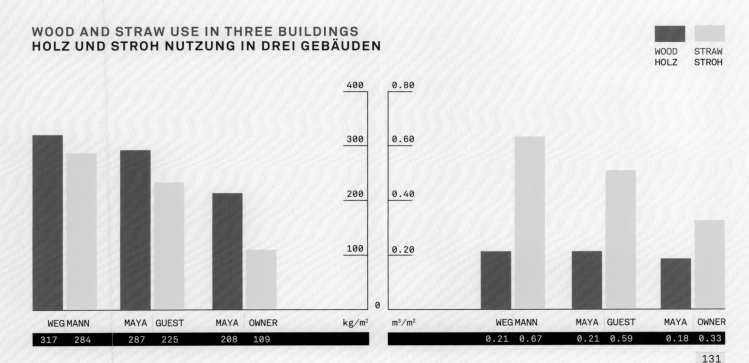

	WEG MANN		MAYA	GUEST		MAYA	OWNER	kg/m²
	317	284	287	225		208	109	

m³/m²		WEG MANN		MAYA	GUEST		MAYA	OWNER
		0.21	0.67	0.21	0.59		0.18	0.33

131

timber panels and a straw-bale envelope, and in the owners' residence with timber frames infilled with straw; while load-bearing straw-bale walls at Glarus – significantly affects the consumption of materials. (→■131) In house Wegmann, 0.21 m³ timber (and wood-based products) and 0.67 m³ straw per cubic metre of inhabitable volume have been employed (or, to put it in another way, 317 kg timber and 284 kg straw per square metre of floor area). In Maya guesthouse, the same values are respectively 0.21 m³ timber and 0.59 m³ straw per cubic metre (or 287 kg timber and 225 kg straw per square metre), and in the owners' house 0.18 m³ timber and 0.33 m³ straw per cubic metre (208 kg timber and 109 kg straw per square metre). These values are high compared with a partially prefabricated wooden house by architects Aichner

das statische System (→§08,09) gibt es einen ernsthaften Streit unter verschiedenen Autoren darüber, ob ein Haus, das im Nebraska-Stil errichtet ist (das heißt aus lasttragenden Strohballenwänden), weniger Holz verbraucht, und ob sein ökologischer Fußabdruck generell kleiner als ein Holzstän-derbau mit Strohdämmung ist. (→B069:126-127,126:78) Um mir selbst eine evidenzbasierte Vorstellung machen zu können, dachte ich es würde Sinn machen, gründliche Berechnungen darüber zu erstellen, wie viel Holz in drei von Schmidts Häusern (Maya Wohnhaus und Bed&Breakfast in Nax, (→■128-130;S.177-183) Haus Wegmann-Gasser in Glarus) (→S.113-119) tatsächlich verwendet wurde und die Ergebnisse miteinander zu vergleichen.
In Nax ist das Verhältnis von Gebäudehülle zu Volumen recht

132

WEGMANN-GASSER HOUSE

address ⌐ Adresse: Eichenstrasse 13,
CH-8750 Glarus/GL
altitude ⌐ Höhe: 486 m
degree-days ⌐ Gradtage: 3143
project ⌐ Entwurf: 2007
construction ⌐ Bau: 2008
main building firms ⌐
Wichtigen Baufirmen:
Bruno Cesato, Glarus
(general contractor ⌐ Baumeister);
Zweifel Holzbau AG, Glarus
(wood construction ⌐ Holzbau);
Atelier Werner Schmidt + Firma Flepp
(straw-bale construction ⌐ Strohbau)
plot area ⌐ Grundstückfläche: 820 m²
heated floor area ⌐
Geheizte Bodenfläche: 181 m²
main window (SW) area ⌐ Fensterfläche
Hauptfassade (SW): 18.5 m²
building cost ⌐ Baukosten:
669,000 CHF [3,700 CHF/m²]

& Seidl at Terenten where 140 kg/m² timber plus 122 kg/m² wood-based products were used, insulating wood-fibre boards excluded. (→B094) In the future, Schmidt plans to drastically reduce the quantity of timber using a false-vault or false-dome structural concept. This will not be beneficial to ecology only: a large part of a project's cost is due to timber structures, which are systematically overdimensioned by engineers and carpenters.

The above calculations would not be complete without considering that in the guesthouse at Nax, there is a large outdoor area, part of which is indispensable to its usability since it includes access to the rooms through a stairway and a gallery. To build these elements, a further 28 m³ timber was used. At house Wegmann, about 5 m³ was used for ancillary portions, including the enclosed entrance porch and storage space on the north side.

hoch, sowohl im Gästehaus als auch im Wohnhaus – jeweils 1,25 und 1,12. Diese Werte resultieren aus den Annahmen unserer Berechnungen und dem speziellen Entwurf dieser Gebäude. Tatsächlich haben wir nur den bewohnbaren, inneren Raum als Volumen bezeichnet, also innerhalb der 80 cm breiten Strohisolierung; während die Fläche der Gebäudehülle von der Außenfassade gemessen ist. Dieselbe Berechnung haben wir beim Haus in Glarus vorgenommen, bei dem sich ein Verhältnis von 1,10 ergibt.

Interessanter ist der Blick auf die Konstruktionstechnik – das Gästehaus ist hauptsächlich aus vorgefertigten kreuzverleimten Holzplatten mit einem Strohballenmantel erbaut und beim Wohnhaus sind es mit Stroh ausgedämmte Holzrahmen, während Haus Wegmann-Gasser aus lasttragenden Strohballenwänden besteht – was den Materialverbrauch signifikant beeinflusst. (→■131) Im Haus Wegmann-Gasser

the entire slope should have been covered with collectors in order to be self-sufficient all year long. Hot water is stored in a 1000 l tank on the first floor. The only inconvenience reported is that the heat it emits is annoying in summer. In the garden there is an underground cistern to collect rainfall but it has never been put in use, as water supply is not really an issue hereabouts.

It is my belief that multi-family load-bearing straw-bale buildings should also be built, not only individual homes: from an ecological point of view the latter are an ambiguous choice, since they inherently consume more in terms of land, building materials, and operating energy. Moreover, sometimes straw-bale houses are holiday homes for rich urbanites who take delight in appearing 'sustainable.' Certainly, this is not the architect's responsibility – Schmidt has designed multi-family buildings and would be ready to work for communities. In fact, many groups have approached him but they were divided. It is hard to initiate a project with a large group; a small founding core with a vision works usually better. In the 'zero carbon' development (→■140-141) Schmidt is now planning together with GrAT and architect Georg Scheicher in Traismauer, Lower Austria, some fifty dwellings – including large houses as well as three-storey row houses – are planned; together with offices, commercial spaces and services. There, at least 70% of the building material – solid wood, clay, and straw – will be issued from within the city limits. To conclude, we must admit that unfortunately both (hand) books and projects concerned with 'alternative' materials still suffer from an American approach that is biased towards new-built single-family houses. This bias is grounded on choices of autonomy, but is not very sustainable either in terms of land consumption or overall environmental impact. We need to focus more on the collective level and on retrofit. (→§10)

Ich bin überzeugt, dass auch lasttragende Mehrfamilienstrohballenhäuser entstehen sollten, nicht nur Einfamilienhäuser: aus ökologischer Sicht sind sie etwas zwiespältig, da sie automatisch einen höheren Verbrauch im Hinblick auf Land, Baumaterial und Betriebskosten haben. Darüber hinaus sind manche Strohballenhäuser Ferienwohnungen von wohlhabenden Städtern, die Freude daran haben, ‚nachhaltig' zu sein. Sicherlich ist dies nicht die Verantwortung des Architekten. Schmidt hat bereits Mehrfamilienhäuser entworfen und wäre bereit, auch für die Gemeinden zu planen. Tatsächlich haben ihn verschiedene Gruppen in der Vergangenheit angesprochen. Es gestaltet sich eher schwierig, ein Projekt mit einer großen Gruppe umzusetzen, eine kleine Gründungsgruppe mit einer klaren Vision funktioniert in der Regel besser. In der ‚ZeroCarbon' Projektentwicklung (→■140-141) arbeitet Werner Schmidt nun zusammen mit der GrAT und dem Architekten Georg Scheicher. Er plant in Traismauer, Niederösterreich, circa 50 Wohnungen, darunter sind große Gebäude und dreigeschossige Reihenhäuser geplant, mit Büros, Gewerbeflächen und einem Informationszentrum. Dort sollen 70% der verwendeten Baumaterialien – Massivholz, Lehm und Stroh – innerhalb der Gemeindegrenzen bezogen werden.

Zusammenfassend muss man zugeben, dass unglücklicherweise sowohl (Hand-)Bücher als auch Projekte, die sich mit alternativen Materialien befassen, noch immer unter dem amerikanischen Ansatz der Einfamilienhaus-Neubau-Methode leiden. Diese Vorliebe basiert auf dem Wunsch nach Autonomie, ist aber nicht besonders nachhaltig im Hinblick auf den Landverbrauch und die Auswirkungen auf unsere Umwelt. Wir müssen den Fokus mehr auf ein gemeinschaftliches Level legen und uns auch auf die Gebäudesanierung konzentrieren. (→§10)

GARTMANN-SGIER HOUSE ⌴ HAUS GARTMANN-SGIER

ADDRESS ⌴ ADRESSE:
Curschetta, CH-7127 Sevgein

ALTITUDE ⌴ HÖHE:
873 m

DEGREE-DAYS ⌴ GRADTAGE:
3561

PROJECT ⌴ ENTWURF:
2000

CONSTRUCTION ⌴ BAU:
2002

**MAIN BUILDING FIRMS ⌴
WICHTIGEN BAUFIRMEN:**
Valaulta Berni AG, Rueun (general
contractor ⌴ Baumeister); Arpagaus,
Cumbel (wood construction ⌴ Holzbau);
Krapf, St.Gallen (glass ⌴ Glas)

**PROJECT MANAGER ⌴
PROJEKTLEITUNG:**
Werner Schmidt + Marc Demont

PLOT AREA ⌴ GRUNDSTÜCKFLÄCHE:
1,027 m²

**HEATED FLOOR AREA ⌴
GEHEIZTE BODENFLÄCHE:**
317 m²

**MAIN WINDOW AREA (S) ⌴
FENSTERFLÄCHE HAUPTFASSADE (S):**
71 m²

BUILDING COST ⌴ BAUKOSTEN (BKP2):
1,250,000 CHF [3,900 CHF/m²]

The plot was large, but building was allowed on only a small portion, and this could not accommodate the amount of volume the clients wanted. It was thus decided to build part of the house underground, and natural lighting became the main theme of the project.

The location does not appear advantageous, since it is on a northern slope. Therefore, quite untypically, the house opens in an uphill direction, towards val Lumnezia, for passive solar purposes. Only a small part of the house overlooks the Rhine valley – the terrace and also the private rooms, to protect from prying eyes.

The entire building is characterised by a quiet, restrained look – the lack of roof overhang on gable fronts, the white rendered walls, windows flush with the external face of the walls, the controlled use of steel plates, and the framework-free glass conservatory convey simple elegance.

Walls are load-bearing (15 cm lime-sand bricks) while the horizontal structure is reinforced concrete slabs.

Interiors are surprisingly bright. The conservatory as well as large, floor-to-ceiling frameless windows on the south façade offer unobstructed views of the Graubünden mountains. Moreover, a 2.5 m diameter lightwell runs through the entire building, in the middle of the plan – a skylight in the roof corresponds to circular, walkable glass portions on each floor. Even the basement receives a lot of light from a glazed, below grade courtyard.

House Gartmann works without active heating, as the south façade ensures strong

Das Grundstück war sehr groß, aber es war nur ein kleiner Teil davon bebaubar, was nicht ausreichte, um all die Raumanforderungen der Kunden zu decken. Daher wurde beschlossen, einen Teil des Gebäudes unter die Erde zu verlegen, und die natürliche Lichtführung wurde zum Hauptthema des Entwurfs.

Die Lage erscheint nicht gerade vorteilhaft, zumal es ein Nordhang ist. Deshalb öffnet sich das Haus, was sehr untypisch ist, zum Hang hin, in Richtung des Val Lumnezia, zum Zwecke der passiven Sonnenenergie. Nur ein kleiner Teil des Gebäudes bietet einen Blick auf das Rheintal – die Terrasse und die privaten Räume, um sie vor fremden Blicken zu schützen. Das gesamte Gebäude ist durch ein ruhiges und zurückhaltendes Äußeres geprägt – das Fehlen der Dachüberstände an den Giebelseiten, die weiß verputzten Wände, die Fenster, die mit der Fassadenebene bündig sind, die bewusste Verwendung von Metallplatten, und die rahmenlose Verglasung des Wintergartens verleihen ihm Eleganz. Die Wände sind lasttragend aus 15 cm starken Kalksandsteinen, während die horizontale Struktur aus verstärkten Betonplatten besteht.

Die Innenräume sind überraschend hell. Sowohl der Wintergarten als auch die rahmenlosen, Geschoss hohen Verglasungen auf der Südseite bieten einen freien Blick auf die Bündner Berge. Des weiteren zieht sich in der Mitte des Grundrisses ein im Durchmesser 2,50 m breiter Lichtschacht durch alle Geschosse – ein Oberlicht im Dach entspricht den kreisrunden, begehbaren Glaselementen auf jedem Stockwerk. Der Keller erhält direktes Tageslicht durch

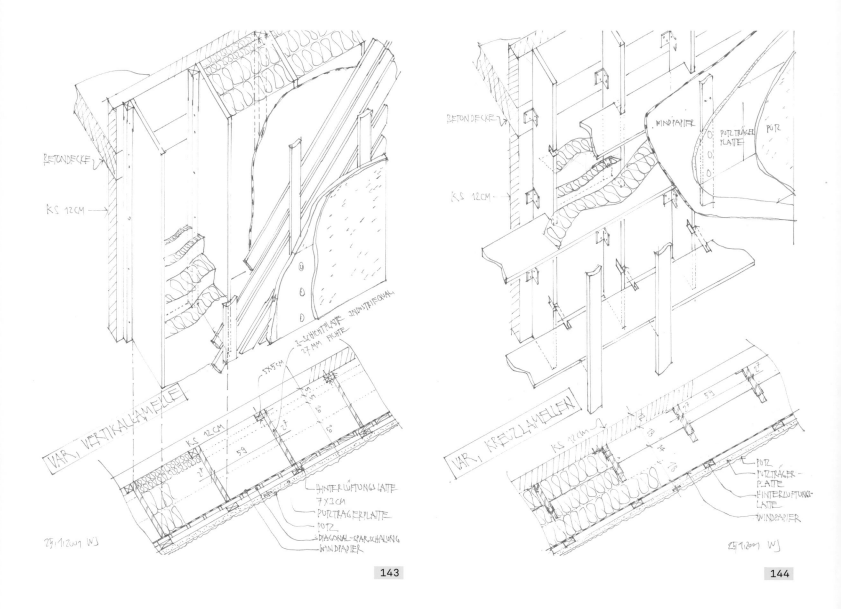

BETONDECKE

KS 12CM

VAR. VERTIKALLAMELLE

KS 12CM

5X5CM

2-SCHICHTPLATTE INDUSTRIEQUAL.

2-SCHICHTPLATTE 27 MM FICHTE

HINTERLÜFTUNGSLATTE 7X2CM

PUTZTRÄGERPLATTE

PUTZ

DIAGONAL-SPARSCHALUNG

WINDPAPIER

25.7.2001 WJ

143

BETONDECKE

WINDPAPIER

PUTZTRÄGER PLATTE

PUTZ

KS 12CM

VAR. KREUZLAMELLEN

KS 12CM

PUTZ

PUTZTRÄGER-PLATTE

HINTERLÜFTUNG-LATTE

WINDPAPIER

25.7.2001 WJ

144

SCALE ⌐ MASSSTAB
1:200

direct solar gains. The rest is done by a
mechanical ventilation system with heat re-
covery. Massive walls serve as a large thermal
storage; such mass is wrapped with a 50 cm
thick layer of EPS (XPS in the lower portion)

einen verglasten Lichthof unterhalb
des Erdniveaus.
Das Haus Gartmann-Sgier kommt ohne
aktive Heizung aus, da die Südfassade hohe
Sonneneinstrahlungserträge liefert.

among which house von Erffa, Schmidt is now designing in Sachsen-Anhalt, which will have half-hidden gardens and places to sunbathe. In any case, outdoor 'rooms' are often provided: that is, outdoor, sheltered spaces – such as deep balconies – placed to the south of the house, which people will use if it is sunny, even in winter.

For passive energy design requirements, Schmidt's residential buildings have a largely glazed south or south-west façade. In some of them, this offers generous views of vegetation, which is reported to have a great therapeutic influence, particularly in conditions of acute stress. (→B036:233,070) The main entrance is preferably placed on the rear (north) side, so that the best view of the outdoors can only be enjoyed once one is already in. Here Schmidt's typical choice is the opposite of what Alexander suggested: "if there is a beautiful view, don't spoil it by building huge windows that gape incessantly at it. Instead, put the windows which look onto the views at places of transition... the view is never visible from the places where people stay." (→B009:134) Actually, I received mixed statements from clients who enjoy idyllic views from very open living rooms: many are enthusiastic, but one farmer said he felt the glazing was too large – "after a working day spent outdoor, you come home looking for protection and inwardness." The balcony parapet – still to be built at the time of my visit – and some plants inside are expected to create the appropriate balance. To avoid the 'picture window' effect, (→B092) Schmidt arranges outdoor elements of the house so that they enter your visual field, therefore letting you perceive – although unconsciously – that you are inside, in spite of the wall-wide window: in house Küng, for instance, you cannot look out without seeing the terrace posts. Further subtle elements to perceptually enclose the view include curtains and creepers. (→■149)

At this point, it is obvious that Schmidt's houses are full of light. The human organism, whose "disinfecting and prophylactic effects have been recognized for over a century,"

gigen Blick ins Grüne, was bekanntlich einen sehr guten therapeutischen Effekt hat, vor allem in Situationen von akutem Stress. (→B036:233,070) Der Haupteingang wird in der Regel auf der Nordseite platziert, somit kann die schönste Sicht nach draußen erst dann von innen genossen werden, wenn man im Gebäude drin ist. Hier ist Schmidts typische Wahl das Gegenteil von dem, was Alexander vorschlägt: „wenn es eine schöne Aussicht gibt, verderben Sie sie nicht, indem Sie große Fenster einbauen, die permanent hinausstarren. Stattdessen platzieren sie das Fenster lieber an Übergangsstellen... die Aussicht ist niemals sichtbar von den Orten, an denen die Menschen sich befinden." (→B009:134) Tatsächlich habe ich sehr unterschiedliche Eindrücke von Bauherren, die den idyllischen Blick von offenen Wohnräumen nach draußen genießen: viele sind begeistert, aber einer der Landwirte meinte, ihm schienen die Verglasungen zu groß – „nach einem ganzen Arbeitstag an der frischen Luft, kommt man nach Hause und sucht Schutz und Geborgenheit." Die Balkonbrüstung, die zum Zeitpunkt meines Besuches noch im Bau war, und einige Grünpflanzen im Inneren, sollen das gewünschte Gleichgewicht schaffen. Um den ‚Fenstergemälde' Effekt zu vermeiden, (→B092) platziert Schmidt Außenelemente, die ins Sichtfeld rücken und einem dadurch unbewusst das Gefühl von Innenraum geben, anstelle des weit offenen Fensters: im Haus Küng zum Beispiel fallen beim Blick nach draußen die Terrassenpfosten ins Sichtfeld. Weitere dezente Elemente, um Öffnungen zu verdecken sind Vorhänge und Schlingpflanzen. (→■149)

An dieser Stelle wird deutlich, dass Schmidts Häuser voller Licht sind. Der menschliche Organismus sehnt sich nach Sonnenlicht, dessen „desinfizierende und prophylaktische Wirkungen seit mehr als einem Jahrhundert bekannt sind" (→B036:200) – es stimuliert die Hypophyse, die Zirbeldrüse und den Hypothalamus. (→B035:31) Schmidt gestaltet seine Gebäude derart, dass das Licht auf strukturierten Oberflächen und mit einer lebhaften Beschaffenheit, wie zum

craves sunlight. (→B036:200) – it stimulates the hypophysis, the pineal gland, and the hypothalamus. (→B035:31) Schmidt specifies buildings so that light is collected by suitably textured surfaces with 'lively' finishes, like those of hand-made plasters (→B036:210) – this allows for a vibrant experience. A similarly stimulating effect is obtained by alternating areas of light and shade, which is good for both optical and hormonal health – see for instance houses Mathis, (→p28-34) with its great variety of light environments, and Gartmann, where a pool of light pierces the entire building. (→■150) More generally, some spatial diversity is recommended to provide for a rich and stimulating living environment. Lacinski and Bergeron argue that "the space should be visually complex, but never jarring. Smooth curves and complex ceiling planes allow the logical mind to wander, giving the other aspects of consciousness a chance to come to the fore." (→B069:293) Also Alexander and Day suggest the design of a progression of different degrees of intimacy, for instance through ceiling height variety. (→B009:127+190,036:217) This is especially true "between rooms which open into each other, so that the relative intimacy of different spaces can be felt." In my opinion this is particularly apparent in some of Schmidt's early works, such as Simon Jacomet's atelier, (→■152;p265-268) and Disentis abbey. (→■031-032) The same would have been experienced in house Bühler-Seiz, (→■415-416) and will be in house Mathis with its rich play of differently shaped and sized volumes. In Gliott house, (→■153;p158-163) one can experience a sequence of entrance spaces (carport, covered hallway, entrance hall); in general, Schmidt thinks it is a good thing to provide a house with sheltered, semi-private spaces. By the way, these are useful in winter as buffers – transition spaces from outdoor to indoor; spaces which are covered but not fully enclosed; spaces which are enclosed but not heated; etc. Also in Cazis church the sequence of spaces is central, to favour a path towards recollection. (→p44-49)

Beispiel bei dem von Hand aufgetragenen Putz, besonders zur Geltung kommt (→B036:210) – eine sehr dynamische Erfahrung. Ein ähnlich stimulierender Effekt wird durch den Wechsel von Licht und Schatten erzielt, was sowohl für das optische als auch das hormonelle Wohlbefinden gut ist – zum Beispiel beim Haus Mathis (→S.28-34) mit seiner großen Vielfalt an verschiedenen Lichtbereichen, und Haus Gartmann-Sgier, (→■150) wo ein Lichtkanal durch das gesamte Gebäude führt.
Generell gilt, ein wenig räumliche Abwechslung wird für ein gesundes, stimulierendes Wohnumfeld empfohlen. Lacinski und Bergeron sind der Meinung, „Raum sollte visuell komplex sein, aber niemals schrill. Weiche Kurven und vielschichtige Deckenebenen erlauben dem Bewusstsein abzuschweifen, während sie anderen Aspekten des Bewusstseins die Möglichkeit geben, in den Vordergrund zu treten." (→B069:293) Alexander und Day schlagen ebenfalls vor, im Entwurf einen Übergang von verschiedenen Intimitätsstufen einfließen zu lassen, so zum Beispiel durch verschieden hohe Decken. (→B009:127+190,036:217) Dies bewahrheitet sich vor allem „bei Räumen, die ineinander greifen, so dass die relative Intimität verschiedener Räume zu spüren ist." Meiner Meinung nach ist dies besonders deutlich in Schmidts frühen Arbeiten, wie zum Beispiel dem Atelier von Simon Jacomet (→■152;S.265-268) und im Kloster Disentis. (→■031,032) Dasselbe gilt für den Entwurf des Hauses Bühler-Seiz (→■415-416) und im Haus Mathis mit seinem Spiel der unterschiedlich geformten und unterschiedlich großen Volumen. Im Haus Gliott (→■153;S.158-163) erfährt man eine Folge von verschiedenen Eingangsbereichen (Carport, überdachter Eingansbereich außen, Eingangsbereich im Innern); im Allgemeinen ist Schmidt vom positiven Effekt überdachter, halbprivater Außenbereiche überzeugt. Im Übrigen sind diese in der Winterzeit als Pufferzonen sehr nützlich – Übergangsbereiche von außen nach innen; Bereiche, die bedeckt aber nicht gänzlich umhüllt sind; Bereiche die geschlossen, aber

sion on the merits of natural materials. (→§04) Sim Van der Ryn affirms that "people are drawn to natural materials because they stand in opposition to the industrial appetite of disassembling the organic, for destroying the soul and spirit inherent in living materials. For a long time, machine-made perfection was the aesthetic standard. Now that may be shifting to an appreciation for the irregularity, the softness, the handmade quality and workmanship of natural building materials." (→B040:xv) It seems to me that this shift is not the result of fashion – indeed it might be linked with a spreading appreciation of organic food and a wider awareness of how hazardous many 'artificial' ones can be. As Day puts it synthetically, "natural materials are life-compatible." (→B036:187) In his opinion, natural materials have the same effect as actual contact with the natural environment, in that they "connect us with life," therefore invigorating and strengthening natural immunity. Some, he adds, "actually have health benefits:" lime is bactericidal; many can buffer temperature and humidity and can absorb pollution. (→B036:190) Another point he makes is very subtle: to surround oneself with deception – for instance, 'fake' materials which pretend to look like something else – cannot be good nourishment for the soul. (→B035:80)

Natural materials and low-tech building methods can also be linked to self-building, or at least to some degree of craftsmanship. Certainly, Schmidt's houses show they are at least partly handmade, sometimes as the result of good old-fashioned hard work. (→§00) In some cases – e.g. Fliri (→■155-156) and Wegmann houses – one can clearly perceive an interaction between perfection and imperfection – for instance between geometrically precise forms and dimensions of timber elements, and gentle undulations and irregular surfaces of rendered straw-bale walls – which reminds of wabi-sabi aesthetic. Leonard Koren describes it as giving preference to simplicity, unrefinement, primitiveness, rawness, and to materials patently vulnerable to atmospheric

biologischem Essen und einem breiteren Bewusstsein dafür, wie gefährlich viele künstliche Produkte sein können. Wie Day es zusammenfassend sagt, „natürliche Materialien sind lebenskompatibel." (→B036:187) Seiner Meinung nach haben natürliche Materialien denselben Effekt, wie der Kontakt mit der Natur, indem „sie uns mit dem Leben verknüpfen" und dadurch unsere natürliche Immunität beleben und stärken. Manche Materialien, fügt er hinzu, „haben tatsächlich gesundheitliche Vorteile:" Kalk ist bakterizid, viele Materialien können Temperatur und Feuchtigkeit regulieren, und können Umweltverschmutzungen aufnehmen. (→B036:190) Ein weiterer Punkt, den er anführt, ist sehr subtil: sich mit Täuschungen zu umgeben – wie zum Beispiel ‚unechte' Materialien, die scheinbar wie etwas anderes aussehen – können keine gute Nahrung für die Seele sein. (→B035:80) Natürliche Materialien und low-tech Bauweisen können mit Eigenbau oder wenigstens zu einem gewissen Grad mit handwerklicher Arbeit in Verbindung gebracht werden. Schmidts Häuser zeigen, dass sie zu einem Teil handgemacht sind, oftmals als Resultat von altbewährter, harter Arbeit. (→§00) In manchen Fällen, wie zum Beispiel den Häusern Fliri (→■155-156) und Wegmann-Gasser, kann man deutlich die Interaktion von Perfektion und Unvollkommenheit sehen; zum Beispiel bei den geometrisch, präzisen Formen und Dimensionen der Holzelemente, und der sanften Wellen und unregelmäßigen Oberfläche der Strohballenwände, die an wabi-sabi Ästhetik erinnert. Leonard Koren beschreibt es als Präferenz der Einfachheit, Unverfeinertheit, Primitivität, Rauheit und der Präferenz von Materialien, die offensichtlich anfällig gegenüber Umwelteinflüssen und menschlicher Manipulation sind – ohne dadurch temporäre oder unfertige Objekte zu erzeugen. (→B067) Wabi-sabi beinhaltet eine intuitive Vorstellung von der Welt, eine Erweiterung der sensorischen Information, ein Entfernen von Überflüssigem, eine Anpassung an die Natur und die Akzeptanz des Vergänglichen und des Alterns – so

elements and human manipulation – without creating temporary or unfinished objects. (→B067)

Wabi-sabi implies an intuitive vision of the world, expansion of sensorial information, removal of superfluousness, adaptation to nature, acceptation of decay and ageing – as the signs of passing time enrich rather than ruin. In fact, natural materials age well, and return "to the earth more slowly and with more grace." (→B040:xv) If I were to comment on the relationship between Schmidt's early works and recent strawbale buildings I would say that the latter tend to emphasise their use value and do not try to stand out of their context, while the former have an exuberant propensity for drawing attention to them.

A further reason for wellbeing is in the absence of mechanical ventilation systems. In spite of consuming very small quantities of thermal energy, in Schmidt's houses windows can be opened – and residents open them – as often as one used to do in ordinary houses. Actually, the quality of indoor air in airtight buildings is often poor because of the presence of chemical and synthetic products, toxins, radon, positive ions, etc., which would be better be removed by aeration, and which mechanical ventilation is not always successful in eliminating. The consequences may range from allergies to metabolism disorders and cancer.

To investigate the aforementioned aspects, I visited a number of houses by Schmidt and interviewed their owners, performing simplified post-occupancy evaluations – and obtaining responses which ranged from very satisfied to enthusiastic. Other buildings were intended as places for the wellbeing of tourists: they are holiday rooms located in beautiful places which induce a slower pace of life and experiences of "inner freedom and expansion." (→B036:186) Such accommodation is meant to make urban souls sample a different, healthier way of living... at least on vacation. It is a fact that tourists find straw-bale houses attractive: the occupancy rate of Fliri's is well above that of other holiday farms in the same

wie die Zeichen der vergehenden Zeit eher bereichernd als ruinierend wirken. In der Tat altern natürliche Materialien sehr gut „gehen langsamer und würdevoller zur Erde zurück." (→B040:xv) Wenn ich das Verhältnis von Schmidts frühen Arbeiten zu den neueren Strohballenbauten kommentieren sollte, würde ich sagen, dass bei letzteren die Betonung auf dem Gebrauchswert liegt und nicht in der Herausstellung aus dem Kontext, während die frühen Arbeiten eine starke Neigung dazu haben, die Aufmerksamkeit auf sich zu ziehen. Ein weiterer Grund für ein sich Wohlfühlen ist das Fehlen von Lüftungsanlagen. Trotz ihres geringen Verbrauchs an thermischer Energie, können in Schmidts Gebäuden die Fenster so oft geöffnet werden, wie man es im alten Haus gewohnt war – und die Bewohner öffnen sie. In der Tat ist die Qualität der Innenluft in luftdichten Gebäuden oftmals bescheiden, auf Grund des Einsatzes von chemischen und synthetischen Produkten, Giften, des Vorkommens von Radon und positiven Ionen, etc., die besser durch Lüften entfernt werden, und die eine Belüftungsanlage selten vollständig eliminiert. Die Konsequenzen reichen von Allergien bis hin zu Stoffwechselerkrankungen und Krebs.

Um die oben genannten Aspekte zu untersuchen, bin ich zu einer Vielzahl von Schmidts Häusern gefahren und habe die Bewohner befragt, habe die Ergebnisse vereinfacht dargestellt und ausgewertet – und ich erhielt daraus Antworten, die von ‚sehr zufrieden' bis ‚begeistert' reichten.

Andere Gebäude sind für touristische Zwecke gedacht: es sind Ferienwohnungen an wunderschönen Plätzen, die ein geringeres Tempo verursachen und die Erfahrungen von „innerem Frieden und Ausweitung" bringen. (→B036:186) Solche Unterkünfte sind dazu gedacht, Städtern eine Kostprobe von einer anderen, gesünderen Lebensart zu geben... zumindest im Urlaub. Es ist ein Tatbestand, dass Touristen Strohballenhäuser anziehend finden: die Bettenauslastung bei Fliris liegt weit über derer von anderen Ferienbauernhäusern im selben Tal (auch dank der ehrlichen, klaren und geschmack-

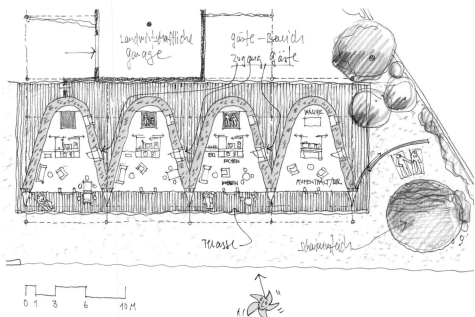

mal self-sufficiency. However, 'emergency' radiant heating has been installed in the bathroom floors, which if necessary can be connected to a solar-heated water tank located in the existing farmhouse. This already provides hot sanitary water.

Besides straw, building materials include fir timber for beams and window frames, untreated wood panels for ceilings and pine timber for external floorings. The indoor floor is pigmented and waxed concrete. Walls are lime-rendered outside and clay-plastered inside (the first coat is of pozzolanic hydraulic lime). No additives, dyes, varnishes or chemical treatments were used to protect the timber.

Each apartment is approximately 40 m². The interior is a sequence of increasing privacy, and decreasing amount of light. The light-flooded living area to the south serves as a kitchen, dining room and living room;

gefüllt mit Strohballen. Weinreben wachsen auf dem Dach, die nicht nur das Gebäude verschönern, sondern es auch im warmen Sommer beschatten, und sie verdecken die angebaute Garage auf der Rückseite.

Die Apartments wurden nach den Prinzipien bioklimatischer Architektur gestaltet, um den Komfort zu maximieren. Dank der gut isolierenden Außenhülle sind sie nahezu autark. Für den Notfall wurde im Badezimmerbereich ein Bodenheizsystem integriert, welches an den Solarspeicher im bestehenden Bauernhaus angeschlossen werden kann. Dieser Solarspeicher liefert auch das nötwendige Warmwasser für das neue Gebäude.

Neben den Strohballen beinhaltet das Gebäude weitere Baumaterialien wie Fichteholz für die Träger und Holzrahmen, unbehandelte Holzplatten für die Decken, und Lärchenholz für die Bodenbeläge im

Außenbereich. Der Boden im Innern besteht aus einem eingefärbtem und gewachstem Hartbetonbelag. Die Wände sind außen mit Kalk und innen mit Lehm (Grundputz aus Trasskalk) verputzt. Das Holz ist gänzlich unbehandelt, frei von Zusätzen, Farbstoffen, Lacken oder chemischer Behandlung. Jedes Apartment besitzt ungefähr 40 m² Fläche. Im Innenraum wird eine Abfolge von unterschiedlich privaten Bereichen und unterschiedlich hohen Lichtmengen erzeugt. Der lichtdurchflutete Wohnbereich im Süden dient als Küche, Ess- und Wohnbereich; von ihm aus blickt man in den Garten. Die in der Mitte platzierte Badebox aus raumhohem, satiniertem Glas lässt nur wenig Licht in den Schlafbereich hindurch. Im nördlichen Teil steht ein einfaches, bequemes Doppelbett: das Bett passt sich der gebogenen Wandform an und schafft dadurch eine geschützte, höhlenartige Atmosphäre. Das Fehlen von Ecken durch die U-Form des Grund-

risses, und der Einsatz von transluzenten Glastrennwänden, lassen den Innenraum als einheitliches Ganzes erscheinen. Natürliche Materialien, einfache Formen und warme Farben schaffen eine freundliches und intimes Umfeld, welches die Sinne anspricht. Hier bekommt man ein Gefühl von Frieden, gewiss auch durch die umliegende Landschaft, aber auch dank der einfachen und schönen Formen des Gebäudes. Die Pergola macht das Umfeld noch einladender und gleichzeitig abgelegener. Die Offenheit in Richtung Süden, wie auch der Gemeinschaftsbereich laden dazu ein, Teil der Ruhe dieses Ortes zu werden. All dies schafft einen angenehmen Ort, an dem man einige ruhige Zeit verbringen kann, im Einklang mit der Natur. In der Tat sind die Wohnungen jetzt fast immer ausgebucht. Es gibt Gäste, die schon sieben Mal dort waren. Auf die Frage, warum sie immer wiederkommen, ist die Antwort, es sei das Gefühl von Wärme, Sicherheit und Friedlichkeit in den Räumlichkeiten.

it overlooks the garden. In the middle, the satin-glass-walled bathroom allows some natural light into the bedroom. To the north there is a simple and cosy double bedroom: the bed is accommodated in the concavity of the apse-shaped wall which creates a protected, cave-like atmosphere. The lack of corners determined by the U-shaped plan, and the use of glass for partition walls make the indoor space an uninterrupted whole. Natural materials, simple shapes and warm colours create a hospitable and intimate environment, which appeals to the senses. Here one feels a sense of peace, certainly thanks to the surrounding landscape, but also due to the simple and beautiful shapes of the building. The pergola makes the environment more welcoming and secluded. The openness to the south, as well as the common living room, however, are an invitation to take part in the serene atmosphere of the place. All this creates a pleasant spot to spend some calm time in tune with nature. In fact, the apartments are now almost always booked. There are guests who have already been there seven times. When asked why they keep coming back, the answer is that it is the feeling of warmth, security, and peace on the premises.

LA DONAIRA

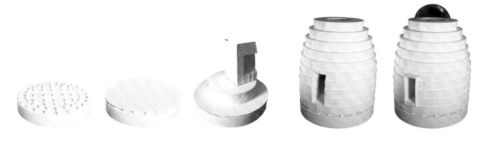

165-169

170-172

The client asked for buildings to accommodate four different functions – country resort, staff rooms, horse stable, and bodega (cellar and winery) – in his hacienda spread over an idyllic area of 270 ha in Ronda, Andalusia. Such functions would be completed by a restaurant to be accommodated in the

Der Kunde wünschte sich Gebäude, in denen vier verschiedene Funktionen untergebracht sind – ein Hotel-Resort mit separaten Unterkünften für die Angestellten, ein Pferdestall und eine Bodega (Weinkeller) – auf seinem idyllischen Landbesitz in Ronda, Andalusien, der sich über eine Fläche von 270 ha

In the introductory essay I have proposed that Schmidt's work has much to do with the condition of marginality, being simultaneously an advantageous position because of the freedom it allows, and a disadvantageous one due to the scarcity of connections. Historically, mountains have been known as refuges of diversity – sometimes even heretical – and places of resistance. But sometimes they have been places of of innovation too.

Better than anyone, Werner Batzing has investigated the identity and perspectives of the Alps. His pages on the survival – or rather the disappearance – of agri-cultural mountain landscapes are among the saddest and most convincing I have ever read. He describes how "the traditional cultural landscape of the Alps is characterised by a dense spatial articulation, where all environmental differences stand out much more clearly than in natural landscape, as its specific variety is emphasised by different forms of exploitation. Therefore, anthropized Alpine landscape turns out to be much more diverse, interesting and, after all, beautiful than natural landscape." In spite of common belief, human intervention there has increased biodiversity (→B015:126+318-321) – at least as long as exploitation was in tune with careful awareness of local limits and characteristics, and subsequently with appropriate, sustainable agricultural practices and a great deal of maintenance labour. (→B015:133) Landscape makes the effort of past generations visible. (→B015:134)

Transformations in agricultural techniques – mechanisation, use of chemicals, pushed specialisation of farms,

Im einleitenden Text habe ich darauf hingewiesen, dass Schmidts Schaffen viel mit Marginalität, dem Arbeiten in einer Nische zu tun hat, was gleichzeitig eine vorteilhafte Position hinsichtlich der Freiheiten, und eine unvorteilhafte hinsichtlich des logistischen Aufwandes darstellt. In der Geschichte sind Berge als Refugium der Vielfalt und Individualität bekannt – manchmal eigenwillig und eigensinnig – und als Orte der Widerstandsfähigkeit. Aber manchmal auch bekannt für Innovation. Werner Bätzing hat besser als kein anderer die Identität und Perspektiven der Alpen untersucht. Seine Seiten zum Thema ‚Überleben' – oder vielmehr Verschwinden – von landwirtschaftlichen Bergregionen, gehören zu den bedrückendsten und überzeugendsten, die ich je gelesen habe. Er beschreibt, wie „die traditionelle Kulturlandschaft der Alpen von einer beengenden, räumlichen Gliederung charakterisiert wird, in der alle ökologischen Unterschiede viel mehr hervortreten, als in einer natürlichen Landschaft, da ihre besondere Vielfalt durch unterschiedliche Formen der Nutzung betont wird. Daher erscheint die von Menschen geprägte Alpenlandschaft viel facettenreicher, interessanter und letzten Endes schöner als Naturlandschaft." Trotz der weit verbreiteten Meinung, hat menschliches Eingreifen dort die Biodiversität erhöht (→B015:126+318-321) – wenigstens so lange, wie die Nutzung mit dem sorgsamen Bewusstsein von lokalen Grenzen und Charakteristiken sowie anschließenden angemessenen, nachhaltigen landwirtschaftlichen Praktiken und einem großen Teil an Instandhaltungsarbeiten einhergeht. (→B015:133) Kulturlandschaft macht die Anstrengungen vergangener Generationen sichtbar. (→B015:134)

192

193

194

195

mountain agriculture is often a marginal activity (**193**: vineyard in Ossola, Italy; **194**: vegetable garden in Trun, Switzerland), or downright transformed into a museum showpiece (**192**: Stübing bei Graz, Austria). It survives, transformed into a pseudo-industrial activity in a few areas (**195**: apple orchard in Vinschgau, South Tyrol)

Berglandwirtschaft stellt oftmals eine Art Nebentätigkeit dar (**193**: Weinberg in Ossola, Italien; **194**: Gemüsegarten in Trun, Schweiz), oder wird geradezu zum Museumsstück deklariert(**192**: Stübing bei Graz, Österreich). Sie überlebt, indem sie in manchen Gegenden zur pseudoindustriellen Tätigkeit umgewandelt wird (**195**: Apfelplantage im Vinschgau, Südtirol)

Transformationen in der Landwirtschaftstechnik – Mechanisierung, Einsatz von Chemikalien, erzwungene Spezialisierung von Betrieben und Gentechnik – haben die Landwirtschaft der Berge aus dem Wettbewerbsmarkt verdrängt. Unter den Hindernissen zu Modernisierung nennt Bätzing: die Kürze des Vegetationszyklus, schwieriger Einsatz von Maschinen auf Grund der Topographie, geringes Interesse der Behörden an Flurbereinigung, schwere Zugänglichkeit und Wartungskosten.

genetic techniques – have pushed mountain agriculture out of market competition. Among the obstacles to modernisation, Bätzing lists: shortness of vegetative cycle, difficult use of machines because of topography, scarce engagement of public authorities for reparcelling, inconvenient accessibility, maintenance costs. (→B015:166-167) In his reconstruction, decline goes through four phases, the fourth being still in the future: abandonment of so-called 'marginal lands;' withdrawal from the variety of farming activities necessary for self-sufficiency and concentration on arable fields and animal breeding; abandonment of fields and some pastures; final demise of mountain agriculture. (→B015:169-174) Bätzing is not optimistic, yet envisages some possibilities to oppose this trend. Among these, farming ancient breeds and growing plants which would offer low yields but extraordinary qualities, and would be adapted to Alpine conditions (→B015:177) – and, more in general, a thorough exploitation of primary local resources in an innovative and sustainable way, merging traditional and contemporary values. (→B015:294+413+427) In his vision, only an innovative mix of different sources of income, an understanding of economic activity as part of realising oneself, and taking responsibility for local environment and development may guarantee a future for Alpine agriculture. (→B015:414+436) Sepp Holzer is an obvious exception to the described trend of decline, yet the rebellious and successful way he displays fits Bätzing's suggestion of multifunctionality and conscious care – as whoever might have visited his farm, the Krameterhof in the Salzburg Alps, can witness. His alternative approach to farming is founded on thinking ecologically and independently (→B054:xiii) and is opposed to training given by agricultural schools which is "focused on fulfilling the demands of agricultural lobbyists" and does not "teach the care and maintenance of nature, but rather its exploitation in the form of maximal yields and monocultures." (→B054:53) South Tyrol is perhaps the luckiest area in the entire Alps,

(→B015:166-167) In seiner Rekonstruktion geht der Rückgang durch vier Phasen, die vierte liegt noch immer in der Zukunft: der Verzicht auf sogenannte ‚Randgebiete'; Rückzug aus der Vielfalt landwirtschaftlicher Tätigkeiten, die für die Autarkie und die Konzentration der Anbauflächen und Viehzucht notwendig sind; Aufgabe von Feldern und Ackerflächen; endgültiger Untergang der Landwirtschaft in den Bergen. (→B015:169-174) Bätzing ist nicht optimistisch, zieht dennoch einige Möglichkeiten in Betracht, um diesem Trend entgegenzuwirken. So das Kultivieren von alten Sorten und der Anbau von Pflanzen, die einen geringen Ertrag dafür aber hohe Qualität bringen, und die an die alpinen Bedingungen angepasst wären (→B015:177) – und im Allgemeinen eine gründliche Nutzung der primären, lokalen Ressourcen auf eine innovative und nachhaltige Art und Weise, mittels Verschmelzung traditioneller und zeitgemäßer Werte. (→B015:294+413+427) Aus seiner Sicht können nur ein innovativer Mix verschiedener Einkommensquellen, ein Verständnis für ökonomische Aktivität als Teil der Selbstverwirklichung und die Übernahme von Verantwortung für das direkte Umfeld und Weiterentwicklung, die Zukunft der alpinen Landwirtschaft garantieren. (→B015:414+436) Sepp Holzer ist das offensichtliche Gegenteil des beschriebenen Rückgangtrends, sein rebellischer und erfolgreicher Weg passt zu Bätzings Vorschlag der Multifunktionalität und bewussten Fürsorge – wie jeder, der seinen Krameterhof in den Salzburger Alpen besucht hat, bezeugen kann. Seine alternative Herangehensweise an Landwirtschaft gründet auf ökologischem und unabhängigem Denken (→B054:xiii) und steht den Ausbildungsmethoden von Landwirtschaftsschulen gegenüber, die „auf die Erfüllung der Forderungen landwirtschaftlicher Lobbyisten fokussiert sind" und die nicht „die Pflege und den Erhalt von Natur, sondern vielmehr ihre Ausbeutung in Form maximaler Erträge und Monokulturen lehren." (→B054:53) Südtirol ist vielleicht dank der politischen Autonomie, die es genießt, und dank der aufgeklärten Politik der autonomen Provinz Südtirol, das glücklichste Gebiet in den gesamten Alpen. Die

made of 3-layer cross-laminated timber panels, are load-bearing. The former bear the roof, while the latter support the floors, also made with (5-layer) cross-laminated timber panels. Timber is left exposed and untreated, as the Gliotts do not seem worried about its ageing – on the contrary, they appreciate the marks history leaves on natural materials. The larch-framed windows were produced by Freisinger in Austria, while the larchwood kitchen was crafted in Sagogn, a nearby village. Cooking is by induction and there is no extractor fan. Beside evening-out moisture and operating as a thermal storage, the unfired brick walls absorb odours – "the day after you can't tell what has been cooked the night before!" they say.

Giusep and Sarah moved in in late 2011 and are already well accustomed to the superior comfort the house offers: the indoor temperature is 22–24°C in the middle of winter, (→■201) while their old house in Laax was draughty, and even if the air temperature was as high, one would feel cold and uncomfortable. On top of it all, the new house shows better performances than Minergie houses, but here one can open the windows during the heating season, since no mechanical ventilation is installed.

Two sensors control the movement of external curtains. (→■206) They are lowered when the indoor temperature is above 23°C, however they are rewound if the wind speed is higher than 25 km/h. The roof overhang is 2.5 m deep. Solar collectors provide hot water. The system is equipped to connect with PV panels, which will be installed when the Gliotts receive the subvention they requested. An electric line was only 160 m away: it hasn't been very costly to extend it, and this allowed to avoid toxic, clumsy and expensive batteries, which would have been needed to

des Dachs auf, und letztere tragen die Zwischendecke, welche aus 5fach Kreuzlagenholz besteht. Das Fichteholz ist naturbelassen und unbehandelt, da Gliotts nicht über dessen Altern besorgt sind – im Gegenteil sie bevorzugen die Spuren, die die Zeit auf den natürlichen Materialien hinterlässt. Die Lärchenholzfenster wurden von der Firma Freisinger in Österreich hergestellt, während die Lärchenholzküche im Nachbarort Sagogn gefertigt wurde. Gekocht wird mit Induktion und es gibt keine Ablufthaube. Neben dem Feuchteausgleich und der Wärmespeicherung, dienen die ungebrannten Lehmsteine vor Zwischen- und Strohwänden als Geruchabsorber – „man kann tagsüber nicht sagen, was am Abend zuvor gekocht wurde!" berichten die Bauherren.

Giusep und Sarah zogen 2011 ein und haben sich bereits an den hochwertigen Komfort, den das Haus bietet, gewöhnt: die Innentemperatur liegt mitten im Winter bei 22 bis 24°C, (→■201) während ihr altes Haus in Laax zugig war und selbst wenn die Lufttemperatur hoch war, war einem kalt und unwohl. Zu guter letzt übertrifft das neue Haus den Minergie Standard bei weitem, und im Gegensatz zu diesen Häusern kann man während der kalten Jahreszeit die Fenster öffnen, da hier keine Lüftungsanlage installiert ist.

Zwei Sensoren kontrollieren die Außenmarkisen. (→■206) Diese senken sich, wenn die Innentemperatur über 23°C liegt, jedoch werden sie eingefahren, wenn die Windgeschwindigkeit mehr als 25 km/h beträgt. Der Dachvorsprung beträgt 2,50 m. Sonnenkollektoren liefern das Warmwasser. Das System ist mit Photovoltaikelementen verknüpft, die installiert werden, sobald Gliotts die beantragten Subventionen erhalten. Die Hauptleitung war nur 160 m vom Haus entfernt: es war nicht sehr teuer, sie zu verlängern, und somit entfiel die Anschaffung

205

206

207

be autonomous (the instantaneous power consumption can be quite high because of the fan used in the stable to dry straw). During the whole winter 2011-12, just 1½ steres of wood have been burnt to heat the two apartments. The stoves were used from Christmas to mid January and again in February during the big chill. The family report that one feels the need to heat the house only on the fourth sunless day: in such a well-insulated house, just a small amount of sun is enough to warm the space up. Sarah and Giusep plan to grow a vegetable garden to the west of the house, next to the kitchen. Here the microclimate is sheltered – on average 2°C higher than on the south side – and a special rock has been placed to allow one to sip aperitifs in the open.

giftiger, sperriger und teurer Batterien, um autark zu sein. Während des gesamten Winters 2011-12 wurden nur 1,5 Ster Holz zum Heizen aller Räume benötigt. Die Holzöfen waren von Weihnachten bis Januar in Betrieb und nochmals im Februar, während der Kälteperiode. Die Familie berichtet, dass man erst am vierten sonnenlosen Tag das Bedürfnis verspürt, das Haus zu heizen. In einem solch gut isolierten Gebäude braucht es nur ein bisschen Sonne um es zu erwärmen. Sarah und Giusep möchten auf der Westseite des Hauses, neben der Küche, einen Gemüsegarten anlegen. Hier ist das Mikroklima geschützt – im Durchschnitt ist es 2 Grad wärmer als auf der Südseite – ein spezieller Stein wurde dort platziert, um einen Aperitif im Freien zu sich nehmen zu können.

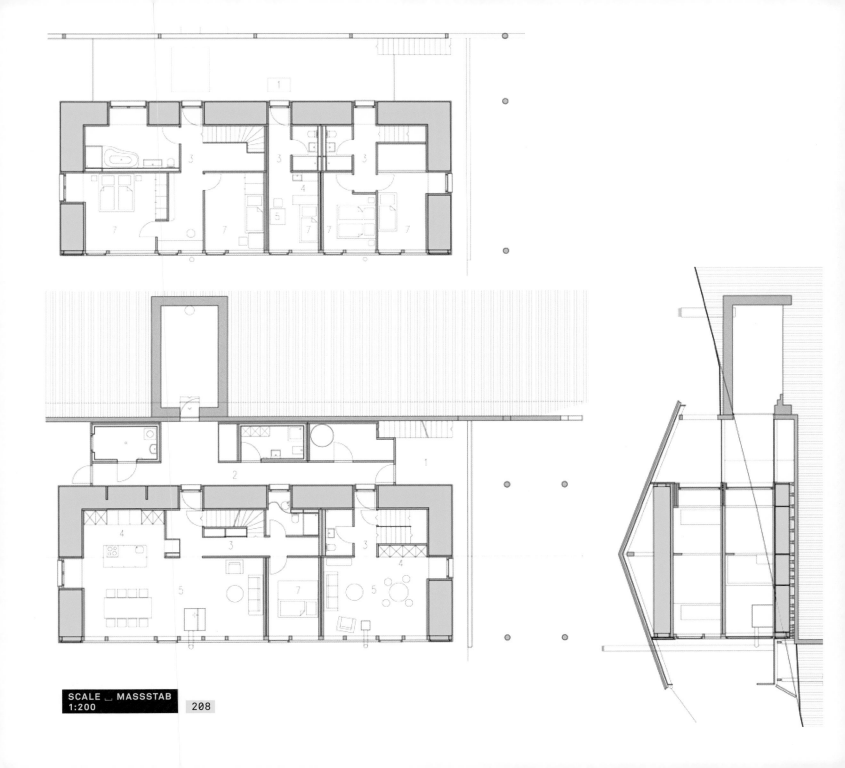

FARM KÜNG ⌐ BAUERNHOF KÜNG

ADDRESS ⌐ ADRESSE:
Söriken 11, CH-5630 Muri/AG

ALTITUDE ⌐ HÖHE:
577 m

DEGREE-DAYS ⌐ GRADTAGE:
3087

PROJECT ⌐ ENTWURF:
2010-11

CONSTRUCTION ⌐ BAU:
2011-12

**MAIN BUILDING FIRMS ⌐
WICHTIGEN BAUFIRMEN:**
Vollenweider, Merenschwand
(general contractor ⌐ Baumeister);
WyliHolz, Muri (wood construction ⌐
Holzbau); Atelier Werner Schmidt +
Firma Flepp (straw-bale construction ⌐
Strohbau)

**PROJECT MANAGER ⌐
PROJEKTLEITUNG:**
Werner Schmidt + Maren Witopil

PLOT AREA ⌐ GRUNDSTÜCKFLÄCHE:
35,886 m²

**HEATED FLOOR AREA ⌐
GEHEIZTE BODENFLÄCHE:**
285 m²

BUILDING COST ⌐ BAUKOSTEN (BKP2):
1,260,000 CHF (4,400 CHF/m²)

Beat Küng's family have been farmers for generations and it was taken for granted that he would take over, but when the time came he felt like changing profession because he was against chemical, industrialised farming methods. Now he his happy with his choice – his poultry farm is not subsidized, but organic farming is faring well. He gets a good profit from eggs and lately also from hen meat.

The farm consisted of a large barn, the old house, and two stables just a hundred meters away. The Küngs wanted to preserve the structure of the complex and to have the house – which over the years had been remodelled and extended several times, and which they esteemed unable to meet contemporary needs – replaced by an ecological building. Beat and his wife Andrea were both interested in straw-bale building, and a friend put them in contact with Werner Schmidt.

The new house was rebuilt on the same site as the old one – in spite of discussions with the municipality that wanted the building to be moved back from the local road –, and was sized on the basis of the volume of the existing house and the maximum permitted building area. It is composed of three parts – the owners' home to the east, a small studio, and the 'retirement apartment' to the west which is now rented to the employee's family. The units have separate entrances, still share the technical facilities and changing room in the middle of the ground floor. In fact, there is a feeling of communitarian spirit among the two families, in keeping with their sympathy for alternative move-

Beat Küngs Familie ist seit Generationen eine Bauernfamilie und es war selbstverständlich, dass er den Hof übernehmen würde, aber als der Zeitpunkt kam, wollte er beinahe den Beruf wechseln, da er gegen den Einsatz von Chemikalien und die industriellen Landwirtschaftsmethoden war. Mittlerweile freut er sich über seine Entscheidung – seine Hühnerfarm wird nicht subventioniert, dennoch läuft die biologische Landwirtschaft sehr gut. Er erwirtschaftet mit Hühnereiern einen guten Gewinn und seit einiger Zeit auch mit dem Hühnerfleisch.

Der Bauernhof bestand aus einer großen Scheune, dem alten Wohnhaus und zwei Ställen, ein paar hundert Meter weiter entfernt. Küngs wollten das Gesamtgefüge des Hofes erhalten und das Bestandsgebäude – welches über die vergangenen Jahrzehnte um- und ausgebaut worden war, und welches ihrer Meinung nach nicht mehr den heutigen Anforderungen entsprach – durch ein ökologisches Haus ersetzen. Beat und seine Frau Andrea waren beide am Strohballenbau interessiert und ein Freund brachte sie in Kontakt mit Werner Schmidt.

Das neue Haus wurde an derselben Stelle errichtet wie das alte – trotz der Diskussionen mit der Gemeinde, die das Haus von der Gemeindestraße zurückversetzt haben wollte – sein Volumen orientiert sich an dem des Bestandsgebäudes und der maximal zugelassenen Ausnützungsziffer. Es setzt sich aus drei Teilen zusammen – die Wohnung des Betriebsleiters auf der Ostseite, ein kleines Studio, und eine Altenteil-Wohnung auf der Westseite, die jetzt an zwei Angestellte vermietet ist. Die Wohnungen haben separate

ments. In 2013, a carport at the rear of north yard has been built, which connects the house with the barn.

Both apartments enjoy a generous view of the countryside through large openings on the south side. They are shaded by the upper floor balcony and a large roof overhang, so that additional devices are unnecessary. The deep balconies on both south and north façades extend the usable, cosy living area. (→ ■209-210)

Perimeter walls are 80 cm wide, and are made of straw bales from Southern Germany. Beat Küng himself produces 6 tonnes of straw per year, but he uses it as animal bedding, while to build the house 40 tonnes were needed. Walls are plastered on both sides – externally with a lime render, while inside a base lime layer

Eingänge, teilen aber den Technikraum und die Umkleide in der Mitte des Hauses im Erdgeschoss. In der Tat spürt man den Gemeinschaftssinn unter den beiden Familien, einhergehend mit ihrer Sympathie für eine alternative Bewegung.

Das Gebäude wird ergänzt durch einen Carport, der sich bis zur Scheune hin erstreckt. Beide Apartments genießen den großzügigen Blick in den Garten durch die großen Fenster im Süden. Sie werden vom Balkon des oberen Geschosses und dem großen Dachüberstand beschattet, so dass ein zusätzlicher Sonnenschutz überflüssig wird. Der tiefe Balkon auf der Nord- und Südseite erweitert die nutzbare und gemütliche Wohnfläche des Hauses. (→ ■209-210)

Die Außenwände sind 80 cm dick und wurden mit Strohballen aus Süddeutschland errich-

is coated with a 2 mm premixed clay finish. The prefabricated interior walls as well as the roof structure are made of 3-layer cross-laminated pine panels. Timber elements have been manufactured locally – this implied higher costs than importing them, but the Küngs felt that this choice made sense, ecologically speaking.

The ground floor is made of black-coloured anhydrite (→■211) which has been oiled after grinding, while the rooms upstairs have a maple board parquet made with timber grown on Beat's own land. The stair rail is made of rough hazelnut stubs. Wet areas are tiled and decorated with mosaics made by Andrea, who also made small artworks disseminated in the house and takes great care to give an Indian touch to some niches the family wanted to be carved in the straw walls: something the architect disapproves of – as they weaken the thermal performance – but which adds to the inhabitants' sense of belonging.

The house is heated by a pre-existing boiler in the barn, from which pipes carry warm water to the underfloor heating system. Vacuum tube collectors on the green roof provide hot domestic water that is stored in a 1,500 l tank. Rainwater is not collected, but while digging for the foundations a spring was discovered, which will be used for watering. A large PV array covers the entire south-facing slope of the barn roof. (→■212)

The Küngs are happy with the house, the only flaw they see is the price. They would have liked to self-build more – they esteem their work saved 120,000 CHF – but they wanted their home finished swiftly. For one year during the construction work, they lived in an old wagon parked in the vegetable garden.

tet. Beat Küng selbst produziert 6 Tonnen Stroh pro Jahr, aber er verwendet es für seine Stallungen, während für den Bau des Hauses 40 Tonnen notwendig waren. Die Wände sind beidseitig verputzt – außen mit Kalkputz, innen wurde der Grundputz aus Kalk mit einer 2mm dünnen Schicht Lehmputz überzogen. Die vorfabrizierten Innenwände sowie die Dachkonstruktion bestehen aus 3fach kreuzverleimten Fichtenholzplatten. Die Holzelemente sind aus heimischem Holz hergestellt – was höhere Kosten als bei importiertem Holz mit sich brachte, aber Küngs waren überzeugt, dass diese Entscheidung aus ökologischer Sicht sinnvoll ist.

Der Bodenbelag besteht aus eingefärbtem Anhydritestrich, (→■211) der nach dem Schleifen geölt wurde, während einige Zimmer des oberen Stockwerkes ein Ahornparkett aus eigenem Holzbestand bekamen. Das Geländer der Innentreppe besteht aus rohen Haselnussstäben. Die Nassbereiche sind gefliest und wurden von Andrea Küng mit Mosaik verziert. Sie erstellte auch kleine Kunstwerke, die übers Haus verteilt sind, und verlieh den Nischen in den Strohballenwänden einen indischen Charakter: diese schwächen zwar etwas die thermische Leistung – tragen aber immens zum Zugehörigkeitsgefühl der Bewohner bei.

Das Haus kann bei Bedarf über eine Fußbodenheizung in den Eingangs- und Nassbereichen zusätzlich erwärmt werden. Das Heizwasser für die Bodenheizung liefert der Stückholzofen im Stallgebäude. Die Vakuumröhrenkollektoren auf dem Gründach liefern das Brauchwarmwasser, welches in einem 1500 l Tank gespeichert wird. Regenwasser wird nicht gesammelt, bei den Aushubarbeiten der Fundamente kam ein unterirdischer Brunnen zu Tage, der nun zum Bewässern des Gartens dient. Auf der Südseite des Scheunendachs wurde zusätzlich eine

212

Photovoltaikanlage installiert. (→■212) Küngs sind sehr glücklich mit ihrem Haus, den einzigen Schwachpunkt, den sie sehen ist der Preis. Sie hätten gerne noch mehr Eigenleistung erbracht, aber sie wollten ihr Haus in relativ kurzer Zeit errichten – sie schätzen, dass ihr aktives Mitarbeiten rund 120.000,- CHF eingespart hat. Während der Bauphase, wohnten sie für ein Jahr in einem alten Bauwagen im Gemüsegarten.

MULTI-PURPOSE HALL BIVIO ⌐ MEHRZWECKHALLE BIVIO

ADDRESS ⌐ ADRESSE:
CH-7457 Bivio/GR

ALTITUDE ⌐ HÖHE:
1769 m

PROJECT ⌐ ENTWURF:
1993

UNBUILT ⌐ NICHT GEBAUT

HEATED FLOOR AREA ⌐
GEHEIZTE BODENFLÄCHE:
681 m²

Lignum GR, the Association for Graubünden Wood, commissioned Werner Schmidt to develop a promotional prototype of an inexpensive hall for sports and events. The project was required to employ the largest possible share of wood, exploiting the different possibilities it offers to building.

The concept Schmidt developed was based on large, modular elements, 9.8 m high. The juxtaposition of seven elements would create a 28 x 26 m plan. The resulting space could accommodate the sports field and/or festival hall in the middle, and secondary areas – such as toilets and cubicles – to the sides, possibly in containers. The roof of such containers could also carry the seats for the public. Shells are extremely efficient structures, particularly to create large, unobstructed spaces. Schmidt's skewed modules were wooden frames consisting of slender ribs and superimposed, diagonally-crossed planking. The whole stuff would have been just 7 to 8 cm thick – the shell structure used for instance in Cazis church, (→p44-49) transposed in wood. The planking would have consisted of *Seitenbretter* (literally, 'side boards'), an abundant by-product of Graubünden sawmills. The modules would have been connected by lattice beams which might have been glazed, and whose top and bottom chords would have reinforced the edges of the adjoining shells.

Schmidt's design was convincing, as it merged function, form and technology in an elegant solution, but unfortunately did not produce any real outcome. An opportunity to build a first specimen – a multi-purpose hall in Bivio – did not advance further than a few preliminary steps.

Die ,Bündnerische Arbeitsgemeinschaft für das Holz' (Lignum GR) beauftragte Werner Schmidt damit, einen verkaufsfördernden Vorschlag für eine günstige Sport- und Eventhalle zu entwerfen. Der Entwurf sollte zum größt möglichen Teil aus Holz gestaltet sein, unter Anwendung unterschiedlicher Konstruktionsmöglichkeiten.

Das Konzept, das Schmidt entwarf, basierte auf großen, modularen Elementen, 9,80 m hoch. Das Nebeneinanderstellen von sieben Elementen erzeugt einen 28 x 26 m umfassenden Grundriss. Die resultierende Fläche könnte eine Sportfeld und/oder eine Festhalle in der Mitte beherbergen, und Sekundärbereiche entlang der Seite schaffen – wie zum Beispiel Toiletten und Kabinen – möglicherweise in Containern. Die Deckel dieser Container könnten die Ränge für die Besucher tragen. Schalen sind extrem effiziente Strukturen, insbesondere um breite, freie Flächen zu schaffen. Schmidts schräg gestellte Module bestehen aus hölzernen Rahmen, feingliedrigen Rippen und einer gekreuzten Diagonalverschalung. Die gesamte Schalenkonstruktion wäre nur 7 bis 8 cm dick – wie in der Kirche Cazis. (→S.44-49) Die Holzverschalung wäre aus Seitenbrettern gefertigt, ein reichlich vorkommendes Nebenprodukt der Bündner Sägewerke. Die Module wären mittels transparenter Shedverglasung verbunden, deren Unter- und Obergurte als verstärkende Schalenränder dienen.

Schmidts Entwurf überzeugte, da er Funktion, Form und Technik in einer eleganten Lösung vereinte, aber unglücklicherweise wurde er nicht umgesetzt. Die Möglichkeit ein erstes Exemplar zu realisieren – die Mehrzweckhalle in Bivio – wurde nicht weiter verfolgt, außer ein paar einleitender Schritte.

STRAW-BALE WALLS + WONDER BOX ⌣ STROHBALLENWÄNDE PLUS WUNDERBOX

Richard Buckminster Fuller was perhaps the first to conceive (in 1936-37) a mass-producible bathroom unit which might be used both as a part of his prefabricated 'Dymaxion House' and in retrofitting existing buildings. (→■214) His design tried to solve the problems of poor hygiene, inefficiency, and high cost of current bathrooms. It would have included bathtub, toilet, sink, integrated lighting, air conditioning, ventilation, and plumbing. All the appliances, pipes, and wires would have been "built-in, limiting on-site construction to mere hook-up." (→B026) The wet cell took up a floor space of 1.5 by 1.5 m and consisted of four main parts, made of stamped sheet metal or moulded plastic. Each part would have been light enough to be carried by two workers and small enough to pass tight staircases and narrow doors.

The almost seamless design also took great care in avoiding places which might favour germ growth or hinder cleaning. Trivial details such as inhibiting the mirror from steaming up, the sink from splattering, and the toilet paper from getting wet had been considered. The project was also very advanced in contemplating dimensions and forms which would have made the care of children and seniors easier, and water-saving devices such as a vapour-gun shower and a waterless composting toilet. (→B027)

Although patented, the *Dymaxion bathroom* was never produced. No luckier destiny had Bruno Munari's project for ELAM shown at the 14th Milan Triennale (1968), (→■215-218) and Joe Colombo's posthumous installation *Unità arredativa globale* (shown at New York's MoMA in the exhibition *Italy: the new domestic landscape*, 1972). (→■219) Both expanded the

Richard Buckminster Fuller war vielleicht einer der Ersten, der sich eine vorfabrizierte Badezimmer-Einheit ausdachte (in 1936-37), die sowohl als Bestandteil seines vorfabrizierten ,Dymaxion House', als auch zur Nachrüstung bestehender Bauten zum Einsatz kam. (→■214) Sein Entwurf versuchte das Problem von schlechter Hygiene, Unwirtschaftlichkeit und hohen Herstellungskosten gewöhnlicher Badezimmer zu lösen. Die Einheit enthielt Badewanne, Toilette, Waschbecken, integrierte Beleuchtung, Klimatisierung, Belüftung und Verrohung. Alle Geräte, Rohre und Kabel sind fix „installiert, und begrenzen die Montage vor Ort auf ein Minimum durch einfaches Anschliessen." (→B026) Die Nasszelle umfasst eine Fläche von 1,5 x 1,5 m und besteht aus vier Hauptelementen, produziert aus gepresstem Metallblech oder geformtem Kunststoff. Jedes Teil ist so leicht, dass es von zwei Personen getragen werden kann und durch enge Treppenhäuser und schmale Türen passt.

Das fast nahtlose Design vermeidet Bakterien fördernde und schwer zu reinigende Stellen. Einfachste Details, wie Schutz des Spiegels vor Beschlagen, Spritzen des Abflusses sowie Nasswerden des Toilettenpapiers, werden berücksichtigt. Das Projekt ist auch im Hinblick auf Abmessungen und Formen, welche Kinder- und Altenpflege erleichtern und wassersparende Apparate, wie eine Sprühdusche und wasserlose Komposttoilette, fortschrittlich. (→B027)

Trotz Patentschutz wurde der *Dymaxion Bathroom* nie in Serie produziert. Auch Bruno Munaris Projekt für ELAM, vorgestellt auf der 14. Mailänder Triennale (1968), (→■215-218) ereilte kein besseres Schicksal, sowie Joe Colombos *Unità arredativa*

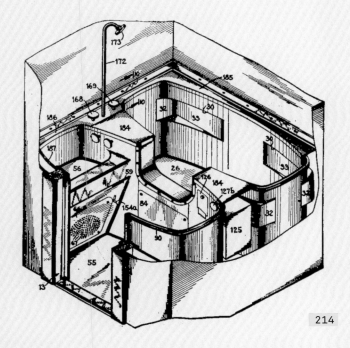

214

idea of a prefabricated furnishing unit and included not only sanitary fittings but all the equipment to support domestic activities, and both were not rooms in themselves but needed a space in which to unpack or deploy. Munari's design was composed by four modules – a 'wet' one including bathroom appliances and the kitchen sink; a four-part container for garments, books, etc.; a kitchen unit including dining board and stools; and a bed/sofa unit. (→B080)
More recently, Allan Wexler designed a number of art installations based on similar principles – packing functions in a small, unified space, encasing everything down to the smallest object. Among these, the *Little office building # 2*, 1987, and the celebrated *Crate House*, 1991, (→■221) compressing "the entire house in an eight foot cube. (…) Kitchen, bathroom, living room, bedroom are each contained in its own

globale (Ausstellung *Italy: the new domestic landscape*, MoMA, New York, 1972). (→■219) Beide entwickelten die Idee einer vorfabrizierten, fertig ausgestatteten Einheit weiter, welche nicht nur Sanitärinstallationen, sondern auch andere häusliche Ausstattungen enthielt. Beide Entwürfe waren keine Räume an sich, sondern Einheiten, welche in einem Raum zur Benutzung aufgestellt werden. Munaris Entwurf war aus vier Modulen zusammengestellt – einem ‚nassen' Bereich, bestehend aus Badezimmerapparaten und der Küchenspüle; einem 4-teiligen Behältnis für Bekleidung, Bücher, usw.; eine Kücheneinheit mit Esstisch und Hockern; und einer Bett/Sofa Einheit. (→B080)
Neueren Datums ist eine Reihe von Installationen von Allan Wexler mit ähnlichen Prinzipien – Funktionen werden in kleine, vereinheitlichte, minimierte Volumen verpackt. Unter

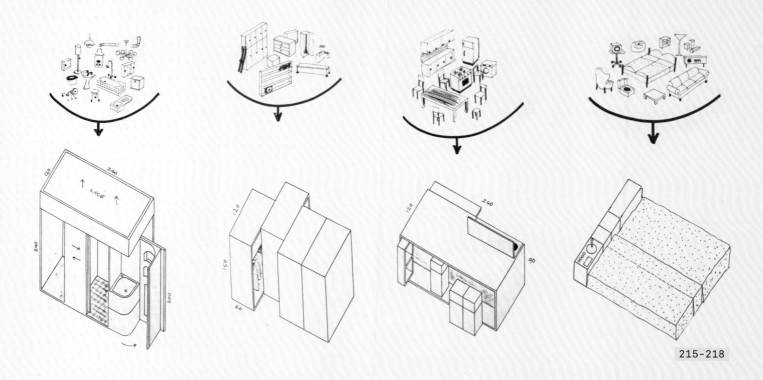

215-218

crate on wheels. (...) When one function is needed its crate is rolled inside [the living space]." (→B118,119)
Hübner and Huster's prefab sanitary units *Sanbau* were designed and produced in 1973-74 by Studenmayer. (→■220) Different series – *Sanbau 2000*, *Sanbau Elementbad für Altbausanierungen*, *Sanbau Mini-Wasch-Dusch-Einheit aus GFK für Kindergärten*, *Sanbau Duschen*, *Sanbau Hospital* – were marketed successfully. According to Peter Blundell Jones, "sales have continued up to the present day." (→B019:31) They were knock-down elements made of glassfibre-reinforced polyester resin. Hübner and Huster's earlier (1972) modular housing system *Casanova* included prefabricated wet-cells. Elements of this system were moulded plastic, octagonal

diesen Arbeiten sind besonders *Little office building # 2*, 1987, und das gefeierte *Crate House*, 1991, (→■221) auffällig. Diese komprimieren „das gesamte Haus in einen 8-Fuss grossen Container. (...) Küche, Bad-, Wohn- und Schlafzimmer sind jeweils in einem eigenen Kasten auf Rädern untergebracht. (...) Benötigt man ein Modul, wird der Kasten einfach ins Innere (den Wohnraum) gerollt." (→B118,119)
Hübners und Husters vorfabrizierte Sanitäreinheiten *Sanbau* sind in den Jahren 1973 und 1974 von Studenmayer gebaut worden. (→■220) Weitere Serien - *Sanbau 2000*, *Sanbau Elementbad für Altbausanierungen*, *Sanbau Mini-Wasch-Dusch-Einheit aus GFK für Kindergärten*, *Sanbau Duschen*, *Sanbau Hospital* – wurden erfolgreich vermarktet. Laut Peter Blundell

shells as large as a room, 3.6 m across. At that time, there was still "optimism about new materials and belief in the economic advantages of mass-production." (→B019:25) To minimise encumbrance and facilitate transport, as early as 1940 Buckminster Fuller had invented "a trailered package of the essential mechanical, kitchen, bath portions of a house to be delivered to the construction site. He called it the *Mechanical Wing*." (→B037) This was to contain "a *Dymaxion bathroom*, with hermetically-sealed waste packaging and chemical disposal apparatus; an energy unit containing diesel engine, air compressor, electrical generator, and hot water heater; and a kitchen and laundry unit, with sink, laundry tub, electric range, refrigerator, and storage space for dishes and silver." (→B038)

I will touch on this point – albeit applied to a much more basic project – examining Schmidt's emergency housing for Pakistan. (→p230-233) What I am concerned about here is discussing his 'straw-bale outer walls plus wonder box' concept, that epitomises his self-sufficient house. To put it very simply, such a house should have a very high-performance envelope – possibly, its area might be minimised adopting a circular plan and even a domed roof – and a container ('wonder box') for wet areas and services for energy, water and air management. From the constructional point of view, the building envelope can be built with simple, even low-tech methods, while the inner, prefabricated unit would include those parts – stairs, cooking implements, baths, etc. – which need to be precisely built, preferably by a joiner. Bathrooms and kitchens should ideally find themselves inside the plan, and not adjacent to straw-bale perimeter walls. This might be one more reason to use prefabricated units.

As such, this concept has not been realised. So far, vonRoll Hydro pavilion is the closest concretisation, but its envelope is technologically very refined (and expensive) because of the functions it must perform. (→■222-223;p50-55) In La Donaira guest rooms, the principle would have found an advanced

Jones: „Der Verkauf läuft bis heute". (→B019:34) Es waren Niedrigstpreiselemente aus Glasfaser verstärktem Kunstharz. Auch Hübner und Husters vorheriges Modul-Haus-System *Casanova* (1972) beinhaltete vorfabrizierte Nasszellen. Die Elemente waren aus geformtem Kunststoff in achteckiger Grundfläche so groß wie ein Raum und einer 3,6 m langen Diagonale. Zu dieser Zeit „es herrschte Optimismus gegenüber neuen Materialien und den wirtschaftlichen Vorzügen der Massenproduktion". (→B019:24)

Um den Aufwand zu reduzieren und den Transport zu erleichtern, erfand Buckminster Fuller schon 1940 ein Container artiges Modul mit dem essenziellen Technik-, Küchen-, und Badteil eines Hauses, welches auf einem speziellen Anhänger auf die Baustelle geliefert werden kann. Er nannte es den *Mechanical Wing*. (→B037) Dieser enthielt ein *Dymaxion bathroom*, mit einer ‚packaging Toilette', die den Urin von den Feststoffen trennt, und diese luftdicht verschweißt; eine Energieeinheit mit Dieselmotor für Druckluftkompressor und Stromgenerator sowie einen Wasserboiler; und eine Koch- und Wascheinheit mit Waschbecken und Waschkessel, Elektroherd, Kühlschrank und Stauraum für Geschirr und Besteck." (→B038)

Berührungspunkte sehe ich – obwohl es sich um ein wesentlich grundlegenderes Projekt handelt – in der Untersuchung von Schmidts Notunterkünften für die Erdbebenopfer in Pakistan. (→S.230-233) Was ich hier besonders zur Diskussion bringen möchte, ist das ‚Strohballenwand + Wunderbox' Konzept, das sein autarkes Haus verkörpert. Einfach gesagt, sollte solch ein Haus eine hocheffiziente Hülle haben – am besten mit minimierter Oberfläche, also eine kreisförmige Grundfläche mit einem Kuppeldach – und einem Container (‚Wunderbox') für Nassbereiche und Gerätschaften für Energie, Wasser, Abwasser und Kühlung. Konstruktiv gesehen kann die Hülle mit einfachen low-tech Methoden gebaut werden, während die innere, vorfabrizierte Einheit – aus Teilen wie Treppe, Kücheneinrichtungen, Bäder, etc. - von Handwerkern präzise

219

220

221

and consistent application. (→p144-149) (Actually, the hypothesis to industrially develop a 'wonder box' unit has been drafted with vonRoll Hydro itself – not only to contain bathroom and kitchen appliances but also the machinery which would operate all the services in an 'autarkic' house →§03). The impossibility of building in the mountains during long, snowy winters has helped the development of woodwork prepared off the building site. In vernacular architecture, prefabrication was already a clever design response to the limits caused by location and climate. In peasant houses, clarity of disposition as well as economy of gestures, money and energy already facilitated the concentration of 'wet services' – in principle, not so differently than in the industrialised, 'designed' counterparts I mentioned above.

Schmidt often uses wood-based prefabricated parts (load-bearing structures, windows and door casements, 'wonder-boxes', etc.) that can be custom produced in winter, in order to keep the on-site building time as short and clean as possible. His job is organised according to the seasons – generally buildings that will be erected the next year are already detailed in the previous one, to allow the winter-time production of what will be needed to assemble them.

In the project Werner Schmidt developed for the Association for Graubünden Wood, the principle of autonomous, prefabricated containers containing services was already present. In subsequent projects, he often used prefabricated elements, e.g. timber wall parts.

In Maya guesthouse, Werner Schmidt has pushed the prefabrication concept to a new limit. The choice was due to the short building time allowed by the high mountain location. During the winter months, the elements were manufactured in Dornbirn by the same enterprise which furnished the prefab parts of Forster+Pfyl twin houses. (→■224-225;p186-189) Notwithstanding the distance and customs duty, the cost was still 25% lower than having them produced in Switzer-

hergestellt werden. Idealerweise stehen diese Einbauten selbständig in der Mitte und berühren die Aussenhülle nicht. Dies ist auch ein weiterer Grund, vorfabrizierte Einheiten zu verwenden.

In dieser Form wurde das Konzept noch nie umgesetzt. Der vonRoll Hydro Pavillon ist jedoch die konkreteste Annäherung an dieses Konzept, aber die Hülle ist hier auf Grund ihrer besonderen Anforderungen sehr speziell und deshalb kostenintensiv. (→■222-223;S.50-55) Beim La Donaira Resort hätte dieses Konzept eine wesentlich weiter entwickeltere und konsequentere Anwendung gefunden. (→S.144-149) (Die Idee eine industrielle ‚Wunderbox' zu bauen, wird tatsächlich von der Firma vonRoll Hydro angedacht – nicht nur eine Küche und ein Bad beinhaltend, sondern auch alle anderen Geräte, um ein autarkes Haus zu betreiben →§03).

Die Schwierigkeit, während langer, schneereicher Winter in den Bergen zu bauen, begünstigt die Entwicklung von vorgefertigten Holzbauteilen. In der traditionellen Architektur war Vorfabrikation schon immer eine kluge Art, um auf die Einschränkungen durch Ort und Klima zu reagieren. Bereits in der bäuerlichen Architektur unterstützt die Klarheit der Einteilung, genauso wie die Sparsamkeit des Ausdrucks, Geldes und der Energie eine Verdichtung der ‚Nasszellen' – im Prinzip nicht grundlegend anders, als bei der oben genannten industrialisierten, ‚gestalteten' Wunderbox.

Schmidt verwendet oft vorfabrizierte Holzelemente (lasttragende Elemente, Fenster- und Türkisten, ‚Wunderboxen', etc.), welche gewöhnlich im Winter hergestellt werden, um die Bauzeit auf der Baustelle so kurz und sauber wie möglich zu halten. Seine Arbeitseinteilung richtet sich nach den Jahreszeiten– in der Regel werden die Gebäude des nächsten Jahres, bereits im Vorjahr detailliert geplant, um eine Vorfabrikation aller für den Aufbau benötigten Teile im Winter zu ermöglichen.

Bereits beim Projektentwurf für Lignum GR von Werner Schmidt war das Prinzip der eigenständigen, vorfabrizierten Container, welche diverse Funktionen enthielten, zugegen. In

222

223

land. The two buildings were erected in just three weeks, and are now open to the public.

The two-storey, elongated building near the road contains eight guest rooms. Each room is constituted by a 20 m² box made of cross-laminated timber panels; the transport of such an oversized load was a design task in itself. Boxes arrived at the site already equipped with a glass box containing the bathroom, and black stone floor tiles. On-site further work processes did not sum up to much more than clay plastering, cabling and installing sanitary appliances. Rooms are entered from the east side, while the large French windows to the west provide an exit to the balcony and offer a view of the mountains. After positioning the wooden boxes, 80 cm-wide straw bales have been placed between the rooms, on the building perimeter, and on the upper face of the last floor. Besides separating acoustically one room from the next, and thermally insulating the building, the straw-bale walls bear the roof load.

The second building, which lies on a slightly lower spot,

den darauffolgenden Projekten verwendete er oftmals vorfabrizierte Elemente wie z. B. Holzelementwände.

Beim Maya Guesthouse hat Werner Schmidt dieses Vorfabrikationsprinzip neu umgesetzt. Die Entscheidung wurde auch im Hinblick auf die Lage in einer hohen Bergregion, welche nur eine kurze Bauzeit ermöglicht, gefällt. Während der Wintermonate wurden die Teile von einer Firma in Dornbirn, Österreich vorfabriziert, welche auch schon die Elemente für die Zwillingshäuser Foster+Pfyl hergestellt hat. (→■224-225; S.186-189) Trotz der Entfernung und Zollgebühren, waren die Herstellungskosten noch immer merklich unter dem Schweizer Niveau. Die beiden Gebäude wurden in nur drei Wochen aufgerichtet, und sind nun für die Öffentlichkeit als Bed & Breakfast zugänglich.

Das zweistöckige, längliche Gebäude zur Straße hin, beherbergt acht Gästezimmer. Jeder Raum besteht aus einer 20 m² großen Holzbox aus Kreuzlagenholz; der Transport einer solch sperrigen Last war ein Herausforderung. Die Boxen erreichten den Bauplatz bereits ausgestattet mit einer gläsernen

224

225

houses the owners' residence on the upper floor, while the kitchen, office, warehouse and a large dining room for guests are located on the ground floor. Here the building method is different: Schmidt has employed for the first time prefabricated – still made-to-measure – straw-bale infill wall panels, which were delivered already plastered on both faces.

Sanitärbox und schwarzen Schiefersteinplatten. Die weiteren Arbeiten vor Ort beschränkten sich auf Feinputz, Anschluss der fertigen Elektroanlagen sowie Endmontage der Sanitärapparate. Die Räume werden vom Osten betreten, während die raumhohen Fenster Richtung Westen einen Austritt auf den Balkon mit seiner großartigen Bergsicht ermöglichen. Nachdem die Holzboxen platziert waren, wurden sie in den Zwischenräumen sowie auf der Außenseite und am Dach mit 80 cm starken Strohballen verpackt. Neben ihrer Funktion der akustischen Trennung und thermischen Isolation der Räume, tragen die Strohwände zu einem großen Teil die Dachlast ab. Das zweite Gebäude liegt an einer etwas tieferen Stelle und beherbergt die Wohnung der Besitzer auf dem Obergeschoss, während Küche, Büro, Lager, und ein großer Speisesaal für die Gäste im Erdgeschoss zu finden sind. Hier ist die Bauweise eine andere: Schmidt verwendet zum ersten Mal vorfabrizierte – maßgefertigte – und mit Stroh gefüllten Wandelemente, welche bereits beidseitig verputzt geliefert wurden.

226

228

227

229

230

231

232

MAYA GUESTHOUSE

address ⌐ Adresse: Linzerbot, CH-1973 Mont Noble-Nax/VS
altitude ⌐ Höhe: 1,282 m
degree-days ⌐ Gradtage: 3308
project ⌐ Entwurf: 2009-11
construction ⌐ Bau: 2012
main building firms ⌐ Wichtigen Baufirmen:
Héritier, Sion (general contractor ⌐ Baumeister); Fussenegger Holzbau GmbH, Dornbirn (wood construction ⌐ Holzbau); Atelier Werner Schmidt + Firma Flepp (straw-bale construction ⌐ Strohbau)
plot area ⌐ Grundstückfläche: 2,614 m²
heated floor area ⌐ Geheizte Bodenfläche: 160 (Bettenhaus) + 175 (Haupthaus) m²
main glazed area (W) ⌐ Fensterfläche Hauptfassade (W): 70 (Bettenhaus) + 27.5 (Haupthaus) m²
building cost ⌐ Baukosten: 2,150,000 CHF (6,400 CHF/m²)

226-229

construction phases of Maya guesthouse (guestrooms building)

226-229

Aufbauphase des Maya Guesthouse (Bettenhaus)

230-232

construction phases of Maya guesthouse (owners' building). In picture 231 the relationship between the two buildings can be understood

230-232

Aufbauphase des Maya Guesthouse (Haupthaus). Im Bild 231 wird der Zusammenhang beider Gebäude deutlich

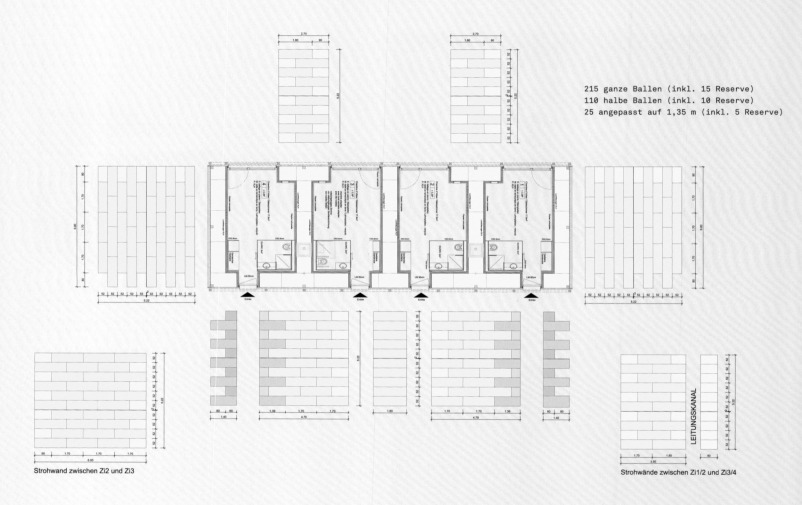

215 ganze Ballen (inkl. 15 Reserve)
110 halbe Ballen (inkl. 10 Reserve)
25 angepasst auf 1,35 m (inkl. 5 Reserve)

Strohwand zwischen Zi2 und Zi3

Strohwände zwischen Zi1/2 und Zi3/4

233

layout of straw bales to be
employed in the construction of
Maya guestrooms building

Strohballenplan für den
Einsatz im Bettenhaus des Maya
Guesthouse

234-242

construction phases of Maya
owners' building

Aufbauschema Haupthaus des Maya
Guesthouse

SCALE ⌐ MASSSTAB
1:200

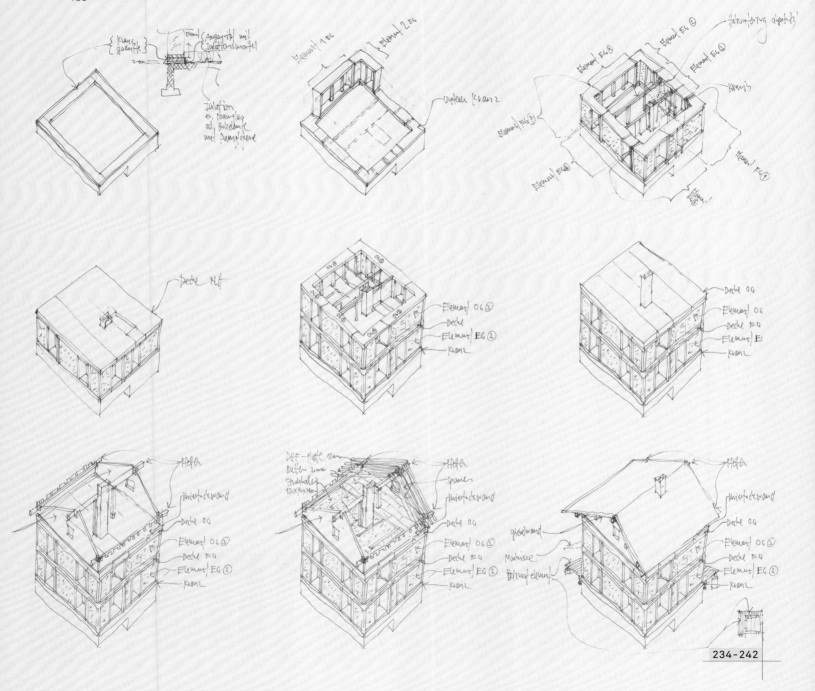

I believe it is interesting to compare the panels Werner Schmidt has designed for this project with ModCell panels. (→B079) Both panels are one-storey high and are timber-framed, so as to form a load-bearing perimeter wall system. Both structural systems can be compared to a platform frame construction, in that the intermediate timber slab is sandwiched in between ground- and first-floor wall panels. ModCell as well as Schmidt's elements may or may not include window frames. Finally, in both systems joints are left exposed and clearly recognisable.

ModCell are a partially standardised product, which has been used in around twenty projects to date, including most recently a scheme of 20 load-bearing 2- and 3-storey houses in Leeds. (→■255-266) Their racking shear resistance, fire resistance, thermal transmittance, and acoustic transmittance have been extensively tested at the University of Bath, in some cases passing "with flying colours." (→B117) They are 490 mm deep (straw bale + render on both sides). Their planar form and rather modest volume make them reasonably transportable. The glulam frame is built first, then straw bales are stacked in and pressed down with a front-end loader. ModCell panels are

Ich denke es wäre interessant, diese Wandelemente von Werner Schmidt mit ModCell Elementen zu vergleichen. (→B079) Beide Außenwandelemente sind einstöckig, lasttragend und holzgerahmt. Beide Systeme können mit einer Holzrahmenkonstruktion verglichen werden, bei welcher die Holzdecke die Außenwände unterbricht, und zwischen den Wandelementen aufliegt. ModCell sowie Schmidts Elemente können Fenster enthalten. In beiden Systemen sind die Elementstöße deutlich sichtbar. ModCell ist ein teilweise standardisiertes Produkt, welches bis heute in circa 20 Projekten zum Einsatz kam, darunter zuletzt ein Entwurf für 20 zwei bis drei geschossige, lasttragende Gebäude in Leeds. (→■255-266) Ihre Zug- und Schwerfestigkeit, ihr Feuerwiderstand, der Wärmedurchgang, und ihre akustische Durchlässigkeit sind gründlich von der University of Bath getestet worden, und haben ‚teilweise sogar mit Bravour' bestanden. (→B117) Sie sind 49 cm stark (Strohballen und Verputz auf beiden Seiten). Ihre flächige Form und ziemlich kleines Volumen macht sie vernünftig transportabel. Zuerst wird der Leimholzrahmen gebaut, dann werden die Strohballen eingestapelt und mit einem Frontlader heruntergepresst. ModCell Wandelemente sind mit rostfreien, vertikalen Stahlstäben inklusive Kreuz und

269

270

271

272

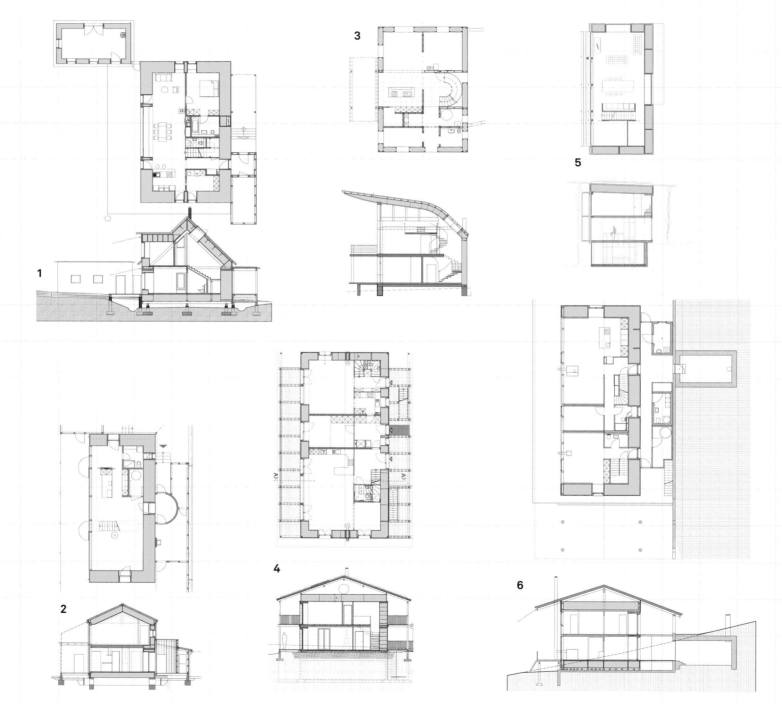

plans and sections of straw-bale buildings

1

2

3

4

5

6

7

8

10

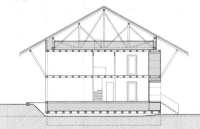

11

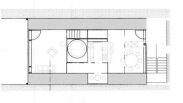

9

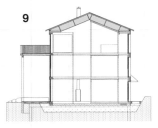

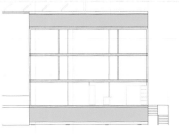

1 Haus Wegmann (2008); load-bearing straw bales ⌣ lasttragende Strohballenbauweise 181 m²; 2 storeys ⌣ Geschosse

2 Haus Schmidlin (2004); load-bearing straw bales ⌣ lasttragende Strohballenbauweise 160 m²; 2 storeys ⌣ Geschosse

3 Haus Dalsant (2003); straw-bale infill in post-and-beam costruction ⌣ Strohballen in Holzständerbau; 250 m²; 3 storeys ⌣ Geschosse

4 Haus Küng (2012); hybrid construction straw bales and cross-laminated timber ⌣ Hybridkonstruktion Strohballen und Kreuzlagenholz; 285 m²; 2 storeys ⌣ Geschosse + cellar ⌣ Keller

5 Haus Bühlmann (2012); timber elements with straw-bale infill ⌣ Holzelemente mit Strohballen; 210 m²; 3 storeys ⌣ Geschosse

6 Haus Gliott (2011); partially load-bearing straw bales ⌣ teillasttragende Strohballenbauweise; 238 m²; 2 storeys ⌣ Geschosse

7 Haus Braun (2002); load-bearing straw bales lasttragende Strohballenbauweise; 110 m²; 2 storeys ⌣ Geschosse

8 Haus Schmid-Hermanutz (2009) partially load-bearing straw bales ⌣ teillasttragende Strohballenbauweise; 120 m²; 2 storeys ⌣ Geschosse

9 Zwillinghäuser Forster + Pfyl (2011); load-bearing straw bales + prefab boxes ⌣ lasttragende Strohballenbauweise + vorfabrizierte Boxen; 190 m²; 3 storeys ⌣ Geschosse + cellar ⌣ Keller

10 Haus Rüesch (2005); load-bearing straw bales ⌣ lasttragende Strohballenbauweise; 150 m²; 2 storeys ⌣ Geschosse

11 ZCV Langhaus (project ⌣ Entwurf); load-bearing straw bales ⌣ lasttragende Strohballenbauweise; 108-162 m²; 2-3 storeys ⌣ Geschosse

plans and sections of straw-bale buildings

12

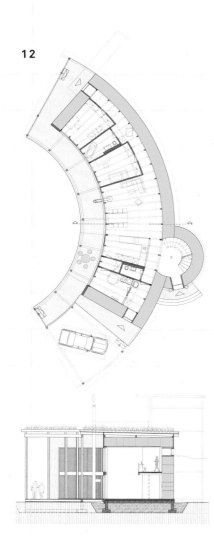

13

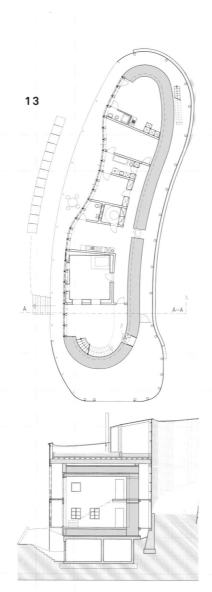

A ◁ ⋯⋯⋯⋯⋯⋯⋯⋯⋯⋯ A—A

A⸜

14

15

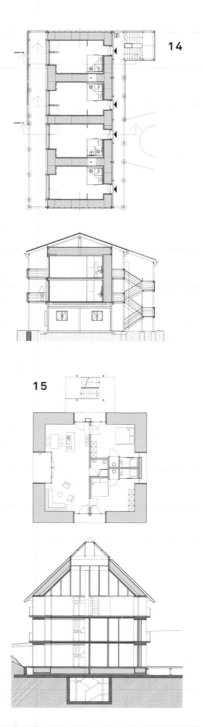

16

18

20

21

19

17

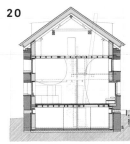

12 Haus von Erffa (ongoing ⌣ laufend); partially load-bearing straw bales ⌣ teillasttragende Strohballenbauweise
251 m²; 2 storeys ⌣ Geschosse

13 Bauernhaus Niederkofler (2007) load-bearing straw bales ⌣ lasttragende Strohballenbauweise
323 m²; 2 storeys ⌣ Geschosse + cellar ⌣ Keller

14 Maya Guesthouse (2012); prefab boxes with load-bearing straw bales ⌣ Vorfabrizierte Boxen mit lasttragende Strohballen (hybrid)
160 m²; 2 storeys ⌣ Geschosse + cellar ⌣ Keller

15 Ferienwohnungen Fliri (2007) load-bearing straw bales ⌣ lasttragende Strohballenbauweise
ca. 400 m²; 3 storeys ⌣ Geschosse

16 Haus Dora (2011); partially load-bearing straw bales ⌣ teillasttragende Strohballenbauweise
186 m²; 3 storeys ⌣ Geschosse

17 Umbau Haus Ervin Jacomet (2011); straw insulation between timber panels ⌣ Strohdämmung in Holzkonstruktion
216 m²; 3 storeys ⌣ Geschosse + cellar ⌣ Keller

18 Maya Haupthaus (2012); straw in prefab elements ⌣ Stroh in vorfabrizierten Elementen
175 m²; 2 storeys ⌣ Geschosse

19 Hauserweiterung Bigliel (2009) straw in prefab elements Stroh in vorfabrizierten Elementen
74 m²; 2 storeys ⌣ Geschosse + cellar ⌣ Keller

20 Umbau Haus Bühler-Seiz (2006) straw insulation of an existing building ⌣ Strohdämmung best. Konstruktion
188 m²; 4 storeys ⌣ Geschosse

21 Haus Oetterli (2010) partially load-bearing straw bales ⌣ teillasttragende Strohballenbauweise
142 m²; 2 storeys ⌣ Geschosse

plans and sections of straw-bale buildings

22

23

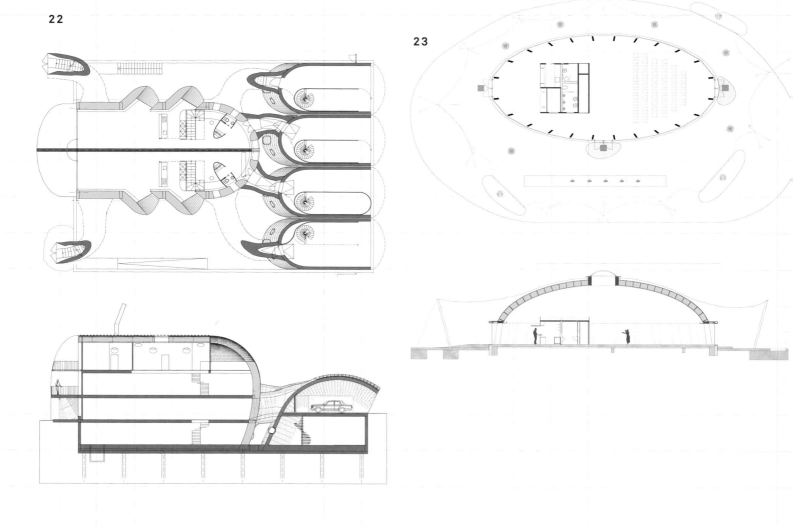

25

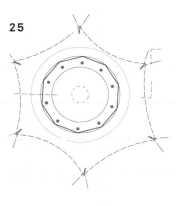

27

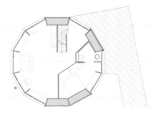

24

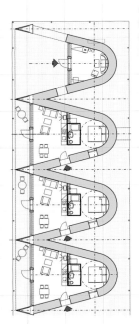

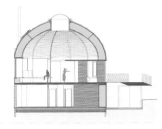

22 „Wellenhaus" (2006)
timber elements with straw infill
⌐ Holzelemente mit Strohdämmung
506 m²; 4 storeys ⌐ Geschosse

23 vonRoll Hydro Ausstellungs-
und Ausbildungshalle (2010)
engineered timber, straw insulation of roof ⌐ Ingenieurholzbau,
Strohdämmung Dach
217 m²; 1 storey ⌐ Geschoss

24 Ferienwohneinheiten
Esserhof (2006)
load-bearing straw bales ⌐
lasttragende Strohballenbauweise
126 m²; 1 storey ⌐ Geschoss

25 ZCV kleiner Infopavillon
(project ⌐ Entwurf)
load-bearing straw bales ⌐
lasttragende Strohballenbauweise
70 m²; 1 storey ⌐ Geschoss

26 Resort La Donaira (2009)
load-bearing straw bales ⌐ lasttragende Strohballenbauweise
23 m²; 2 storeys ⌐ Geschosse

27 Haus Camenzind (2013)
timber elements with
straw-bale infill ⌐
Holzelemente mit Strohballen
148 m²; 2½ storeys ⌐ Geschosse

28 Haus Ochoa (2010); partially
load-bearing straw bales ⌐ teillasttragende Strohballenbauweise
134 m²; 2 storeys ⌐ Geschosse

28

26

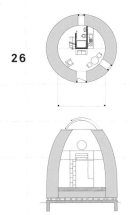

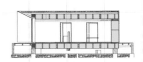

STRAW-BALE BUILDING À LA WERNER SCHMIDT ⎵
STROHBALLENBAU À LA WERNER SCHMIDT

"Strawbale building makes sense. It offers us a radical way to solve many of the issues facing construction with respect to thermal efficiency, carbon footprint and cost. (...) Working with straw (...) is simple, flexible, imprecise and organic."
Barbara Jones (→B061:9)

"converts' enthusiasm is not a sound or rational basis for choosing a building material, since this is not holistic in approach"
Tom Woolley (→B126:72)

„Die Strohballenbauweise macht Sinn. Sie bietet uns eine radikale Möglichkeit, Probleme zu beheben, die beim Bau im Hinblick auf thermische Effizienz, Ökologischen Fußabdruck und Kosten auftreten (...) Das Arbeiten mit Stroh (...) ist einfach, flexibel, ungenau und ökologisch."
Barbara Jones (→B061:9)

„Der Enthusiasmus von Befürwortern ist keine Grundlage oder vernünftige Basis, um ein Baumaterial zu wählen, da dies keinen ganzheitlichen Ansatz darstellt."
Tom Woolley (→B126:72)

All materials offer possibilities to the builder. Schmidt says: "there are no bad materials, just erroneously utilised." (A statement which echoes Leon Battista Alberti's: "The good builder is not so much concerned with choosing the most adapted materials, as he is to making the most appropriate and fruitful use of those being available to him"). (→B007) Schmidt has used various materials both for structural and insulation purposes – those used for the latter include polyurethane foam, rock wool, cellulose, EPS, foam glass, wood fibre board, cork, expanded clay, and vacuum-fused fumed silica. It was his experience with various materials that convinced him to give preference to straw, as its characteristics best adhere to his principles. Schmidt's choice, far from stemming from an ideological parti-pris, is grounded on an holistic understanding of ecological building, much more demanding than just meeting low-energy consumption requirements.

Straw is appropriate for creating healthy living environments (→§05) and minimising the ecological impact of the building process – from construction to disposal. (→§04) Schmidt's goal is to realise pleasant, autonomous buildings, (→§03) and "The first step is always to eliminate the heating, and if you want to do so you need a thick insulation. If this is done with conventional insulation materials, it is very expensive because the production of these materials is dependent on rising energy prices. In straw-bale building it is not relevant, from a cost perspective, if one uses 50 or 120 cm insulation." (→B064) To put it in another way, 'Passivhaus' standards are attained at a much lower cost than with conventional solutions. According to Schmidt, a single-family, jumbo-

Alle Materialien bieten dem Gestalter Möglichkeiten. Schmidt sagt: „es gibt keine schlechten Materialien, nur falsch eingesetzte." (ein Statement, welches Leon Battista Albertis ähnelt: „Der gute Planer ist nicht so sehr damit beschäftigt, das geeignetste Material zu wählen, sondern zieht den angemesssendsten und fruchtbarsten Nutzen aus den Materialien, die ihm zur Verfügung stehen"). (→B007) Schmidt hat verschiedenste Materialien verwendet, sowohl für konstruktive als auch isolierende Zwecke – hier sind Polyurethanschaum, Steinwolle, Zellulose, EPS, Schaumglas, Holzfaserplatten, Kork, Blähton, Vakuumisolationsplatten zu nennen. Es war seine Erfahrung verschiedener Materialien, die ihn von den Vorzügen des Strohs überzeugten, da dessen Eigenschaften am besten mit seinen Prinzipien übereinstimmen. Schmidts Wahl, weit entfernt von einer ideologischen Sichtweise, gründet auf einem ganzheitlichen Verständnis der ökologischen Bauweise, welches er vielmehr als gesamtheitliche Verpflichtung, denn als bloße Erfüllung der Anforderungen an einen niedrigen Energieverbrauch sieht.

Stroh eignet sich für das Schaffen von gesunden Lebensräumen, (→§05) und für die Minimierung der ökologischen Auswirkungen des Bauprozesses – von dem Errichten bis zur Entsorgung. (→§04) Schmidts Ziel ist es, angenehme, autonome Gebäude zu realisieren, (→§03) und „Der erste Schritt ist immer, die Heizung wegzulassen, und wenn man das will, braucht man eine dicke Isolierung. Wenn man dies mit konventionellen Isolierungsmaterialien macht, ist dies sehr teuer, da die Produktion dieser Materialien von den steigenden Energiepreisen abhängt. Interessant ist dabei, dass die Stärke der Isolation im Falle ei

straw-bale house may be built at about 1,200 to 2,200 €/m²
anywhere in Europe – except in Switzerland where prices
are definitely higher. In fact, the price of straw bales is lower
than that of any other insulating material. (The price varies
widely according to region and to the crop year. On average,
in Central Europe straw costs about 18 €/m³ – approximately
0.13 €/kg. The price may more than double including transport). On the other hand, the labour cost / material cost ratio
is larger than with other building techniques. In a straw-bale
house the only expensive products are advanced-technology
parts such as triple-glazed windows and PV arrays, as well
as some glued timber elements.

Among the advantages Schmidt has found in straw-bale
construction, the following are worth mentioning:
- derivation from a renewable and globally abundant resource. One can use straw to build a house on the same f
ield whence it was harvested the previous year, while a
human life-span is needed to grow a tree suitably sized
for construction.
- carbon sequestration. According to Wilhelm, 1 kg straw
binds 2.12 kg CO_2. (→B018)
- excellent bio-compatibility before, during and after operational life. No harmful consequences to the health of
inhabitants and to the environment in general have ever
been reported.
- biodegradability: when not (re)usable they can be burnt or
dumped with no consequence for the environment.
- very low embodied energy: 0.18–0.35 MJ/kg, (→B077:29)
whereas the embodied energy of synthetic insulating materials such as EPS, XPS and PUR is around 72–109 MJ/kg.
(→B049) Since 1.2 m straw equals 0.9 m EPS as long as thermal conductivity is concerned, one square metre of insulated
wall would cost 40–140 MJ in the first case, 1,800–2,100 MJ
in the second. (→B008)
- good thermal insulation value. The λ value given for straw
bales by the Fachverband Strohballenbau Deutschland e.V.

ner Strohballenkonstruktion für die Kosten praktisch keine Rolle spielt." (→B064) Mit anderen Worten, der ,Passivhausstandard'
kann mit einem viel geringeren Kostenaufwand erreicht werden,
als bei konventionellen Lösungen. Gemäß Schmidt, ein Einfamilienhaus mit Jumbostrohballen kann für 1200 bis 2200 €/m²
überall in Europa gebaut werden – mit Ausnahme von der
Schweiz, wo die Preise definitiv höher sind. In der Tat ist der
Preis für Strohballen tiefer als der jedes anderen Isolationsma-
terials. (Der Preis variiert je nach Region und Ernteertrag stark.
Im Durchschnitt kostet in Mitteleuropa Stroh 18 €/m³ – ungefähr 0,13 €/kg. Der Preis kann sich inklusive Transport mehr
als verdoppeln.) Auf der anderen Seite ist das Arbeitskosten zu
Materialkosten Verhältnis größer als bei anderen Bautechniken.
In einem Strohballenhaus sind die einzigen teuren Produkte
moderne Technikelemente wie Dreifachverglasung, Photovoltaikanlagen oder verleimte Holzelemente.

Die Vorteile, die Schmidt beim Strohballenbau sieht, sind folgende:
- Ursprung einer erneuerbaren und weltweit reichlich vorkommenden Quelle. Praktisch kann man ein Haus auf demselben
Feld bauen, auf dem das Stroh im Vorjahr geerntet wurde,
während es ein Menschleben lang dauert, bis ein Baum die
entsprechende Größe erreicht hat, um eine Holzkonstruktion
daraus machen zu können.
- Kohlenstoffbindung. Gemäß Wilhelm bindet 1 kg Stroh
2,12 kg CO_2. (→B018)
- Exzellente Biokompatibilität vor, während und nach dem
Gebrauch. Keine schädlichen Auswirkungen auf die Gesundheit
der Bewohner und auf die Umwelt im Allgemeinen wurden
je beobachtet.
- Biologische Abbaubarkeit: wenn es nicht (wieder)verwendet
wird, kann man es verbrennen oder wegwerfen ohne die
Umwelt zu belasten.
- Sehr wenig Graue Energie: 0,18 bis 0,35 MJ/kg, (→B077:29)
wohingegen die Graue Energie von synthetischen Isolationsmaterialien wie EPS, XPS und PUR bei ungefähr 72 bis 109 MJ/
kg liegt. (→B049) Da, was die Wärmeleitfähigkeit betrifft, 1,20 m

(FASBA) (→B041) is 0.045 W/mK, considerably lower than that given by other authors. (→B077:18)
- inherently massive walls, deriving much of their stability and strength from simple geometry. (→B040:76) They are among the few insulation materials which are capable of standing upright, independent of a supporting structure – indeed they can bear a load. (→§09)
- latent heat storage. According to Minke, (→B077:19) the heat capacity of straw is much lower than those of structural materials but higher than those of insulating materials.
- very good fire resistance if appropriately protected by a plaster layer. (→B041,117) Straw is classified as B2 (normally flammable material) according to DIN 4102 standard.
- low water vapour diffusion resistance factor, as was the rule in traditional building methods.
In Europe, just a few laboratories – among which GrAT, the University of Bath, Braunschweig Technical University, HTW Chur, CSTB [Centre Scientifique et Technique du Bâtiment] – have developed tests on straw bales, and there is still much disagreement about the values – even about basic dimensions. (→B126:83) Assigned values are often conservative, for the benefit of industrial products; (→B025) in fact, real performances obtained making use of natural materials are often better than predicted from calculation. Moreover, laboratory tests were often conducted on low- (90 kg/m³) or mid- (120 kg/m³) compressed small bales, usually employed in the USA and elsewhere.
These are among the main reasons why Schmidt aims to perform a series of tests on 'jumbo' bales – i.e. 240 x 120 x 70–90 cm – at the gbd Lab GmbH in Dornbirn. (→■273) Values such as λ, μ, compressive strength, etc., would be measured on 140 kg/m³-compressed bales as such, and on unplastered as well as plastered walls made of these bales. Tests would scientifically investigate jumbo bales characteristics, that are expected to be different from those of usual, small ones. Tests will be performed on both bales made of entire straws

Stroh 0,90 m EPS entsprechen, würde 1 m² isolierte Wand 40 bis 140 MJ für ersteres und 1800 bis 2100 MJ letzteres Material bedeuten. (→B008)
- Guter thermischer Isolationswert. Der λ-Wert, der vom Fachverband Strohballenbau Deutschland e.V. (FASBA) (→B041) angegeben wird, liegt bei 0,045 W/mK, tiefer als der Wert von anderen Autoren. (→B077:18)
- Inhärente, massive Wände, abgeleitet von ihrer Stabilität und Festigkeit einfacher Geometrie. (→B040:76) Sie gehören zu den wenigen Isolationsmaterialien, die aufrecht stehen können, unabhängig von eine m statischen Element – in der Tat können sie Last aufnehmen. (→§09)
- Latente Wärmespeicherung. Gemäß Minke (→B077:19) ist die Wärmekapazität von Stroh viel niedriger, als die Werte statischer Materialien, aber viel höher als die von Isolationsmaterialien.
- Sehr gute Feuerwiderstandsfähigkeit, wenn entsprechend durch eine Putzschicht geschützt. (→B041,117) Stroh ist als B2 eingestuft (normal entflammbar) gemäß des DIN 4102 Standards.
- Geringer Wasserdampfwiderstandsfaktor, wie es die Regel in der traditionellen Bauweise der Fall war.
In Europa haben nur wenige Labore – darunter GrAT, University of Bath, Technische Universität Braunschweig, HTW Chur, CSTB (Centre Scientifique et Technique du Bâtiment) – Strohballentests entwickelt, und es gibt nach wie vor Uneinigkeit zu den Werte – sogar zu den grundlegenden Dimensionen. (→B126:83) Bestimmte Werte sind oftmals konservativ, zu Gunsten von Industrieprodukten; (→B025) in der Tat sind die Erfahrungen, die durch den Einsatz von natürlichen Materialien gemacht werden, oftmals hilfreicher als Berechnungen. Vielmehr wurden die Tests oft an gering (90 kg/m³) oder mittel (120 kg/m³) gepressten Ballen durchgeführt, in der Regel in den USA und anderswo verwendet.
Das ist der Grund, weshalb Schmidt auf eine Reihe von eigenen Tests an Jumboballen – zum Beispiel 240 x 120 x 70 bis 90 cm – abzielt – am gbd Lab GmbH in Dornbirn. (→■273) Werte, wie λ,

and of fragments (the length they are cut for animal bedding). Werner Schmidt hypothises that λ might be better with chopped stalks, whereas whole straws offer a better grip for plastering. Another advantage is that the newest balers automatically put a chip in jumbo bales, containing data such as production place, date, moisture, etc. Jumbo bales are also favoured by farmers, as they can be more rapidly moved and stocked than small bales.

Obviously, building with jumbo bales means according preference to fully or partly load-bearing walls. These are Schmidt's favourite techniques – although sometimes he designs timber-frame buildings where small bales (50 cm thick or less) are just used as insulating infill. Schmidt asserts the load-bearing and partly-load-bearing ("hybrid") techniques are "the simplest and best method[s] of construction in terms of my goals. (…) A loaded straw-bale wall is condensed by the weight of the building," (→B081:9) while if the wall is not loaded, over time the straw insulation will perhaps settle down, creating a thermal bridge at the top.

Moreover, in load-bearing straw-bale walls the number of layers is minimised. As Bruce King has remarked, "a plastered [load-bearing] straw bale assembly is structure, insulation, air barrier, finish, and fire resistance all in one – as opposed to most building materials, which typically perform one or two of the requisite functions of a building enclosure." (→B063:xxv) Other advantages include ease and rapidity of construction. Schmidt specifies 120 cm-wide bales wherever possible, because in one hour 7-8 bales can be craned in place, independently of their size. Therefore, while 80 cm-wide bales provide 5-6 m² of wall, 20 m² can be erected from 120 cm bales in the same amount of time.

On the other hand, the adoption of jumbo bales severely limits self-building, as they need to be craned. Furthermore, the envelope of a jumbo-bale building is quite thick, which is no problem in suburban homes but might be a constraint in other cases. On this point, Schmidt observes that walls may

µ, Druckfestigkeit, etc. würden an 140 kg/m³ gepressten Ballen als solche und an unverputzten und verputzten Wandelementen aus diesen Ballen getestet. Tests würden die Eigenschaften von Jumboballen wissenschaftlich untersuchen, die sich erwartungsgemäß von den gewöhnlichen, kleinen Ballen unterscheiden werden. Tests würden sowohl an Ballen mit langen Halmen als auch Ballen mit gehäckseltem Stroh (wie für Tiereinstreu) durchgeführt werden. Werner Schmidt vertritt die Hypothese, dass der λ–Wert bei gehäckseltem Stroh besser sein würde, während die langen Halme sich für das Verputzen besser eignen. Ein weiterer Vorteil ist, dass mit den neuesten Strohballenpressen die Jumboballen mit einem Chip versehen werden, auf dem Daten wie Herstellungsort, Datum, Feuchte, etc. gespeichert sind. Jumboballen werden von Bauern überdies bevorzugt, da weniger Arbeit anfällt für das Be- und Entladen der Transportmittel und sie zudem besser gestapelt werden können.

Offensichtlich bedeutet das Bauen mit Jumboballen eine Bevorzugung von lasttragenden und teillasttragenden Wänden. Diese sind Schmidts bevorzugte Technik – obwohl er manchmal auch Gebäude mit Holzrahmenkonstruktion entwirft, in denen kleine Ballen (50 cm dick oder weniger) lediglich als Isolierung dienen. Schmidt sagt, dass die lasttragende und teillasttragende „die einfachste und besten Baumethoden sind in Bezug auf meine Ziele. (…) Die Wände verdichten sich selber durch das Gewicht des Gebäudes." (→B081:9)

Außerdem wird in lasttragenden Strohballenwänden die Zahl der einzelnen Wandschichten minimiert. Wie Bruce King es sagt, „verputztes [lasttragendes] Strohballenbauteil ist Statik, Isolation, Winddichtigkeit, Oberfläche und Brandschutz in einem – im Gegensatz zu den meisten Baumaterialien, die in der Regel ein oder zwei Anforderungen an eine Gebäudehülle erfüllen." (→B063:xxv)

Weitere Vorteile sind die Leichtigkeit und Schnelligkeit des Aufbaus. Schmidt verwendet wo immer möglich 120 cm breite Ballen, da in einer Stunde 7 bis 8 Ballen unabhängig von ihrer Größe per Kran platziert werden können. Während 80 cm breite

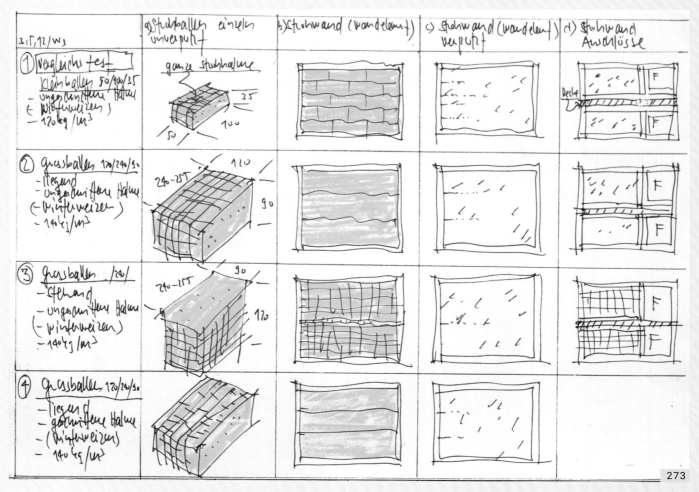

273

take a lot of space, but this approximately equals the area which would be occupied by central heating room, oil-fuel or pellet tank, etc. that can be omitted thanks to the superinsulation.

Schmidt points out that "a straw bale house with a wooden structure, i.e. with straw only as insulation, could use another ecological insulation material between the timbers as well. It is actually a conventional construction, just with a differ-

Ballen eine Wandfläche von 5 bis 6 m², ergeben 120 cm breite Ballen in derselben Zeit eine Fläche von 20 m².

Auf der anderen Seite schränkt die Verwendung von Jumboballen das Selberbauen sehr ein, da man einen Kran benötigt. Des weiteren ist die Hülle eines Jumboballengebäudes sehr dick, was in ländlichen Gegenden kein Problem darstellt, aber in anderen vielleicht doch einschränkt. Diesbezüglich bemerkt Schmidt, dass die Wände vielleicht viel Platz in Anspruch

ent insulating material. The realisation of a [fully or partly] load-bearing straw bale building necessitates a completely different design principle." A change of attitude is required from the builders' side too, because during construction "the house moves and reacts to what you do. (…) Most engineers and craftsmen have a hard time during the first confrontation with such a design – there are no computer programs that expect these changes during construction, you can put away your meter stick with millimetres marked on it, etc. It demands craftsmanship and common sense. This kind of design frees us from our obsession with precision everywhere, even in places where it is not needed." (→B064) Similar remarks apply to Gion Caminada's log houses, whose success partly depends on his cooperation with a great structural engineer like Jürg Conzett. A discussion of the structural concept of Schmidt's straw-bale buildings is to be found in the next chapter. (→§09)

Schmidt has been refining solutions from one project to the next. Luckily enough, for the time being "the non-proprietary nature of straw bale building has kept innovation, refinement, and failures out in the open to learn from." (→B063:xxiv) Straw-bale building designers form networks, and exchange information among themselves and with the world at large. Schmidt is no exception, as I have already remarked in the introductory essay. (→§00) In the following pages I will try to describe how a straw-bale building 'à la Werner Schmidt' is made.

nehmen, aber dass dies ungefähr der Fläche entspricht, die für ein Heizungsraum, Öl- oder Pelletstank, etc. benötigt würde, die dank der Superisolierung überflüssig werden.

Schmidt weist darauf hin, dass „ein Strohballenhaus mit einer Pfosten-Riegel-Konstruktion, bei der Stroh nur als Isolationsmaterial zum Einsatz kommt, auch ein anderes ökologisches Dämmmaterial zwischen dem Holz eingesetzt werden könnte. Es ist tatsächlich eine konventionelle Konstruktion, nur mit einem anderen Isolationsmaterial. Die Realisierung eines lasttragenden [oder teillasttragenden] Strohballenhauses bedingt ein völlig anderes Entwurfsprinzip." Eine Veränderung der Einstellung der Bauherren ist ebenfalls erforderlich, denn „es (das Haus) reagiert auf kleinste Gewichtsunterschiede (…) Normale Ingenieure und Handwerker haben meistens bei der ersten Konfrontation mit einer solchen Bauweise große Mühe; es gibt keine Computerprogramme, die diese Veränderungen rechnen; beim Bauen kann man den Meterstab mit seinen Millimetern nur beschränkt einsetzen, etc. Es ist handwerkliches Geschick und gesunder Menschenverstand gefragt. Diese Bauweise befreit uns von unserem krankhaften Zwang, unserer Besessenheit überall Genauigkeit zu realisieren, auch dort wo sie gar nicht notwendig ist." (→B064) Ähnliches gilt für Gion A. Caminadas Blockhäuser, deren Erfolg teilweise von der Kooperation mit dem Statikingenieur Jürg Conzett abhängt. Eine Diskussion über das statische Konzept von Schmidts Strohballenhäusern findet sich im nächsten Kapitel. (→§09)

Schmidt hat seine Lösungsansätze von Projekt zu Projekt verfeinert. Glücklicherweise solange „der Strohballenbau nicht urheberrechtlich geschützt ist, sind Innovationen, Verfeinerungen und das Scheitern möglich, um daraus zu lernen." (→B063:xxiv) Strohballenbauarchitekten bilden Netzwerke und tauschen untereinander und mit der Welt ihre Erfahrungen aus. Schmidt ist keine Ausnahme, wie ich bereits in der Einleitung erwähnt habe. (→§00) Auf den folgenden Seiten möchte ich versuchen zu beschreiben, wie ein Strohballenhaus ‚à la Werner Schmidt' gemacht wird.

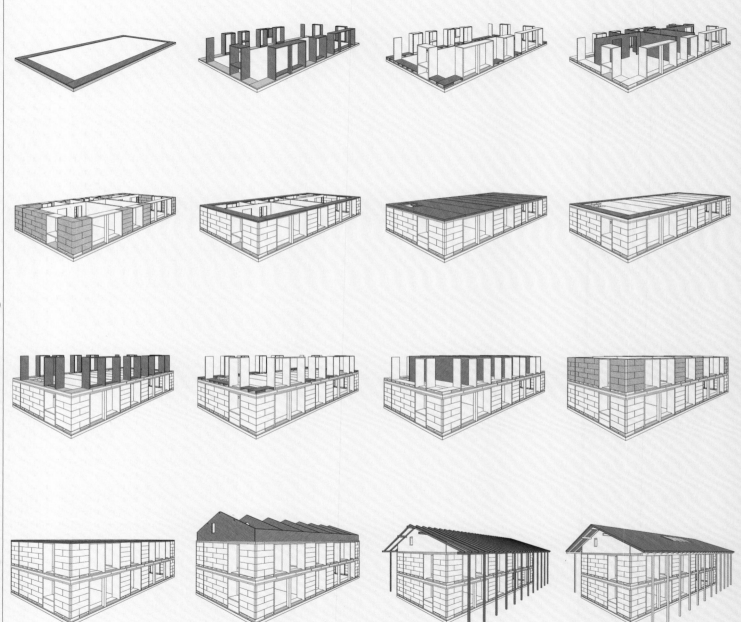

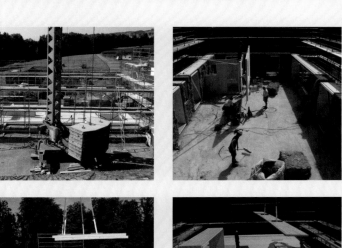

275-290

building sequence of house gliott

291-314

1. Currently, there are few manufacturers of building-grade bales. Schmidt is an opponent of the current trend towards certifying straw bales for building use. Such certification is superfluous, and the result might be bales which cost 3 to 5 times more and are not easily available. Being an experienced connoisseur, his opinion is that the project should be adapted to the quality and dimensions of available straw bales, and that a straw bale builder must be able to respond to it properly.

1. Derzeit gibt es einige wenige Hersteller von Baustrohballen. Schmidt ist ein Gegner des überflüssigen Zertifizierungstrends für Strohballen für den Hausbau, da zertifizierte Ballen das 3 bis 5fache kosten und sie nicht kurzfristig verfügbar sind. Als erfahrener Strohballenbauer ist er der Meinung, dass sich ein Projekt an der Qualität und den Dimensionen des verfügbaren Strohs orientieren muss. Der Strohballenbauer muss in der Lage sein, darauf richtig zu reagieren.

315

2. Almost always, the timber laminated products Schmidt uses contain glue. He does not like this very much, and in the future he would like to do without it. Apart from its toxicity, it is guaranteed for 20 years only. At Fliri's, for floors he used brettstapel elements: lumbers are connected by diagonal timber dowels, without any glue.

316

2. Die Holzelemente, die Schmidt verwendet, beinhalten fast immer Kleber. Dies mag er nicht sonderlich und möchte daher künftig versuchen, darauf zu verzichten. Abgesehen von seinem toxischen Potenzial, wird für den Kleber nur 20 Jahre garantiert. Bei Fliri verwendete er Brettstapelelemente: Hölzer werden mit diagonalen Holzdübeln verbunden, ohne Kleber.

317

3. The quality of Schmidt's buildings is also the result of the cooperation with a small, trustworthy building firm – Flepp SA, from Disentis. They have long experience in the refurbishment of historical buildings, which calls for an empirical approach to face unpredictables. This attitude is very fruitful in straw-bale building, and Schmidt tends to involve this company in many of his projects, as they are accustomed to his ways and have appropriate machinery. At least three people experienced with straw-bale construction are requested at every building site. Working instructions are detailedly discussed beforehand.

3. Die Qualität von Schmidts Gebäuden ist auch das Resultat seiner Zusammenarbeit mit einem kleinen, vertrauensvollen Bauunternehmen – Firma Flepp SA aus Disentis. Sie haben viel Erfahrung mit der Sanierung historischer Gebäude: diese verlangen eine empirische Annäherung, um allem Unvorhergesehenen entgegen treten zu können. Diese Haltung ist sehr hilfreich beim Strohballenbau, und Schmidt involviert sie gerne in seine Projekte, zumal sie an seine Arbeitsweise gewöhnt sind und die entsprechenden Maschinen besitzen. Drei Personen mit Strohballenbauerfahrung sind auf der Baustelle notwendig. Arbeitsanweisungen werden vorher detailliert besprochen.

318

4. Cellars are usually avoided and excavations are kept to a minimum. Schmidt observes that it would be interesting to use a single large stone for each pier foundation, as suggested by Gloor. (→B047:82-83) So far, foundations have always been reinforced concrete: using other materials is still a goal for his future work.

5. A lower drainage is provided both to protect against rising damp and to allow any water that might be found in the walls and floor to drain away. Schmidt is in accordance with whoever recommends that waterproof layers be avoided, as they would hold moisture inside. (→B061:59-60) Recently he happened to employ foam glass gravel in contact with the ground – as in Küng house – but still prefers a continuous ventilated element underneath the house – as in Gliott house. In principle, both methods allow the use of straw in ground floors. The second allows timber ground floors to constitute a planar structure and therefore support the walls.

6. Over floor bales, an 8-15 cm anhydrite or concrete layer may be cast on a separating membrane. Dark grey anhydrite may be polished and waxed to be used as flooring, otherwise may function as a subfloor, often with a flagstone or other dark flooring on top of it. Haggard, Cooper and Rennick report that dark surfaces have created glare problems by producing too much contrast with windows; (→B040:49) but none of Schmidt's clients I have met has reported such inconvenience.

4. Unterkellerungen werden normalerweise vermieden, damit der Aushub auf ein Minimum reduziert wird. Schmidt fügt hinzu, es wäre interessant, einzelne große Steine anstelle der einzelnen Fundamente zu verwenden, wie auch von Gloor vorgeschlagen. (→B047:82-83) Bis jetzt wurden Fundamente immer mit Beton gegossen: andere Materialien einzusetzen bleibt sein Ziel für künftige Projekte.

319

5. Eine Sickerleitung sorgt dafür, um sowohl vor aufsteigender Feuchtigkeit zu schützen, als auch jegliches Wasser, das in der Nähe der Wände und Böden auftauchen könnte, abfließen zu lassen. Wasserdichte Schichten sind gemäß Schmidt zu vermeiden, da sie die Feuchte im Innern zurückhalten könnten. (→B061:59-60) In letzter Zeit hat er öfters Schaumglasschotter zum Erdreich hin eingesetzt – wie beim Haus Küng – aber er bevorzugt nach wie vor unterlüftete Häuser – wie beim Haus Gliott. Im Prinzip erlauben beide Methoden den Einsatz von Stroh in Bodennähe.

6. Über dem Strohboden kann ein 8-15 cm starker Anhydrit- oder Zementboden, mit einer Folie als Trennschicht, eingebracht werden. Dieser Boden kann geschliffen und geölt werden, um als Fertigboden genutzt zu werden, andernfalls dient er als Unterboden, oftmals mit dunklen Steinplatten belegt. Haggard, Cooper und Rennick berichten, dass dunkle Oberflächen zu Blendungen führen können, da sie einen zu starken Kontrast zu den Fenstern bilden (→B040:49) – aber keiner von Schmidts Kunden, die ich getroffen habe, berichtete von solchen Unannehmlichkeiten.

320

321

7. In principle, the building's dimensions are co-ordinated on the basis of the bales, in order to minimise cuts. But in practice, the actual dimensions of bales – and in particular their length – does not correspond exactly to the nominal ones, therefore one ought to be ready to manage these irregularities during construction.

7. Im Prinzip beruhen die Gebäudedimensionen auf der Ballengröße, um das Schneiden zu minimieren. Aber in der Praxis entsprechen die angenommenen Maße nicht exakt mit den tatsächlichen Dimensionen – vor allem in der Länge – daher muss man in der Lage sein, vor Ort auf diese Unregelmäßigkeiten zu reagieren.

8. Schmidt employs "temporary braces at corners and along long lengths of walls to provide a guide to keep everything vertical" during construction, as Jones suggests. (→B061:79) Nevertheless, with straw bales it is not possible to obtain the same precision as with conventional methods, and Schmidt accepts this.

322

8. Schmidt setzt während des Aufbaus temporäre Anschläge wie beim Backsteinmauerwerk ein, um das Gebäude an den Ecken gerade zu halten, wie auch Jones es vorschlägt. (→B061:79) Beim Strohballenbau kann man nicht die gleiche Genauigkeit realisieren, wie bei konventionellen Baumethoden.

9. If straw bales are load-bearing, time is needed for them to displace under load. Schmidt's experience is that the full creep – up to about 30 cm per floor according to the straw quality – will occur in the first 4–8 weeks, thus finding the permanent configuration: At Fliri's, this took two months. Where the structure is just partly load-bearing, the creep time can be controlled, but straw will not be compressed as much as in load-bearing buildings. According to Schmidt, haste can be counter-productive, as it entails a higher risk of plaster cracking.

9. Wenn die Strohballen lasttragend eingesetzt werden, braucht es Zeit damit sie sich unter der Last setzen können. Nach Schmidts Erfahrung ist die vollständige Setzung nach 4 bis 8 Wochen erreicht – etwa 10 bis zu 30 cm pro Geschoss, abhängig von der Belastung und der Strohqualität – und findet so einen permanenten Zustand: beim Haus Fliri dauerte es zwei Monate.
In teillasttragenden Konstruktionen kann man die Setzungszeit steuern, normalerweise wird das Stroh nicht so stark gepresst wie in den lasttragenden Konstruktionen. Gemäß Schmidt kann diese Eile jedoch kontraproduktiv sein, da es eine höhere Gefahr bei der Rissbildung im Putz mit sich bringt.

323

10. Tying the roof to the foundation – recommended with small bales (→B126:83,063:215) – is also used in Schmidt's system, to contrast wind hazard. At Fliri's, wall plates were connected to base plates with a perforated metal band, while at Braun's a metal strand placed inside a tube (to avoid problems caused by possible condensation) was used.

10. Das Dach mit den darunter liegenden Geschossen oder der Bodenplatte zu verbinden ist zu empfehlen bei kleinen Ballen (→B126:83,063:215) und auch bei Schmidts system mit großen Ballen, um den starken Windkräften widerstehen zu können. Bei Fliri wurden an Wand- und Bodenkranz Platten befestigt mit perforierten Metallbändern oder überkreuzten Metallstangen (in Röhren, um Kondensation zu vermeiden).

324

11. Pinning was used where small bales were employed, as in the second floor of Schmidlin house. Pins can be either wood or bamboo. Another current practice of strawbale building – connecting the base plate to the first course of bales with wooden stubs (→B061:82) to avoid horizontal displacement – is implemented using steel nails.

325

11. Holz- und Bambusstäbe wurden im zweiten Stock beim Haus Schmidlin-Jeker verwendet (kleine Ballen). Eine weitere gängige Praxis im Strohballenbau, um die erste Strohballenreihe mit der Grundplatte zu verbinden (→B061:82) und somit das horizontale Verschieben zu verhindern, ist das Einschlagen von Stahlnägeln in den Holzkranz.

326

12. Bruce King suggests precompressing small-bale walls in case of "severe loading such as seismic or high snow loads." (→B063:89) In Schmidt's opinion, precompression is not needed with jumbo bales, since they are denser to start with, and will be even more compressed when loaded in any case. Compression straps have been used in some early projects such as Esser, Braun, and Schmidlin; they were enveloped with mesh and then plastered. Schmidt has dropped this method because straps cannot be cut away, are a redundant cost, entail a lot of work, and may produce cracks in the plaster.

12. Bruce King schlägt vor, kleine Strohballen vorzupressen, falls sie „starken Lasten, wie seismischen und Schneelasten, ausgesetzt sind." (→B063:89) Nach Schmidts Meinung ist das Vorpressen bei kleinen Ballen manchmal sinnvoll, bei Jumboballen ist es nicht notwendig, da diese stärker gepresst sind und bei der lasttragenden Konstruktion die Pressung automatisch erfolgt. Spanngurte wurden in manchen früheren Projekten wie Esser, Braun-Dubuis und Schmidlin-Jeker eingesetzt. Schmidt hat diese Variante wieder verworfen, da die Spanngurte nicht mehr entfernt werden können, sie bringen unnötige Kosten, und können Risse im Putz verursachen.

13. In case straw bales are really load-bearing, Schmidt leaves a settlement gap above windows and doors boxes. This space is filled with loose straw after settlement under load; window frames can only be built when dimensions are stable. This was the case with Fliri house. In later buildings, such as Maya guesthouse, this method is superseded; prefabrication frees one from creeping issues. In both cases, Schmidt uses full-depth window boxes. In partly load-bearing buildings window and door boxes are exploited as piers and bracing. (→§09)

13. Im Fall, dass Strohballen tatsächlich lasttragend sind, lässt Schmidt einen Abstand über den Fenster- und Türkisten. Dieser Abstand wird mit losem Stroh ausgestopft, nachdem sich die Ballen unter Last gesetzt haben; realisiert man die Fenster ohne Fensterkisten, kann das Fenster erst gemessen und bestellt werden, wenn der Setzungsprozess abgeschlossen ist. Dies war beim Haus Fliri der Fall. In späteren Gebäuden, wie dem Maya Guesthouse, wird diese Methode abgelöst; die Vorfabrikation befreit von den Setzungsproblemen. In beiden Fällen verwendet Schmidt Fensterkisten über die komplette Wandtiefe. Bei teillasttragenden Konstruktionen werden Fenster- und Türboxen als Pfeiler und Aussteifungen genutzt. (→§09)

327

14. In most cases, windows are wooden-framed and triple-glazed. To avoid thermal bridges around windows, Schmidt uses cork, sheep wool, or wood fibre panels against the outer side of the framework. Shutters are never provided, as customary in the region.

328

14. In den meisten Fällen, sind die Fenster aus Holzrahmen und Dreifachverglast. Um Wärmebrücken um die Fenster zu vermeiden, benutzt Schmidt als Überisolation der Fensterrahmen Korkplatten oder Holzfaserplatten, ausgestopft mit Schafwolle, gegen die Außenseite der Rahmen. Fensterläden sind in der Regel nicht enthalten.

329

15. Moisture and waterproof membranes are avoided. Schmidt designs 'breathable' building envelopes, without being troubled about detailing an increasing vapour permeability of the wall from the inside to the outside, as theory would require. (→B069:42) In his opinion, what counts is that any moisture that might be found in jumbo-bale walls can escape when summer comes, following the same principle as in traditional architecture built with natural materials.

15. Dampf- und wasserdichte Membranen werden so gut es geht vermieden. Schmidts Gebäudehüllen sind immer ‚dampfoffene' Konstruktionen, ohne im Speziellen darauf zu achten, dass die innere Haut dampfdichter ist als die äußere, wie die Theorie es sagt. (→B069:42) Nach seiner Meinung, ist es nur wichtig, dass der Wasserdampf durch das Material aufgenommen werden kann und dass diese Feuchtigkeit im Verlaufe des Jahres die Konstruktion wieder verlässt. Bei der traditionellen Architektur und deren natürlichen Materialien war und ist das immer so.

330

16. Load-bearing walls are plastered two to eight weeks after creeping has stopped. As all authors recommend, Schmidt gives the straw bales a 'haircut' before rendering.

16. Lasttragende Strohballenkonstruktionen werden zwei bis acht Wochen nachdem sich die Setzung eingestellt hat verputzt. Wie alle Autoren empfehlen, gibt auch Schmidt den Gebäuden zuerst einen ‚Haarschnitt' vor dem Grundputzauftrag.

17. Jones states that plastering over meshes "is totally unnecessary and a waste of time," (→B061:97) but Schmidt uses them anyway, to reduce the risk of cracking. A number of authors – including Jones (→B061:73+83) and Minke – recommend not inserting metal elements in bales and plasters, to reduce the environmental impact and above all to inhibit condensation and rusting. Usually, Schmidt employs galvanised steel mesh, sometimes fibreglass or vegetal fibres: he claims he has never experienced problems as a result of using metal.

331

17. Gemäß Jones ist das Verputzen über ein Netz „eine völlig unnütze Zeitverschwendung", (→B061:97) aber Schmidt benutzt sie dennoch, um Haarrisse zu vermindern. Eine Vielzahl von Autoren, inklusive Jones (→B061:73+83) und Minke – schlagen vor, keine Metallelemente in die Ballen und den Putz zu stecken, um die Umwelt zu schonen und um Kondensation und Rosten zu verhindern. Normalerweise verwendet Schmidt ein verzinktes Hühnergitter, manchmal Fiberglas oder pflanzliche Fasern: er sagt, er habe nie Probleme auf Grund des Hühnergitters bekommen.

18. After the application of each coat, render is protected from sun and wind to prevent premature drying. Plastering comes in three or four coats, whose total thickness may be 20–50 mm. On the outer face of the perimeter walls, Schmidt generally employs lime plasters. Sometimes, he has walls limewashed, as at Gliott's; on other occasions, pigments may be added to the last coat of lime, according to the clients' taste. The outer skin is untreated. The inner face of perimeter walls is clay- or lime-plastered.

18. Der Putz wird nach dem Aufbringen jeder Schicht abgedeckt, um ihn vor Sonne und Wind zu schützen und ein zu schnelles Austrocknen zu vermeiden. Der Putzaufbau ist drei- bis vierlagig (Anspritz, 1. Lage Grundputz, eventuell 2. und 3. Lage Grundputz und Fertigputz); insgesamt 2 bis 5 cm. Auf der Außenseite der Außenwände, verwendet Schmidt in der Regel Kalkputz. Manchmal lässt Schmidt die Wände auch kalken wie beim Haus Gliott; bei anderen Projekten, wurden der letzten Putzschicht Pigmente beigemischt, gemäß dem Wunsch der Bauherren. Die äußere Schicht ist oft unbehandelt. Im Innern wird die Strohwand mit Lehm oder Kalk verputzt.

332

333

19. In traditional architecture, large, uninter-rupted plaster surfaces were seldom used; cornices and mouldings served to minimise the risk of cracking. Straw-bale buildings are also similar to traditional (masonry) ones in this respect. Lacinski and Bergeron suggest applying a new coat of limewash or patching the cracks every spring. (→B069:49) Nonetheless, it is unrealistic to assume that owners will do it, and after all the render in most of Schmidt's houses does not show signs of decay.

19. In der traditionellen Architektur wurden große, ununterbrochene Putzoberflächen selten verwendet; Gesimse und Leisten dienten dazu, die Rissbildung zu verhindern. Strohballenhäuser ähneln den traditionel-len Steingebäuden unter diesem Aspekt. Lacinski und Bergeron schlagen vor, jeden Frühling eine neue Schicht Kalkschlemme anzubringen oder die Risse nachzubessern. (→B069:49) Nichtsdestotrotz ist es sehr unwahrscheinlich, dass die Bewohner dies tun. Der Alterungsprozess hat dem Verputz bis heute nichts anhaben können.

20. Air tightness is obtained with plaster and adequate detailing at joints (openings, electrical junction boxes, etc.). If required, buildings are tested with the blower door method.

334

20. Die Winddichtigkeit wird durch den Putz und sachgerechte Ausführung der Stöße erreicht (Öffnungen, Elektrokabelleitungen, etc.). Schmidt testet seine Gebäude auf Wunsch mit dem Blow-Door-Test.

21. As is the tradition in straw-bale building, 'truth windows' are often used.

21. Wie es im Strohballenbau Tradition ist, wird häufig ein Strohfenster 'truth windows' eingebaut.

335

22. Intermediate floors differ from one building to the next. For instance, in house Braun, the floor is made of cross-laminated timber panels, which function as flooring as well; at Fliri's, the brettstapel structure is topped by fleece, sound insulation mat, membrane, anhydrite subfloor, and brick flooring; at Schmidlin's, wooden beams carry the flooring and the space between them is filled with an earth screed. As a rule, first floors interrupt the perimeter walls forming a ring beam, like in platform frame construction.

22. Die Zwischenböden unterscheiden sich von einem Gebäude zum anderen. Zum Beispiel beim Haus Braun-Dubuis ist es eine verleimte Brettstapeldecke, die auch als fertiger Bodenbelag dient; beim Haus Fliri ist die unverleimte Brettstapeldecke mit einem Vlies (Rieselschutz), einer Trittschalldämmung, einer Membran und einem Anhydritboden sowie Lehmplatten abgedeckt; bei Schmidlin-Jeker besteht die Zwischendecke aus einer Holzbalkendecke. In der Regel unterbricht ein Holzkranz die Außenwand wie in der Rahmenbauweise.

336

23. Not load-bearing, partition walls are often constructed with unfired bricks to maximise humidity regulation; at Gliott's, they are left unplastered. Minke has observed that in a room with unfired, unplastered brick walls the RH value stays quite steadily around 50%, all year long. (→B078)

337

23. Nicht lasttragende Zwischenwände sind oft aus luftgetrockneten Lehmziegeln errichtet, um die Feuchteaufnahme zu maximieren; bei Gliott sind sie unverputzt. Minke hat beobachtet, dass in Räumen mit ungebrannten und unverputzten Lehmziegelwänden der RH-Wert das ganze Jahr über ziemlich konstant um 50% herum bleibt. (→B078)

338

24. Roofs are almost always pitched (or domed, as in the case of vonRoll pavilion and Camenzind house), and may contain a very thick straw-bale insulation layer or not. If not, this is placed above the last floor and the attic is not inhabitable; if so, their timber structure is similar to those Schmidt often employs for ground floors. As several authors recommend, the roof structure lays evenly on the load-bearing or 'hybrid' wall system, through a roof plate. (→B077:55)
For roofing, Schmidt has used metal sheets, roof tiles, FRC boards, etc. In a few cases, like house Bühlmann, the roof is flat. At completion in spring 2013, it will be a green roof.

24. Dächer sind oftmals als Giebeldächer ausgebildet (oder Kuppeln, wie zum Beispiel beim vonRoll Pavillon und Haus Camenzind), und können eine dicke Strohballendämmung enthalten. Wenn nicht, dann sitzt die Dämmschicht oberhalb der letzten Deckenplatte und der Dachraum ist belüftet (Kaltdach). Wie einige Autoren empfehlen, liegt die Dachkonstruktion mittels Holzkranz und Deckenplatte eben auf der lasttragenden oder teillasttragenden Außenwand auf. (→B077:55) Für das Dach verwendet Schmidt Blech, Ziegel, Faserzementplatten, etc. In manchen Fällen, wie im Haus Bühlmann ist es ein Fachdach. Bei seiner Fertigstellung im Frühjahr 2013 wird es ein Gründach bekommen.

25. Schmidt does not employ mechanical ventilation. Feist has observed that 70% of the air changes that are usually calculated or even prescribed are actually needed to expel toxic substances from the indoor environment, 20% to drive excess moisture out, and just 10% to change stale air. (→B043) Schmidt holds that in a healthy house such those he builds, the first problem does not exist and the second is regulated by clay plasters and other porous materials such as wood: therefore it is sufficient to open the windows every now and then.

25. Schmidt verwendet meistens keine Zwangsentlüftungen. Feist stellte fest, dass 70% der Luftumwälzung, die normalerweise berechnet und teilweise vorgeschrieben ist, gebraucht wird, um giftige Substanzen aus den Innenräumen abzuführen, 20% um Feuchtigkeit abzuführen und lediglich 10% um verbrauchte Luft zu erneuern. (→B043) Schmidt ist überzeugt, dass in einem gesunden Haus wie er es baut, oben genanntes gar nicht in Erscheinung tritt und die Feuchte mittels Lehmputz und anderer offenporiger Materialien wie Holz reguliert wird: daher ist es ausreichend, das Fenster ab und zu zu öffnen.

339

26. Combustion in stoves is obtained collecting fresh air from the outside. The uptake is placed outside as much as possible, because although well insulated it can bring cold inside, and under special meteorological conditions cold air risks being sucked inside.

340

26. Die Frischluftzufuhr für die Holzöfen wird durch Öffnungsklappen nach außen, möglichst im Boden unterhalb des Ofens platziert, gewährleistet. Da es unter bestimmten Wetterbedingungen zu einem Ansaugen der kalten Luft kommen kann, ist es wichtig, dass diese Klappen verschließbar sind.

341

27. In kitchens I sometimes encountered induction cookers and I imagined this was to avoid consuming oxygen from the indoor environment, but Werner Schmidt told me that actually this was the choice of some of his clients. In other cases, in fact, there are ordinary gas cookers. Usually there are no suction fans in kitchens and bathrooms. Carbon filters are used instead, to even moisture out and absorb bad odours.

27. In der Küche fand ich meist Induktionsoder Elektroherde vor und ich nahm an, der Grund hierfür sei ein Vermeiden des Sauerstoffverbrauchs, allerdings erzählte mir Schmidt, dass dies die freie Wahl der Kunden sei. In einigen Fällen gab es gewöhnliche Gasherde. Normalerweise wird auf Absaugungen in Küche und Bad verzichtet. Stattdessen kommen Aktivkohlefilter zum Einsatz um sogar Feuchtigkeit und unangenehme Gerüche zu absorbieren.

28. Ideally, systems should be conceived so that pipings run inside the building, not in straw-bale walls. (→B077:58) Schmidt would prefer to chase pipings into partition walls, but clients usually want a more ramified electrical system. This implies not only pipings chased in straw-bale walls, but also slightly higher costs. Pipes and sockets are insulated – the latter with PUR. In house Bühlmann, pipings run in a central conduit inside every floor, from which all wires extend. This layout is rational as well as inexpensive.

28. Idealerweise sollten Systeme so konzipiert sein, dass Rohrleitungen innerhalb der isolierten Gebäudehülle verlaufen und nicht in den Strohballenwänden. (→B077:58) Schmidt bevorzugt das Führen der Leitungen in Trenn- oder Versorgungswänden, aber die Kunden wünschen häufig ein verzweigtes Elektrosystem. Dies bedeutet nicht nur das Führen von Leitungen in den Strohwänden, sondern auch höhere Kosten. Leitungen und Buchsen werden isoliert. Im Haus Bühlmann verlaufen die Rohre in einem zentralen Kabelkanal auf jedem Geschoss, von wo aus die Kabel abgezweigt werden. Dieses Konzept ist sowohl rational als auch günstig.

342

29. Any straw leftovers – both trimmings and whole bales – are given to local farmers. Construction site waste is limited: at Schmidlin's the total was as small as 2 m³, including straw which was given to the client's brother, who is a farmer.

343

29. Alle Strohreste, sowohl vom Trimmen als auch ganze Ballen, werden an Bauern vor Ort abgegeben. Baustellenabfälle sind begrenzt: bei Schmidlin-Jeker handelte es sich gerade mal um 2 m³, inklusive des Strohs, das dem Bruder des Kunden, der Bauer ist, gegeben wurde.

30. Schmidt has never happened to extend a straw-bale building, but he thinks that in principle his designs might allow for future changes. Extensions might be realised removing plaster and joining (new) timber on (existing) timber, as in traditional houses.

30. Schmidt konnte bislang noch kein Strohballenhaus erweitern, aber er meint, dass dies im Prinzip bei seinen Entwürfen möglich wäre. Erweiterungen könnten durch das Entfernen des Putzes und Anfügen von (neuem) Holz an (bestehendes) Holz ausgeführt werden, wie es in traditionellen Gebäuden der Fall ist.

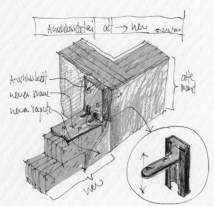

344

I chose house Schmidlin as an appropriate example to show Schmidt's straw-bale building method, as it still used the load-bearing wall technique. (→■345) Of course, every building is different, but here a number of features can be easily spotted. Thomas Schmidlin was the first client to commission a straw-bale house to Werner Schmidt after the wide coverage of Braun house. The land was available, and the program for the family of three – a couple and their daughter – was clear. Schmidt designed a low-tech house which exploits the maximum building area allowed. Aspects such as embodied energy, reduction of waste production during construction, reduction of operating energy, etc. were of great concern both to the client and the architect.

The building stands on a perimeter frost wall made of reinforced concrete. Cross-laminated timber panels placed vertically – with 50 cm thick straw bales between them (total thickness of ground floor slab 0.66 m, U = 0.084 W/m²K) – constitute the ground floor slab, which has a 70 cm-high air space underneath. Ground floor walls consist of jumbo bales (total thickness 1.27 m, U = 0.037 W/m²K). They were plastered outside with triple-reinforced lime render and inside with 2–5 cm-thick clay plaster made with earth obtained from the excavation, to which some sand was added, as it was too clayey. The interior face has been finished with a thin coat of industrially produced clay plaster, which in some cases was waxed. Different, agreeable hues were used for each room, (→■352) as suggested by the site engineer Rainer Hettenbach, who is also a clay specialist and a member of IG Lehm.

Earth from the excavations was also used as screed in the intermediate floor, to give it thermal mass and improve acoustic insulation. This is a more conventional fir joist construction with upper boarding, which is left visible from underneath. The attic outer wall is also load-bearing straw bales – this time regular-size, as the compressive stress is also smaller (total thickness 0.56 m, U = 0.088 W/m²K). The

Ich habe das Haus Schmidlin-Jeker als angemessenes Beispiel gewählt, um Schmidts Strohballenbauweise zu zeigen, zumal es die lasttragende Strohballentechnik aufweist. (→■345) Natürlich ist jedes Gebäude unterschiedlich, aber hier können einige Merkmale einfach dargestellt werden. Thomas Schmidlin war der nächste Kunde, nach einer langen Zeitspanne zum Haus Braun-Dubuis, der ein Strohballenhaus bei Werner Schmidt in Auftrag gab. Das Land war vorhanden und das Programm für eine dreiköpfige Familie – Elternpaar mit einer Tochter – stand. Schmidt entwarf ein low-tech Haus mit der maximal möglichen netto Geschossfläche. Aspekte wie die Graue Energie, Reduzierung von Abfall während der Bauphase, Reduzierung der Betriebskosten, etc. waren für die Bauherren und den Architekten von großer Bedeutung.

Das Gebäude steht auf einem umlaufenden Frostriegel aus armiertem Beton. Bodenelemente aus stabverleimten Holzplatten sind darauf platziert – mit 50 cm dicken Strohballen gefüllt (der gesamte Bodenaufbau beträgt 0,66 m, U = 0,084 W/m²K) – und bilden die Bodenplatte mit einer 70 cm hohen Unterlüftung. Die Erdgeschosswand besteht aus Jumboballen (Gesamtdicke 1,27 m, U = 0,037 W/m²K). Sie ist von außen mit einem dreilagigen vernetzten Kalkputz, und innen mit einem 2 bis 5 cm starken Lehmputz verputzt. Dieser Lehmputz wurde aus der Erde des Aushubs gewonnen, und da die Erde zu ‚fett' war musste sie mittels Sand ‚magerer' gemacht werden. Die Oberflächen erhielten einen Fertigputz aus einer dünnen, industriell hergestellten Lehmputzschicht, die in manchen Fällen gewachst ist. Jeder Raum erhielt einen unterschiedlichen, angenehmen Farbton, (→■352) gemäß den Vorschlägen des Bauleiters Rainer Hettenbach, Architekt und Mitglied der IG Lehm und daher Spezialist auf diesem Gebiet.

Das Erdmaterial des Aushubs wurde auch als Schüttung in der Zwischendecke eingesetzt, um ihr thermische Masse zu geben und die Akustik zu verbessern. Die Zwischendecke ist aus einer konventionellen Balkenlage aus Tannenholz. Die Außenwand des Dachgeschosses ist ebenfalls aus kleinen lasttragenden

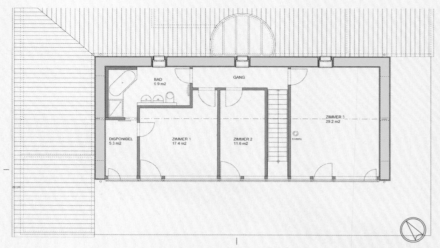

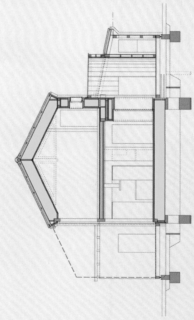

SCHMIDLIN-JEKER HOUSE

address ⌴ Adresse: Breitenbachweg 22,
CH-4246 Wahlen/BL
altitude ⌴ Höhe: 410 m
degree-days ⌴ Gradtage: 3027
project ⌴ Entwurf: 2004
construction ⌴ Bau: 2004-05
main building firms ⌴ Wichtigen Baufirmen:
Franz & Co. Baugeschäft AG,
Büsserach (general contractor ⌴ Baumeister);
Daniel Blaser AG, Reinach (wood construction ⌴
Holzbau); Atelier Werner Schmidt + Firma Flepp
(straw-bale construction ⌴ Strohbau)
plot area ⌴ Grundstückfläche: 594 m²
heated floor area ⌴ Geheizte Bodenfläche: 160 m²
main glazed area (SW) ⌴ Fensterfläche Hauptfassade
(SW): 61 m²
building cost ⌴ Baukosten: 839,000 CHF (5,200 CHF/m²)

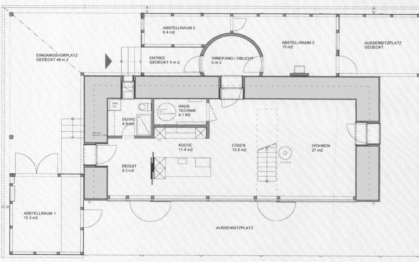

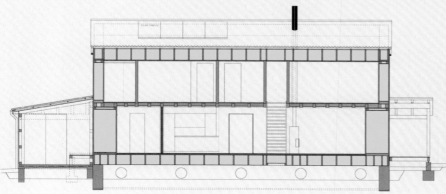

347

roof consists of prefabricated straw-infilled timber elements (total thickness 0.62 m, U = 0.079 W/m²K). Windows (whose frame is aluminium outside, larch inside) and doors have a U-value of 0.76 W/m²K.

A 4-kW stove is provided, as in winter it is likely that the sun does not shine for more than two days. On a yearly basis, approximately 2 steres of wood are burnt. 80% of the hot water is produced by 3.6 m² solar thermal collectors and fed into a 860 l tank; the rest is heated electrically. In spite of this, Thomas Schmidlin says his electrical power consumption rates have been consistently lower by 70% than those of his neighbours.

Rain water is dispersed on site, which allows one to avoid paying the tax for using the urban drainage system.

A meteo-controlled 15 x 3.2 m awning shades the completely glazed south-west façade – but this is not completely effective on summer afternoons when some overheating can occur. On the other hand, even during the harsh February of 2012, indoor temperatures as high as 26°C were registered during those days when the sun shone. Thermal mass and natural ventilation cooling allow a balanced, pleasant climate throughout the year. Since 'breathable' materials were employed for the building envelope, some openings in the

Strohballen – hier normale Größe, da die Drucklast ebenfalls kleiner ist (Gesamtdicke beträgt 0,56 m, U = 0,079 W/m²K). Die Fenster (deren Rahmen außen aus Aluminium, innen aus Holz sind) und die Türen haben einen U-Wert von 0,76 W/m²K.

Ein 4 kW Ofen steht zur Verfügung, da die Sonne im Winter häufig bis zu vier Wochen nicht scheint. Im Jahr werden ungefähr 2 Ster Holz verbrannt. 80% der Warmwassers wird von 3,6 m² thermischen Sonnenkollektoren produziert und in einem 860 l Speicher geführt; der Rest wird elektrisch erwärmt. Trotzdem sagt Thomas Schmidlin, dass sein Stromverbrauch konstant 70% tiefer als der seiner Nachbarn sei. Regenwasser wird oberflächlich auf dem Grundstück versickert, was Nutzungsgebühren für das städtische Abwassersystem einspart.

Eine wettergesteuerte 15 x 3,2 m Markise verschattet die gänzlich verglaste Südwestfassade – welche in den Sommermonaten nicht gänzlich ausreicht, wenn es manchmal zu einer Überhitzung kommt. Die Innentemperaturen lagen selbst im kalten Februar bei Sonnenschein bei 26°C. Thermische Masse und Lüftungsfenster für Nachtauskühlung sorgen für ein ausgeglichenes, angenehmes Raumklima über das ganze Jahr hinweg. Da atmungsaktive Materialien in der Gebäudehülle verwendet wurden, reichen einige Öffnungen zur Unterlüftung im Erdgeschoss aus, um die Luftzirkulation zu gewährleisten.

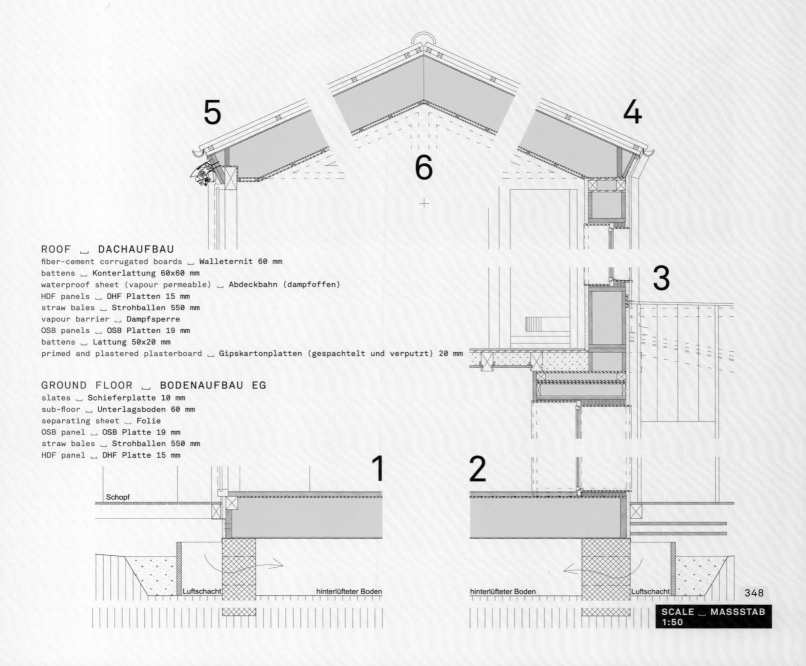

ROOF ⌣ DACHAUFBAU

fiber-cement corrugated boards ⌣ Walleternit 60 mm
battens ⌣ Konterlattung 60x60 mm
waterproof sheet (vapour permeable) ⌣ Abdeckbahn (dampfoffen)
HDF panels ⌣ DHF Platten 15 mm
straw bales ⌣ Strohballen 550 mm
vapour barrier ⌣ Dampfsperre
OSB panels ⌣ OSB Platten 19 mm
battens ⌣ Lattung 50x20 mm
primed and plastered plasterboard ⌣ Gipskartonplatten (gespachtelt und verputzt) 20 mm

GROUND FLOOR ⌣ BODENAUFBAU EG

slates ⌣ Schieferplatte 10 mm
sub-floor ⌣ Unterlagsboden 60 mm
separating sheet ⌣ Folie
OSB panel ⌣ OSB Platte 19 mm
straw bales ⌣ Strohballen 550 mm
HDF panel ⌣ DHF Platte 15 mm

Schopf

Luftschacht   hinterlüfteter Boden

hinterlüfteter Boden   Luftschacht

348

SCALE ⌣ MASSSTAB
1:50

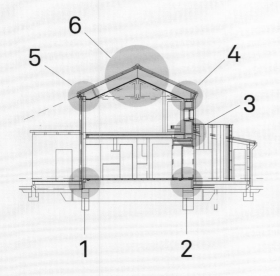

WALLS ⌐ WANDAUFBAU

interior final rendering (vapour permeable) ⌐ Deckputz innen (dampfoffen) 5 mm
lime base plaster ⌐ Kalkgrundputz 30-50 mm
straw-bale walls ⌐ Strohballenmauerwerk 1200 mm (ground floor ⌐ EG)
                                                   500 mm (first floor ⌐ OG)
lime base plaster ⌐ Kalkgrundputz 30-50 mm
exterior final rendering (vapour permeable) ⌐ Deckputz aussen (dapfoffen) 5 mm

FIRST FLOOR ⌐ BODENAUFBAU

timber boards flooring ⌐ Riemenboden 20 mm
sound insulation layer ⌐ Trittschall 10 mm
OSB panel ⌐ OSB Platte 19 mm
joists sw. ⌐ Balkenlage Fl 260x160 mm
clay screed ⌐ Schüttung aus Lehm
trickle protection ⌐ Rieselschutz
grooved base panel sw. ⌐ Blindboden Fl Platte (genutet) 27 mm

349

350

351

352

airspace under the ground floor are enough to ensure air circulation. No mechanical ventilation system is provided. Thanks to the large glazed exterior surface and also to the glazed upper part of the partition walls of the first floor, house Schmidlin is full of light. "I cannot feel at ease in usual rooms anymore," the owner says. "They all seem too dark to me."

Coaxial electric cables were used to avoid electrosmog. Plaster meshes are made of plastic to avoid Faraday effects. The plan recalls that of house Wolf-Bearth in many respects, the most evident being the L-shaped ancillary, unheated shed which lays adjacent to the house. It has a simple, mostly non-insulated larch structure and serves as carport, entrance, storeroom, and also as an outdoor sitting room. In addition, the L-shaped wing helps protect the main building from northern winds. (→■349) The timber used to build the larder is untreated and unvarnished – and still pleasantly smells of wood.

According to a survey by three high-school students (→B096)

Es gibt keine Lüftungsanlage.

Dank der großen verglasten Außenfassade und der teilweise verglasten Trennwände im Obergeschoss, ist das Haus Schmidlin-Jeker voller Licht. „Ich fühle mich in gewöhnlichen Räumen nicht mehr wohl" – sagt der Besitzer – „Sie wirken auf mich alle zu dunkel."

Koaxiale Elektroleitungen wurden zur Vermeidung von Elektrosmog eingesetzt. Das Putzgitter ist aus Kunststoff, um den Faradaysischen Effekt zu verhindern. Der Grundriss erinnert in vielen Aspekten an den vom Haus Wolf-Bearth. Am offensichtlichsten ist der L-förmige, unbeheizte Anbau, der an das Haus anschließt. Er hat eine hauptsächlich unisolierte Holzkonstruktion, und dient als Carport, Eingang, Stauraum und als Außensitzbereich. Zusätzlich schützt der L-förmige Flügel das Haupthaus vor den Nordwinden. (→■349) Das Holz, das für den Bau der Speisekammer eingesetzt wurde, ist unbehandelt und unlackiert – und riecht nach wie vor angenehm nach Holz.

Gemäß eine interdisziplinären Studie von FH-Studentinnen (→B096) kostet das Haus – mit allen Systemen und Anschlüs-

the house – complete with systems and fittings – cost 50 CHF/m³ less than the average in the neighbouring houses, not to mention its much lower running costs. The Schmidlins say they paid exactly the price of a prefabricated, Minergie-standard wooden house of the same size – but the performances they got are superior, corresponding those of a Minergie-P house which would have cost 10–15% more. Even after 6 years, the owner is enthusiastic and proud ("it is pleasant, and it works!" he repeats) and actively promotes the choice he made. No damage has occurred so far, except for an early air-tightness problem with window frames, which was demonstrated to be the fitter's fault.

In sum, following Werner Schmidt's method one can get an excellently-performing house for a relatively low price. Still, one might think that straw-bale building is an élite choice. This impression would have been reinforced had the four-storey apartment buildings for two clients been built. Both were to stand in an exclusive residential area on the shores of Lake Zurich. The one Schmidt usually refers to as 'Wellenhaus' (literally, 'Wave House') because of its curvy forms, would have sat on the shore itself, and would have included four large, luxury units. (→■353-354) The other one, for the Häring-Braschler family, would have had winding, amoeba-shaped floor plans and partially protruding terraces and balconies. (→■355-356)

Apart from these special cases one can argue that, if implemented by companies, a straw bale house costs about the same as a conventional house. This the opinion of Tom Woolley, for instance, who says that although they have "been portrayed as the ultimate solution to 'cheap,' environmentally friendly building (...), straw bale buildings are rarely cheaper than the conventional, particularly if they are built properly." (→B126:72) Schmidt too judges that actually the construction of a straw-bale house costs about the same as a comparable conventional one: the advantage is lower operating costs. But if one

sen – im Durchschnitt 50,- CHF/m³ weniger als die Nachbarhäuser, ganz zu schweigen von den viel geringeren Betriebskosten. Die Schmidlins sagen, dass sie genau den Preis wie für ein vorgefertigtes Minergie-Standard Holzhaus derselben Größe – aber die Leistung liegt höher, korrespondierend mit einem Minergie-P Haus, welches 10 bis 15% mehr gekostet hätte. Auch nach 6 Jahren ist der Besitzer enthusiastisch und stolz („es ist angenehm und es funktioniert!" sagt er) und wirbt aktiv für die Entscheidung, die er getroffen hat. Bis jetzt trat kein Schaden auf, bis auf ein Dichteproblem an den Fenserrahmen, der sich als Fehler des Herstellers herausstellte.

Folgt man, in der Summe betrachtet, Werner Schmidts Methode, kann man ein hocheffizientes Haus zu einem relativ geringen Preis realisieren. Dennoch könnte man denken, dass der Strohballenbau eine sehr spezielle Entscheidung darstellt. Dieser Eindruck hätte sich verstärkt, wenn die viergeschossigen Apartment Häuser für zwei Kunden gebaut worden wären. Standort der beiden Projekte wäre ein exklusives Wohngebiet am Ufer des Zürichsees gewesen. Das eine Haus, das Schmidt wurde auf Grund seiner Wellenformen als ‚Wellenhaus' bezeichnet, wäre mit vier großen Luxuseinheiten ausgestattet direkt am Seeufer platziert gewesen. (→■353-354) Der Entwurf für die Familie Häring-Braschler hatte geschwungene, amöbenartige Grundrisse mit auskragenden Balkonen und Terrassen. (→■355-356) Abgesehen von diesen Spezialfällen, könnte man meinen, dass einen Strohballenhaus, wenn durch Unternehmen umgesetzt, ungefähr gleichviel kosten wie konventionelle Häuser. Dies ist zum Beispiel Tom Wooleys Meinung, der sagt, dass obwohl sie „als die ultimative Lösung für ‚günstige', umweltfreundliche Häuser (...) dargestellt werden, Strohballenhäuser selten günstiger sind als konventionelle, speziell dann wenn sie angemessen gebaut sind." (→B126:72) Schmidt ist der Meinung, dass der Bau eines Strohballenhauses in etwa gleich viel kostet wie ein konventionelles Haus. Der Vorteil sind die minimalen Betriebskosten: Wenn die Kosten

353

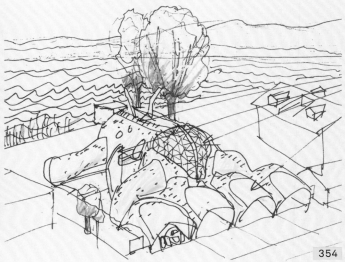

354

wants to save some building costs rather than construction time, the best thing is to superimpose a bale on top of the other and wait for creep to develop fully under load. This is the method he favours, both because it is the 'truest' to the straw-bale building approach and because the resulting building will be healthier (for the lack of glues in wood-based products) and have a lower embodied energy. On the other hand, when a building needs to be finished in a short time, straw may tend to be used just as insulating infill in a prefabricated timber construction, which is more expensive. However, it must be remarked that the construction system only partially affects the final cost, which depends more largely on finishes, equipment and labour; see the wide range of costs per square metre in the projects here illustrated. A load-bearing straw-bale DIY building tends to be inexpensive, and requires design for simple assembly due to the large share of manual labour involved – see for instance the work of Amazonails (now StrawWorks) in the UK and the Red Feather Development Group in the Hopi nation.

wichtig sind und weniger die Bauzeit maßgebend ist, ist es besser einen Ballen über den anderen zu stapeln und die Setzung unter der vollen Last abzuwarten. Dies ist die Methode, die er bevorzugt, weil sie die ehrlichste Herangehensweise an die Strohballenbauweise ist, und weil das daraus resultierende Gebäude gesünder ist (weniger Kleber durch hölzerne Materialien) und einen geringeren Anteil an Grauer Energie beinhaltet. Soll hingegen das Gebäude in einer kurzen Zeit erstellt werden, wird das Stroh eher als Füllmaterial in vorfabrizierten Holzkonstruktionen eingesetzt, die teurer sind. Jedoch muss angemerkt werden, dass die Konstruktion nur einen Teil der Gesamtkosten ausmacht, die weit mehr auch von der Oberflächenbeschaffenheit, der Ausstattung und Arbeit abhängen: dies zeigt die breite Kostenspanne pro Quadratmeter der hier aufgeführten Projekte. Ein lasttragendes Strohballengebäude tendiert dazu günstig zu sein; und erfordert ein einfaches Montageprinzip auf Grund des hohen Anteils an möglicher Eigenleistung – vergleiche die Arbeit von Amazonails (jetzt StrawWorks) in Großbritannien und die Red Feather Development Group im Hopi Reservat. Schmidt

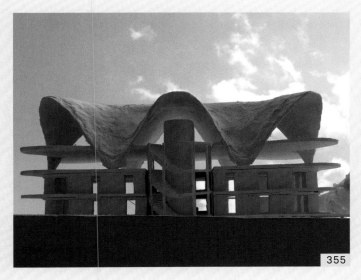

355

356

Schmidt designed Fliri house for self-help, and both he and his clients often take part to the building process to some degree. (→p242-255) Now, he is working a great deal on the development of the concept of a really inexpensive, low-tech solution: a 'casa cabana' made of jumbo bales, whose building envelope would be almost without timber; the roof would be a straw-bale false dome (like in Apulian trulli) or false vault, protected by a detached, waterproof membrane like in vonRoll pavilion. (→■045-046,049,222) All services would be contained in a 'wonder box' technical unit (→§07) placed inside the living volume. This concept is the development of the trulli-like living units designed for La Donaira. (→p144-149)

Design for emergency is just an extreme case of dealing with the much broader matter: Is design meant for luxury or necessity? Of course, Victor Papanek, as well as Italian democratic designers of past decades, has already answered this question more than convincingly, (→B085,074) but it seems that every new generation must address the issue

entwarf Haus Fliri für das Einbringen von Eigenleistung der Bauherren, generell sind sowohl er als auch seine Bauherren zu einem bestimmten Grad am Bauprozess beteiligt. (→S.242-255) Im Moment arbeitet er an der Entwicklung einer wirklich günstigen, low-tech Lösung: einem ‚Casa Cabana' aus Jumboballen, dessen Außenhülle nahezu ohne Holz auskommt – das Dach wäre ein Kraggewölbe oder falsches Gewölbe aus Strohballen (wie in den Apulischen Trulli), geschützt durch eine wasserfeste Membran wie beim vonRoll Pavillon. (→■045-046,049,222) Alle Anschlüsse wären in einer technischen Einheit der ‚Wunderbox' enthalten, (→§07) die innerhalb des Wohnbereichs platziert wäre. Dieses Konzept ist die Weiterentwicklung der Trulli ähnlichen Wohneinheiten, die für La Donaira entworfen wurden. (→S.144-149)

Entwurfskonzepte für Katastrophen sind ein extremer Fall des Umgangs mit viel weitreichenderen Belangen, ist der Entwurf als Luxus oder als Notwendigkeit gedacht? Natürlich hat Victor Papanek, ebenso wie andere italienische demokratische Ge-

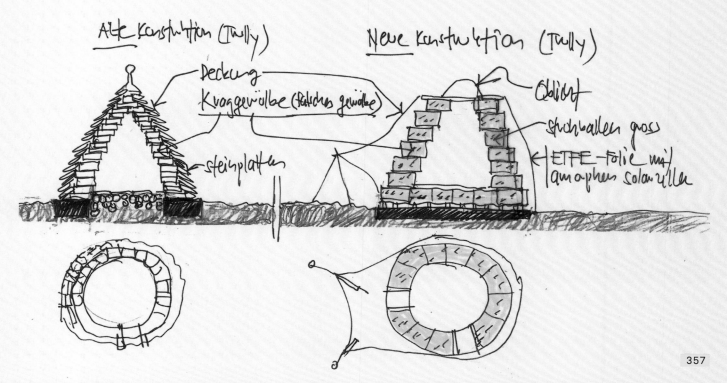

357

anew, as many designers have – perhaps understandably – a tendency to work for wealthy clients.

At present, we are experiencing a newly-born wave of social commitment in design issues – even more widespread among young architects. The global success of Rural Studio or Architecture for Humanity, (→B083,010) to name but the most famous cases, is an indication of such a trend. Obviously, by the 20th century, and most of all during and shortly after WWII, mass-production-oriented design had already tried to exploit the potential of industry to produce low-cost houses through the prefabrication of standardised, modular components. One just needs to think of Buckminster Fuller's and Prouvé's work. (→B115)

The main goal was to produce basic, inexpensive housing,

stalter der vergangenen Jahrzehnte, diese Frage bereits mehr als überzeugend beantwortet, (→B085,074) aber es scheint, dass jede neue Generation sich dieser Frage wieder stellen muss, da viele Gestalter – durchaus verständlich – für eine wohlhabende Klientel arbeiten.

Zur Zeit erfahren wir eine neu entstandene Welle der sozialen Verpflichtung bei Designthemen – besonders verbreitet unter jungen Architekten. Der globale Erfolg von Rural Studio oder Architecture for Humanity, (→B083,010) um nur die bekanntesten zu nennen, sind ein Indikator für eine solche Bewegung. Offensichtlich hat ein an Massenproduktion orientiertes Design bereits im 20. Jahrhundert, und vor allem während und nach dem 2. Weltkrieg, versucht, das Potenzial der Industrie zu nutzen, um günstige Häuser zu produzieren mittels Vorfabrikation

irrespective of considerations for local society or culture, as human 'needs' were assumed to be the same everywhere (or worse, because diversity was discarded as 'irrational'). Perhaps the only aspect which was sometimes given attention to was climate. Of course, in the case of emergency housing much ingenuity was employed to develop easy packaging, delivery, and assembly solutions.

It was authors like Fathy, Friedman, Illich, Segal, and Turner (→B042,046,058,073,111) who showed that a new approach including the ability to let the 'recipients' speak for themselves, and to recognise diversity, was called for. This was both for the sake of efficacy and respect – to the point that in most advanced situations architects (without renouncing their role) are now conceived as agents, participatorily cooperating with those they are trying to help. (→B012) This clearly goes hand-in-hand with a broader understanding of cultural and social relativity, with an engagement for people's empowerment, and with the development of an 'appropriate technology' approach. (→B123,052)

Of course, catastrophes (natural and man-made) happen again and again, and intelligent solutions for emergency shelter are required more than ever, as many are still too expensive or cumbersome to be realistically produced in large amounts and quickly delivered wherever necessary. In some instances, where local organisations or groups of people can operate, it makes more sense to transport – perhaps by helicopter – only the most advanced equipment and make use of local materials and processes for the rest. This is the approach Schmidt happened to embrace when he was confronted with the problem of transitional buildings.

von standardisierten, modularen Komponenten. Es sei hier an Buckminster Fullers und Prouvés Arbeiten gedacht. (→B115) Das Hauptziel war die Herstellung von grundlegenden, kostengünstigen Behausungen, unabhängig von sozialen oder kulturellen Überlegungen, in der Annahme, das menschliche ‚Bedürfnisse' überall dieselben sind – oder weil Vielfalt als ‚irrational' angesehen wurde. Vielleicht war der einzige Aspekt, der nicht ungeachtet blieb, die klimatischen Bedingungen. Natürlich wurde im Fall der Notunterkünfte viel Einfallsreichtum eingesetzt, um einfache Verpackung, Lieferung und Montagelösungen zu entwickeln.

Es waren Autoren wie Fathy, Friedman, Illich, Segal, und Turner, (→B042,046,058,073,111) die die Notwendigkeit nach einem neuen Ansatz aufzeigten, der die Möglichkeit der Selbstbestimmung der ‚Empfänger' mit einschließt und die Vielfalt berücksichtigt. Sowohl aus Gründen der Wirksamkeit und des Respekts – bis zu dem Punkt, dass in den meisten fortgeschrittenen Situationen die Architekten (ohne ihre Rolle aufzugeben) nun als Agent gesehen werden, unter mitwirkender Zusammenarbeit derer, denen sie helfen möchten. (→B012) Dies geht eindeutig Hand in Hand mit einem breiteren Verständnis für kulturelle und soziale Relativität, mit einem Engagement für die Stärkung der Menschen und mit der Entwicklung eines angemessenen Technikansatzes. (→B123,052)

Selbstverständlich geschehen Katastrophen (natürliche oder von Menschen generierte) immer wieder überall, und intelligente Lösungen für Notunterkünfte werden mehr denn je benötigt, zumal viele noch immer zu teuer und umständlich sind, um in großen Zahlen realisiert und schnell an den Einsatzort gebracht zu werden. In einigen Fällen, wo lokale Organisationen und Menschengruppen agieren können, macht es Sinn, nur das notwendige modernste Zubehör – vielleicht mittels Helikopter – zu liefern und den Rest mit Hilfe von lokalen Materialien und Verfahren zu realisieren. Dies ist der Ansatz, den Schmidt verfolgen konnte, als er mit der Problematik von Notunterkünften konfrontiert wurde.

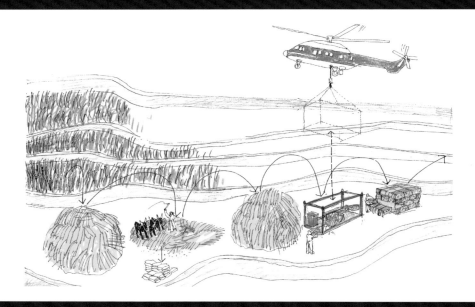

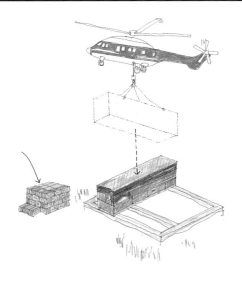

358

After the devastating earthquake of 2005, Werner Schmidt was contacted by Aga Khan's Foundation chief helicopter pilot, who asked him to develop a sustainable, earthquake-resistant building design for Azad Kashmir, a mountain area of northern Pakistan. (→B002,003,004,005,006) Such buildings would also protect from heat and cold, and issues such as cooking, water supply and disposal of waste water needed to be solved as well – possibly by a donated, airborne 'technical package.'

In similar situations, however, it is important to use as much local material as possible. Schmidt observed that rice was grown in the region, (→■364-366) and that rice straw was mostly burned. His design would therefore include walls made of rice straw bales, locally formed with simple hand-presses.

Nach dem verheerenden Erdbeben im Jahre 2005 kam Schmidt über einen Freund in Kontakt mit dem Chefpiloten der Aga Khan Foundatiaon. Sie baten ihn, ein nachhaltiges, erdbebensicheres Gebäudekonzept für Azad Kashmir, eine Bergregion in Nordpakistan, zu erstellen. (→B002,003,004,005,006) Derartige Gebäude wären zudem ein Schutz vor Hitze und Kälte, und Themen wie Kochen, Wasserversorgung, Schmutzwasserent-sorgung müssten ebenfalls gelöst werden – wenn möglich durch ein aus der Luft angeliefertes ‚Technikpaket'.

In solchen Situationen ist es wichtig, so viel wie möglich lokale Materialien einzusetzen. Schmidt wusste, dass in der Gegend Reis angebaut wird, (→■364-366) und dass das Reis-stroh meistens verbrannt wird. Sein Entwurf enthielt daher Wände aus Reisstrohballen,

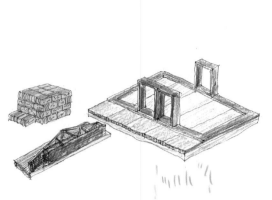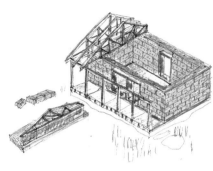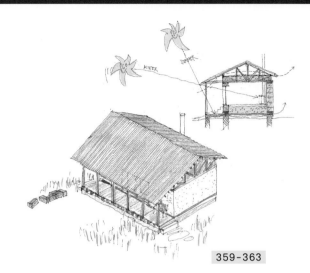

359-363

(→ ■358) Bales would perform as load-bearing structure and insulation. To enhance earthquake resistance, Schmidt detailed an ingenious albeit very basic way of making the walls also take out-of-plane loads, behaving as a spring which dissipates kinetic energy. (→ ■367) Walls would be prestressed vertically and also horizontally – which is totally uncommon – by means of ties connecting external 'pinning' bamboo sticks at every straw bale course. Both vertical precompression straps and bamboo poles would be buried in the (local earth, or lime) plaster.

It was foreseen to deliver a kit by helicopter, containing floor panels, door and window boxes and roof trusses, all wooden, as well as corrugated metal roofing. Such products would have been manufactured

vor Ort mittels Handpressen gepresst.
(→ ■358) Die Ballen wären als lasttragendes Element und als Isolierung eingesetzt. Um die Erdbebensicherheit zu verbessern, entwickelte Schmidt eine geniale und einfache Möglichkeit, wie die Wände die Erdbebenkräfte aufnehmen können. Die kinetische Energie wird über die Strohballen diagonal wie eine Art Feder abgegeben. (→ ■367) Die Wände wären vertikal vorgespannt, ebenso horizontal – was völlig unüblich ist – mit Hilfe von Bändern, die zwischen senkrechten Bambusstäben an der Innen- und Außenseite der Strohballenwand in jeder Ballenreihe gespannt sind. Sowohl die vertikalen Vorspannungsbänder als auch die Bambusstäbe würden unter der Putzschicht (aus Kalk oder Lehm) verschwinden.
Es war geplant, mittels Helikopter einen

364

365

366

in Switzerland and donated, as to allow the construction of 500 buildings. A team would have gone to Pakistan to train local people and build public buildings such as schools, community centres or hospitals with them. Having gained the experience, residents would then have been able to subsequently build their own homes, also using building products processed by local craftsmen. Although not put into practice, Schmidt's project seems particularly adapted to the context, at least from a technological point of view. The most internationally quoted test about the earthquake resistance of load-bearing straw-bale structures was (success-fully) performed in 2009 by PAKSBAB (Pakistan Straw Bale and Appropriate Building) at the University of Nevada, Reno. (→B084)

Bausatz bestehend aus Bodenplatten, Türen und Fensterkisten und Nagelbinder aus Holz sowie Wellbleche für die Eindeckung zu liefern. Diese Elemente wären in der Schweiz produziert und gespendet worden, um den Bau von 500 Gebäuden zu ermöglichen. Ein Team wäre nach Pakistan gereist, um Einheimische zu schulen und gemeinsam mit ihnen öffentliche Gebäude, wie Schulen, Gemeindezentren und Krankenhäuser zu errichten. Nachdem die Bewohner Erfah-rungen gesammelt hätten, würden sie sich nach und nach ihre eigenen Häuser bauen, ebenfalls mit dem Einsatz lokal hergestellter Elemente.
Obwohl dieser Entwurf nicht umgesetzt wur-de, scheint Schmidts Konzept besonders gut an den Kontext angepasst, wenigstens vom technologischen Standpunkt aus betrachtet. Der international meist zitierte Erdbeben-test zur lasttragenden Strohballenbau-weise wurde 2009 von PAKSBAB (Pakistan Straw Bale and Appropriate Building) an der University of Nevada, Reno (erfolgreich) durchgeführt. (→B084)

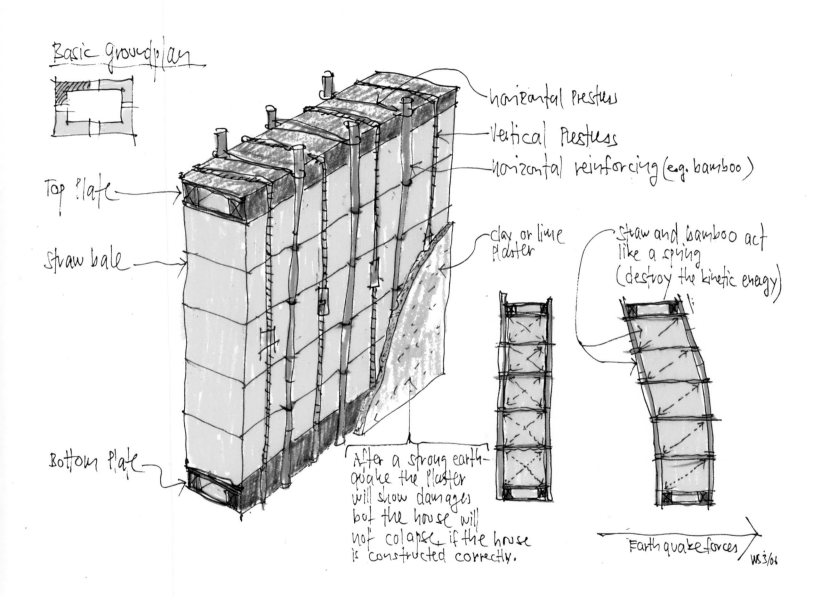

Basic groundplan

Top plate

straw bale

Bottom plate

horizontal Prestress

Vertical Prestress

horizontal reinforcing (e.g. bamboo)

clay or lime plaster

straw and bamboo act like a spring (destroy the kinetic energy)

After a strong earth-
quake the plaster
will show damages
but the house will
not collapse if the house
is constructed correctly.

Earthquake forces

WS 3/06

STRUCTURAL CONCEPT ⌐
STATIKKONZEPT

Should one comply with the rules or anticipate them? David Eisenberg – who more than many others has strived to reform building regulations – thinks that what they essentially do is maintaining the status quo, not creating favourable conditions to sustainability. (→■368) His opinion is that "We need to design a fully integrated regulatory system based on system principles and goals. The first principle should be that buildings should first do no harm." Eisenberg is committed to promoting a cultural change in codes and in code officials, as he advocates a broader understanding of safety which should encompass immediate aspects – such as structural safety – as well as long-term ones, so that buildings can be "safe for their occupants and the other inhabitants of earth, both current and future." (→B040:27)
Such a cultural change needs to be backed by information on the "viability of the proposed alternatives." (→B040:29) Unfortunately, unconventional solutions are often required to pass through time-consuming and expensive evaluation and certification processes, just because they do not conform to expectations raised (or imposed) by industrial standards. (→B040:28) This should not surprise anyone, since "the greatest influence on building codes is the building industry itself. Industry proposes the majority of code changes, pays for the research and testing to back its claims, spends the most time and money supporting those code changes." (→B040:25-26) Eisenberg also argues that "traditional, non-industrial materials and building systems were rejected mostly because of labor-intensity, not because they're inferior or dangerous." But, King adds, as laboratory tests are expensive, "materials

Sollte man die Normen einhalten oder sie antizipieren? David Eisenberg – der mehr als andere bemüht war, Bauvorschriften zu reformieren – glaubt, dass Normen im Grunde nur den Status quo aufrecht erhalten, jedoch keine günstigen Bedingungen für Nachhaltigkeit schaffen. (→■368) Er ist der Meinung, dass „wir ein komplett integriertes Regelsystem basierend auf Systemgrundsätzen und Zielen entwerfen müssen. Das erste Prinzip sollte sein, dass Gebäude nicht verletzen." Eisenberg hat sich dem Vorantreiben eines kulturellen Wandels der Regulierungen und Regulierungsinstanzen verschrieben, indem er für ein breiteres Verständnis von Sicherheit plädiert, welches unmittelbare und umfassende Aspekte beinhalten sollte – wie zum Beispiel statische als auch langfristige Sicherheit – so dass Gebäude „für ihre Bewohner und andere Menschen sicher sind, sowohl jetzt als auch in der Zukunft". (→B040:27)
Solch eine kultureller Wandel muss durch Informationen über die „Realisierbarkeit der vorgeschlagenen Alternativen" (→B040:29) abgesichert werden. Leider müssen unkonventionelle Lösungen oft durch zeitaufwändige und teure Bewertungs- und Zertifizierungsverfahren passieren, nur weil sie nicht den Erwartungen, die von Industriestandards geformt (oder auferlegt) wurden, entsprechen. (→B040:28) Dies sollte niemanden überraschen, denn „den größten Einfluss auf Gebäudenormen hat die Bauindustrie selbst. Die Industrie schlägt die Mehrheit der Normänderungen vor." (→B040:25-26) Eisenberg argumentiert auch, dass „traditionelle, nicht industrielle Baustoffe und Bausysteme meist wegen der Arbeitsintensität abgelehnt wurden, nicht weil sie minderwertig oder gefährlich sind"; King fügt hinzu, da Labortest teuer sind, „werden

and systems with no financial backing (…) tend to be undertested or remain untested, and therefore dismissed by the modern building community." (→B040:72) This applies to many natural materials, straw included. In sum, certificates and norms are meant to protect common good and they do it – but in doing so they also promote the interests of the more advanced enterprises and tend to inhibit innovation.

As long as the issuing of permits to straw-bale buildings is concerned, in Switzerland the law is very simple. Municipalities just worry that planning regulations are met in terms of distances from roads and boundaries, height, maximum building area, etc., and the fire police is the only body which will scrutinise a project from the constructional point of view. Architects and/or engineers take full responsibility for their work. As Peter Braun told me, "Obviously, the building will have to stand up. Is possible instability just local failure, or will it provoke a chain reaction? This is one of the aspects the structural engineer is called to anticipate." (→B024)
The European picture is not homogeneous: In countries like France and Switzerland it is enough to declare that the material used will be able to perform as required by regulations; in France it is even illegal to reject a project on the basis of the building material. In the UK and other countries, different kinds of suitability evidence are being accepted – from international tests passed to previous permits issued by authorities in other jurisdictions.
In Italy straw-bale load-bearing buildings are not allowed anymore, since straw is not listed among legal structural materials (DM 14.01.2008 "Norme tecniche sulle costruzioni"). Therefore, to build the Fliri holiday apartments one should now obtain a one-off certificate of suitability from the national technical council – a lengthy and costly procedure. In Germany, unregulated building products such as straw bales must obtain a certificate (AbZ or AbP), otherwise an individual (case-by-case) approval must be requested from the

Materialien und Systeme ohne finanzielle Unterstützung (…) in der Regel nicht gut genug getestet oder bleiben ungetestet, und werden damit von der modernen Gebäudelobby abgelehnt." (→B040:72) Dies gilt für viele natürliche Materialien, wie auch das Stroh. Zertifikate und Normen sollten dem Wohl der Gesellschaft dienen, was sie auch tun – aber indem sie dies tun, verhindern und blockieren oftmals dringend notwendige Innovationen, da sie die Interessen besser gestellter Unternehmen stützen.

Solange es um die Erteilung von Genehmigungen von Strohballenhäusern geht, ist das Gesetz in der Schweiz sehr einfach. Die Gemeinden achten darauf, dass bei der Planung die Vorschriften in Bezug auf Straßen- und Grenzabständen, Höhen, maximale Bebauungsfläche, etc. eingehalten werden, und die Feuerpolizei überprüft ein Projekt nur aus brandschutztechnischer Sicht. Architekten und/oder Ingenieuren übernehmen die volle Verantwortung für ihre Arbeit. Wie Peter Braun mir erklärte: „Das Gebäude muss stehen bleiben. Ist eine mögliche Instabilität nur ein lokales Versagen, oder wird diese eine Kettenreaktion auslösen? Dies ist einer der Aspekte, die der Statiker ermitteln muss." (→B024)
Die Meinung vieler Europäer ist hier nicht einheitlich: In Ländern wie Frankreich und der Schweiz reicht es aus zu bestätigen, dass das verwendete Material in der Lage ist, die erforderlichen Vorschriften zu erfüllen; in Frankreich ist es sogar verboten, ein Projekt aufgrund des Baustoffes abzulehnen. In Großbritannien und anderen Ländern werden verschiedene Tauglichkeitsnachweise akzeptiert – von internationalen Tests bis hin zu ausgestellten Genehmigungen von Behörden in andern Ländern.
In Italien sind lasttragende Strohballengebäude nicht mehr zulässig, da Stroh nicht unter den rechtlich anerkannten Baumaterialien geführt wird (DM 14.01.2008 „Norme tecniche sulle costruzioni"). Würde man also zum heutigen Zeitpunkt für die Fliri Ferienwohnungen nochmals ein Baugesuch

368

RISKS TO FUTURE GENERATIONS

Climate Impact

Embodied Energy

Pollution

Toxicity of Materials

Nutrification of Water

Healt Island Effect

Fire Safety
Structural Integrity
Means of Egress
Light
Ventilation
Heat
Water and Wastewater
Electrical & Gas
Energy Efficiency

Externalized Costs
to Society

Resource Depletion

Dependence on
Non-Renewable Energy

Loss of Habitat

Loss of Biodiversity

Loss of Agricultural Land

Increased Trasportation

369

CaRPE's straw-bale house in
Vers-chez-les-Blanc/VD

CaRPE Strohballenhaus in
Vers-chez-les-Blanc/VD

369

370

State construction supervision agency. In 2008, a 'General appraisal certificate' [Allgemeines bauaufsichtliches Prüfzeugnis – AbP] was issued for load-bearing, space-enclosing outer wall construction. (→B041,077:72) Schmidt's Schmid-Hermanutz house (→■370) is load-bearing at least to a large extent – according to Peter Braun, who performed the structural consultancy, load is taken 60% by straw bales, 40% by 16x16 cm timber studs. But since the latter might theoretically take the entire load, the permit was issued.

Engineer Peter Braun from Fribourg is the brother of the first client who commissioned Werner Schmidt with a straw-bale house. Braun's structural analyses have been playing a relevant role in promoting the acceptation of straw-bale building in Switzerland, and he regularly cooperates with architects who use straw bales in their projects, such as CArPE (Collectif d'Architecture Participative et Ecologique, Lausanne) whose approach is more low-tech and low-cost than Schmidt's. (→■369)
Braun studied 'rural engineering' (now renamed as 'environmental engineering') at the ETHZ: this study course included subjects such as biology, timber construction, and pedology, which were not taught elsewhere. He has worked as a carpenter, civil engineer, and for five years as a consultant at the Canton Fribourg office for historical monuments. Now he is one of the partners of an engineering and architectural practice.
Sertorio observes that regulations have been progressively substituting knowledge: (→B100:154) well, Braun is a rare case of engineer who does not hide behind a computer or a standard and who takes responsibility for his judgements – such responsibility is not easy to bear, but on the other hand it allows the freedom to develop new ways. He does not like certificates of any sort, as they tend to conceal the designer's responsibility. For example, according to the Minergie protocol even a 1,000 m² house for two persons can

stellen, bräuchte man ein einmaliges Eignungszertifikat des nationalen Technikrates – ein langwieriger und kostenintensiver Vorgang. In Deutschland müssen ungeprüfte Baumaterialien wie Strohballen ein Zertifikat erhalten (AbZ oder AbP), ansonsten muss eine Einzelgenehmigung von der Staatlichen Baubehörde angefordert werden. Im Jahr 2008 wurde für lasttragende, raumabschließende Außenwandkonstruktionen ein „Allgemeines bauaufsichtliches Prüfzeugnis" – AbP erstellt. (→B041,077:72) Schmidts Haus Schmid-Hermanutz (→■370) ist eine teillasttragende Strohballenkonstruktion – gemäß Peter Braun, der die statische Berechnung machte, wird die Last zu 60% über die Strohballen und zu 40% über die 16 x 16 cm dicken Holzstützen abgetragen. Aber theoretisch könnten auch die Holzstützen die gesamte Last tragen und somit wurde die Genehmigung erteilt.

Ingenieur Peter Braun aus Freiburg ist der Bruder des ersten Kunden, der Werner Schmidt mit einem Strohballenhaus beauftragte. Brauns Statikanalysen spielten für die Förderung der Akzeptanz von Strohballengebäuden in der Schweiz eine wichtige Rolle, und er arbeitet regelmäßig mit Architekten zusammen, die Strohballen in ihren Projekten verwenden, wie CArPE (Collectif d'Architecture Participative et Ecologique, Lausanne), deren Ansatz noch mehr in Richtung low-tech und low-cost geht als bei Schmidt. (→■369)
Braun studierte ‚Kulturtechnik' (jetzt in ‚Umwelttechnik' umbenannt) an der ETHZ: Dieses Studium beinhaltete Fächer wie Biologie, Holzbau und Bodenkunde, die anderswo nicht unterrichtet wurden. Er hat als Zimmermann, Bauingenieur und fünf Jahre lang als Berater für die Kantonale Denkmahlpflege des Kantons Freiburg gearbeitet. Jetzt ist er Partner in einem Ingenieur- und Architekturbüro.
Sertorio bemerkte, dass Normen schrittweise zum Ersatz von Wissen werden: (→B100:154) Braun ist ein seltener Fall eines Ingenieurs, der sich nicht hinter einem Computer oder einer Norm versteckt, und der Verantwortung für sein Urteil übernimmt –

be certified as eco-compatible. The label merely requires certain insulation standards to be met, and various technical measures to be taken. However, the whole footprint of the house is not measured. Urs Braun's house in Disentis is practically a zero-energy house. Still, since few systems were installed – e.g., double-flux mechanical ventilation is absent – it could not be certified, nor did the owners want it to be.

Braun's structural approach is based on risk analysis (allowable deformations), in his opinion an "experimentally clean" method. (→B024) He clearly states that a structural designer must differentiate "between load-bearing capacity, which must be guaranteed, and serviceability, which can be negotiated to a certain extent." (→B045:113) "Since one cannot see forces," he explains, "one must establish a model," but this will not be enough to guarantee the success of the structure, as this is achieved by a mix of calculation, experience, and fine-tuning on the building site. The latter has been the result of Schmidt's work, whom Braun likes to cooperate with, also because "he can reason as an engineer." (→B024)
So far, tests could not determine an ultimate strength value for straw bales. In Braun's opinion, the limit load must be over 15 t/m^2, the value obtained at the HTW Chur. (→B055) However, the structural behaviour is determined by the modulus of elasticity, which is approximately 0.4–0.6 N/mm^2 according to both FEB Kassel (→B068) and HTW Chur. Thus, according to Peter Braun's models, a 3 m-high, 80 cm-wide straw-bale wall can bear a maximum load of about 6 t/m^2. At higher loads, the wall buckles. This means in practice that at loads of 3 t/m^2 there is a safety factor of 2, which is sufficient. King asserts that "neither the straw bale walls nor the plaster skins could perform in the same structural fashion individually; the sum is greater than its parts" (→B063:21) and Braun agrees, as his experience makes him think that the (1–2 cm thick) transition layer where straw is intimately mixed with plaster is crucial in determining the whole structural

eine solche Verantwortung ist nicht leicht zu tragen, aber andererseits ermöglicht diese Herangehensweise neue Wege zu entwickeln. Er mag keine Zertifikate jeglicher Art, zumal sie dazu neigen, die Verantwortung des Gestalters zu kaschieren. Zum Beispiel gilt nach dem Minergie Statuten ein 1000 m^2 Haus für zwei Personen als eco-kompatibel. Das Label erfordert lediglich die Einhaltung bestimmter Dämmwerte und das Ergreifen verschiedener technischer Maßnahmen. Jedoch wird der Ökologische Fußabdruck des gesamten Gebäudes nicht gemessen. Urs Brauns Haus in Disentis ist praktisch ein Nullenergiehaus. Da auf die Installation von Systemen wie zum Beispiel einer Zwangsentlüftungsanlage mit Wärmerückgewinnung verzichtet wurde, kann das Haus nicht zertifiziert werden, was in diesem Fall aber auch nicht beabsichtigt war.

Brauns statischer Ansatz basiert auf der Risikoanalyse (zulässige Verformungen), seiner Meinung nach eine „experimentell besenreine" Methode. (→B024) Er betont, dass der Statiker unterscheiden muss „zwischen Tragfähigkeit, die gewährleistet sein muss, und Funktionstüchtigkeit, die zu einem gewissen Grad verhandelbar ist." (→B045:113) „Da man Kräfte nicht sehen kann – erklärt er – muss man ein Modell erstellen" aber das wird nicht ausreichen, um die statische Sicherheit des Bauwerks zu garantieren, da dies durch eine Mischung aus Berechnungen, Erfahrung und Feinabstimmung auf der Baustelle erreicht wird. Dies ist das Ergebnis von Schmidts Arbeit, mit welchem Braun gerne zusammenarbeitet, auch weil „er als Ingenieur gesunden Menschenverstand walten lassen kann." (→B024)
Brauns Ansicht nach muss die Grenzbelastung bei über 15 t/m^2 liegen, dieser Wert wurde an der HTW Chur erreicht. (→B055) Allerdings ist das statische Verhalten vom Elastizitätsfaktor (E-Modul) bestimmt, der etwa 0,4 bis 0,6 N/mm^2 beträgt gemäß FEB Kassel (→B068) und HTW Chur. So kann gemäß Peter Brauns Modell eine 3 m hohe, 80 cm breite Strohhallenwand eine maximale Last von etwa 6 t/m^2 aufnehmen.

system's behaviour. Although not modelised, the recognition of this phenomenon implies a different understanding of straw-bale walls than as sandwich panels or weak stressed-skin panels, like King suggests, (→B063:66-68) because the solutions Braun has been developing with Schmidt differ from USA load-bearing systems in two relevant issues: 1) bales are denser; 2) they are larger and therefore walls are thicker. Ring beams are dimensioned to rest on straw bales only, therefore the vertical load carried by plaster must first pass through them.

Braun assessed 40 kN/m as the permissible load for a 120 cm-thick wall. This was obtained halving limit load – as in timber structures – and is very close to the value given by FASBA. Facts seem to demonstrate that the theoretical value stipulated by Braun was still conservative. For his brother's house in Disentis, Peter Braun designed the structure so that operating load did not exceed 30 kN/m^2, whilst the plaster's function was mostly to brace the wall. Actually, under the heavy snowfall of winter 2006, total loads were 23 kN/m (dead load) + 19 kN/m (live loads) = 42 kN/m, which gives that load in plaster has been as high as about 0.18 N/mm^2 – as apparently such overload could not be carried by straw bales. In fact, straw is elastic: If it took the weight of snow, the house would theoretically compress in winter and spring back again in summer. Actually, no movement is apparent. This means that the snow load is entirely taken by the plaster, or that the combination of the two materials can actually carry more than theoretically expected.

As we will soon see, house Fliri showed even better structural performances: 1 linear metre of straw-bale wall, plastered on both sides can carry 1+3+1 tonnes instead of 1+0.2+1 as according to the American construction method and structural model. Braun thinks that the major static issue is not maximum admittable load, but creep control, so that a satisfactory horizontality is obtained.

Also for this reason, then, structural analyses must be

Bei höheren Lasten beult die Wand aus. Dies bedeutet in der Praxis, dass bei Lasten von 3 t/m² ein Sicherheitsfaktor von 2 besteht, welcher ausreichend ist.

King behauptet „weder die Strohballenwände noch die Putzschichten können für sich allein dieselbe statische Beschaffenheit aufweisen; die Summe ist größer als die einzelnen Teile", (→B063:21) und Braun stimmt dem zu, da ihm seine Erfahrungen zeigen, dass die (1 bis 2 cm dicke) Übergangsschicht, wo Stroh und Putz ineinander greifen, entscheidend ist für das gesamte statische Verhalten. Obwohl dies noch nicht im Modell gezeigt, stellt die Erkenntnis dieses Phänomens ein anderes Verständnis von Strohballenwänden dar, als bei Sandwichplatten oder wenig beanspruchten Außenschalung, wie King schreibt, (→B063:66-68) weil sich die Lösungen, die Braun mit Schmidt entwickelt hat, von lasttragenden Systemen aus den USA in zwei relevanten Fragen unterscheiden: 1) die Ballen sind dichter, 2) sie sind größer und daher sind die Wände dicker. Holzkränze sind so dimensioniert, dass sie auf den Strohballen auflagern, somit wird die vertikale Last erst über die Strohballen auf den Verputz übertragen.

Braun nimmt 40 kN/m als die zulässige Last für eine 120 cm dicke Wand an. Dies wurde bei einer halbierten Grenzbelastung erreicht – wie im Holzbau – und ist sehr nahe an dem Wert, der von der FASBA angegeben wird. Die Fakten scheinen zu belegen, dass der von Braun festgelegte theoretische Wert noch konservativ ist. Für das Haus seines Bruders in Disentis, entwickelte Peter Braun das statische Konzept so, dass die Betriebslasten 30 kN/m² nicht überschreiten, während der Putz in erster Linie als Verstärkung und Aussteifung der Wände dient. Tatsächlich lag im Winter 2006 unter starkem Schneefall die gesamte Belastung bei 23 kN/m (Eigengewicht) + 19 kN/m (Nutzlasten) = 42 kN/m, was für den Putz eine Belastung von 0,18 N/mm² ergibt – scheinbar konnte diese ‚Überlastung' nicht durch die Strohballen abgetragen werden. Stroh elastisch ist: wenn das Stroh das Gewicht des Schnees im Winter und Frühjahr aufnimmt, setzt sich das Haus, und im Sommer geht

performed and verified for three building phases: 1) straw-bale walls only; 2) finished construction (dead load only); 3) construction in operating conditions. Rendering at the end of phase 2 stabilises the building and prevents further creep. Temporary loads (e.g. sand and clay mortar bags) were moved onto the floors to keep them horizontal as they displaced down, and also to precompress the walls a bit. (→■371-376) Braun does not think prestressing straw-bale walls is necessary. In principle, there is no need to tie the straw-bale walls to the foundations either, as the straw-bale insulating layer above the last floor weighs 80–100 kg/m², and the usual wind load in Switzerland is 80 kg/m². At Fliri's however, rafters at the building corners were tied to the foundation by tension strands. On one hand this allowed to straighten the building out, on the other it reinforced it against strong winds.

From a structural point of view, Schmidt's most interesting projects are houses Braun and Fliri, both born out of the close cooperation with Peter Braun.

In the attic of house Fliri there were already two holiday apartments, but for a long time the owner has wanted to expand such activity onto a plot next to his farmstead, where 100 m² were still available for construction. The new building was to be made of natural materials and constructed around human needs – not to demand that people adapt to it, as is what happens with much 'design' architecture. This building was to contain two more holiday apartments and Mr. Fliri's own *atelier d'artiste*.
One of his clients told him of Dalsant house, another farmstead Margareta Schwarz and Werner Schmidt had just built in the same region. After a telephone conversation with the owner, Richard Fliri decided this was the approach he was looking for, and called Schmidt to commission a 3-storey building. Also given the extreme constraints imposed

es theoretisch wieder zurück. Tatsächlich ist keine Bewegung erkennbar. Dies bedeutet, dass die Schneelast vollständig vom Putz oder die erhöhte Belastbarkeit aus der Kombination der Strohballen mit Verputz abgefangen wird. Wie wir bald sehen werden, zeigt das Haus Fliri noch bessere statische Leistungen: 1 Laufmeter Strohballenwand, beidseitig verputzt, kann 1+3+1 anstelle von 1+0,2+1 Tonnen tragen, wie es die amerikanische Bauweise und deren Statikmodell darstellt. Braun ist der Meinung, dass das große statische Problem nicht die maximale Belastbarkeit ist, sondern die Kontrolle über das Setzungsverhalten, so dass eine zufriedenstellende Horizontalität erreicht wird.
Aus diesem Grund müssen statische Analysen für drei Bauphasen durchgeführt und nachgewiesen werden: 1) nur für die Strohballenwand, 2) für die fertige Konstruktion (nur Eigengewicht), 3) für den Bau während der Benutzung. Das Verputzen am Ende der Phase 2 stabilisiert das Gebäude und verhindert ein weiteres Setzen. (→■371-376) Darüber hinaus wurden temporäre Lasten (Lehmputz und Sand) auf den Stockwerken verteilt, um sie während des Setzungsprozesses waagrecht zu halten, und um die Wände nach unten zu pressen.
Braun ist nicht der Meinung, dass das Vorspannen der Strohballenwand nötig sei. Im Prinzip ist es auch nicht notwendig, die Strohballenwand an die Fundamente zu binden, zumal die Dachkonstruktion mit der isolierenden Schicht aus Strohballen 80–100 kg/km² wiegt, und die üblichen Windlasten in der Schweiz 80 kg/m² betragen. Allerdings wurde beim Haus Fliri die Dachkonstruktion mittels Rispenbändern mit den Fensterlaibungen des Dach- und Obergeschosses zusammengehängt. Einerseits konnte das Gebäude somit ausgerichtet, und andererseits gegen starke Windkräfte verstärkt werden.

Vom statischen Gesichtspunkt sind Haus Braun und Haus Fliri Schmidts interessantesten Projekte, beide sind in enger Zusammenarbeit mit Peter Braun entstanden.

243

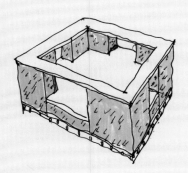

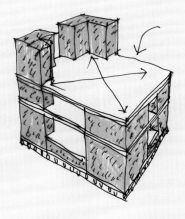

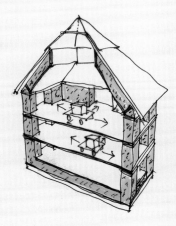

371-376

371-373

building phase I of Fliri house:
laying load-bearing straw-bale
external walls, wall- and roof-
plates, floors, roof

Aufbauschema I zu Haus Fliri:
Setzen der lasttragenden Stroh-
ballenaußenwände, Holzkränze,
Zwischendecken und des Daches

374-376

building phase II of Fliri house:
laying brick partition walls,
window sideboards, plasters

Aufbauschema II zu Haus Fliri:
Aufmauern der Innenwände aus
Tonziegeln, Setzen der Fenster-
laibungen und Aufbringen des
Verputzes

377

FLIRI HOLIDAY FARM

address ⌐ Adresse: Langtaufers 84A,
I-39027 Graun im Vinschgau/BZ
altitude ⌐ Höhe: 1850 m
degree-days ⌐ Gradtage: 5010
project ⌐ Entwurf: 2001-07
construction ⌐ Bau: 2007
building firms ⌐ Baufirmen: Richard Fliri (self builder ⌐ Baumeister);
Erich Fliri, Taufers im Münstertal (wood construction ⌐ Holzbau);
Werner Schmidt (straw-bale construction ⌐ Strohbau)
plot area ⌐ Grundstückfläche: 60,000 m²
heated floor area ⌐ Geheizte Bodenfläche: 276 m²
building cost ⌐ Baukosten: 456,000 € (1,700 €/m²)

by the high mountain location, Schmidt would not have achieved such a successful result without a substantial co-operation with Peter Braun, with whom he associated for the second time in a challenging project; architectural and structural concept are two sides of the same entity. Schmidt worked out several layouts, and his client always opted for the simplest. Also the building process was to be as simple as possible, since the owner wanted to be able to self-build the house with the help of his brother, making use of minimum equipment. In the end, architect and engineer came up with a clear and simple form – a square plan almost rigorously symmetrical, surmounted by a pyramidal, shingled roof (the typical roof in the area was covered with long shingles, *Legschindeln*). (→■377) This solution fits the primordial appearance of the valley, and somehow recalls the Romanesque towers so common in Vinschgau – giving the new building some local flavour, in spite of the fact that vernacular farms are typically gabled (the traditional roof typology was a *Schwardach*) and have an elongated plan. The two lower floors would contain a holiday apartment each

Im Dachgeschoss des bestehenden Hauses Fliri gab es bereits zwei Ferienwohnungen, doch seit langem wollte der Bauherr weitere Ferienwohnugnen auf dem Grundstück neben seinem Hof errichten. Das neue Gebäude sollte aus natürlichen Materialien bestehen und die menschlichen Bedürfnisse erfüllen – derart, dass die Menschen sich nicht anpassen müssen, wie es häufig bei solch einer „design" Architektur der Fall ist. Dieses Gebäude sollte zwei weitere Ferienwohnungen und das Atelier des Bauherren beherbergen.
Einer seiner Kunden erzählte ihm vom Haus Dalsant-Pernter, ein weiterer Bauernhof, den Margareta Schwarz und Werner Schmidt gerade in der Region Südtirol gebaut hatten.
Nach einem Telefongespräch mit dem Eigentümer, kam Richard Fliri zu dem Schluss, dass dies der Ansatz war, nach dem er so lange gesucht hatte, und beauftragte Schmidt mit der Planung von einem drei geschossigen Gebäude. Angesichts der extremen Einschränkungen durch die hohe Lage in den Bergen, hätte Schmidt wohl ohne die enge Zusammenarbeit mit Peter Braun, der zum zweiten Mal in ein solch herausforderndes Projekt involviert wurde, nicht so ein

– their envelope is constituted by massive L-shaped walls placed at the corners, and large openings in between them, which give access to terraces where the sheltered guests can enjoy the sun and the views – while the owner's atelier was to be located under the roof, and illuminated by a skylight at the top. (→■382,387)

The approval process took several years: the Municipality of Graun immediately issued a permit, but since the house was to be built in an environmental protection zone, the project had to be approved by the Province too – there, it was repeatedly rejected in spite of changes and additions. Finally the permit was obtained, and Richard Fliri was also granted some subventions, both for the development of mountain agriculture and the preservation of landscape. It must be noted that none of the permit-issuing authorities involved in the process never raised any objections regarding the building technique.

"Calculations were my duty but Werner ought to understand enough to be able to correct the imperfections which might occur during construction," remembers Peter Braun. "Starting from a risk analysis, we have developed an experimental approach which defines different intervention scenarios in case of unattended behaviour of the construction.

"We soon abandoned the idea of letting loads rest entirely on the straw bales: the loads were more than double than in Disentis; moreover, the internal partition walls had to be built in any case, and could easily be reinforced so as to perform a structural function." (→B023) Braun and Schmidt designed a system where the collaboration of different parts – L-shaped exterior walls formed of jumbo bales, window boxes made of timber panels, and interior solid brick walls – has allowed the attainment of a considerable height: this is probably the tallest load-bearing straw-bale building, at least in Europe. (→■381) Finally, continues Braun's explanation, "The roof needed to be quite pointed – at least 45° – to draw away some of the snow." (→B045:112) In fact, it is reported that

erfolgreiches Ergebnis erlangen können; das architektonische und statische Konzept gehen Hand in Hand. Schmidt erarbeitete zwei Varianten, eine runde und eine quadratische. Der Bauherr entschied sich für die quadratische Variante. Auch der Bauprozess war so einfach wie möglich gehalten, da der Bauherr in der Lage sein wollte, sein Haus mit minimaler Ausrüstung und mit Hilfe seines Bruders selber zu bauen. Am Ende kamen der Architekt und der Ingenieur mit einer klaren und einfachen Form – ein quadratischer Grundriss, streng symmetrisch, mit einem pyramidenförmigen Holzschindeldach. (→■377) Diese Lösung passt zum ursprünglichen Erscheinungsbild des Tals und erinnert an die oft auftretenden, romanischen Türme im Vinschgau – was dem neuen Gebäude lokales Flair einverleibt, trotz der Tatsche, dass die heimischen Höfe typischerweise ein Giebeldach vorweisen (der traditionelle Dachtypus ist ein *Schwardach*) und einen länglichen Grundriss haben.

In den beiden unteren Stockwerken befinden sich die Ferienwohnungen – deren Hülle besteht aus massiven L-förmigen Wänden, die an den Ecken platziert worden sind und große Öffnungen in der Mitte bilden, die den Zugang zu den Terrassen bieten, wo die Gäste geschützt die Sonne und die Aussicht genießen können. Während das Atelier des Bauherrn sich unter dem Dach befindet und durch das 15 m² große Oberlicht an der Spitze des Daches viel Tageslicht erhält. (→■382,387)

Die Baugenehmigung dauerte mehrere Jahre: die Gemeinde Graun erteilte unverzüglich eine Genehmigung, aber da das Haus in einer Schutzzone errichtet wurde, musste das Projekt auch von der autonomen Provinz Südtirol genehmigt werden – dort wurde es immer wieder trotz Abänderungen und Anpassungen abgelehnt. Schließlich wurde das Projekt genehmigt und Richard Fliri wurden einige Zuschüsse gewährt, sowohl für die Entwicklung der Berglandwirtschaft als auch für den Erhalt der Landschaft. Es sei hier erwähnt, dass keine der beteiligten behördlichen Instanzen je etwas an der Bauweise selbst auszusetzen hatte.

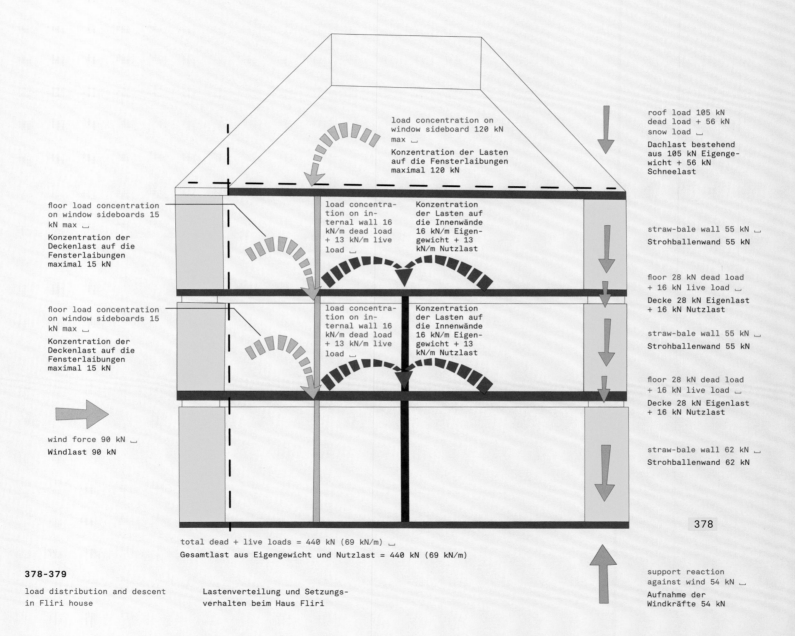

load concentration on
window sideboard 120 kN
max ⌐

Konzentration der Lasten
auf die Fensterlaibungen
maximal 120 kN

roof load 105 kN
dead load + 56 kN
snow load ⌐

Dachlast bestehend
aus 105 kN Eigenge-
wicht + 56 kN
Schneelast

floor load concentration
on window sideboards 15
kN max ⌐

Konzentration der
Deckenlast auf die
Fensterlaibungen
maximal 15 kN

load concentra-
tion on in-
ternal wall 16
kN/m dead load
+ 13 kN/m live
load ⌐

Konzentration
der Lasten auf
die Innenwände
16 kN/m Eigen-
gewicht + 13
kN/m Nutzlast

straw-bale wall 55 kN ⌐
Strohballenwand 55 kN

floor 28 kN dead load
+ 16 kN live load ⌐

Decke 28 kN Eigenlast
+ 16 kN Nutzlast

floor load concentration
on window sideboards 15
kN max ⌐

Konzentration der
Deckenlast auf die
Fensterlaibungen
maximal 15 kN

load concentra-
tion on in-
ternal wall 16
kN/m dead load
+ 13 kN/m live
load ⌐

Konzentration
der Lasten auf
die Innenwände
16 kN/m Eigen-
gewicht + 13
kN/m Nutzlast

straw-bale wall 55 kN ⌐
Strohballenwand 55 kN

floor 28 kN dead load
+ 16 kN live load ⌐

Decke 28 kN Eigenlast
+ 16 kN Nutzlast

wind force 90 kN ⌐
Windlast 90 kN

straw-bale wall 62 kN ⌐
Strohballenwand 62 kN

378

total dead + live loads = 440 kN (69 kN/m) ⌐
Gesamtlast aus Eigengewicht und Nutzlast = 440 kN (69 kN/m)

378-379

load distribution and descent
in Fliri house

Lastenverteilung und Setzungsverhalten beim Haus Fliri

support reaction
against wind 54 kN ⌐

Aufnahme der
Windkräfte 54 kN

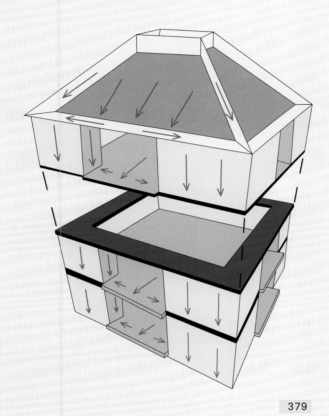

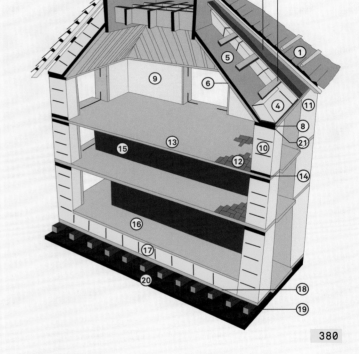

379

380

1 shingle roofing ⌐
Schindeleindeckung

2 waterproof layer ⌐
Sparschalung

3 timber battens ⌐
Konterlattung Gerüstbretter

4 straw-bale insulation ⌐
Strohballenisolierung

5 timber-board decking ⌐
Dreischichtplatten

6 rafters ⌐
Dachsparren

7 skylight ⌐
Oberlicht

8 roof plate ⌐
Dachplatten

9 internal clay-plaster ⌐
innerer Lehmputz

10 load-bearing straw bales ⌐
lasttragende Strohballen

11 external lime-plaster ⌐
äußerer Kalkputz

12 brick flooring ⌐
Tonziegelboden auf Fließestrich

13 brettstapel floor ⌐
Brettstapeldecke

14 wall plate ⌐
Kranz

15 brickwork partition wall ⌐
Trennwände aus Tonziegeln

16 cast plaster flooring ⌐
Fließestrich

17 straw-bale insulation
+ separating layer ⌐
Strohballenisolierung + Folie

18 timber decking ⌐
Holzeindeckung

19 concrete beams ⌐
Betonpfähle

20 concrete slab ⌐
Betonplatte

21 horizontal metal rods
connecting the rafters ⌐
horizontaler Ring aus Flacheisen
zur Verbindung der Haupteck-
träger

381

"the earliest straw houses had hipped roofs. (...) It's a very stable design, very well suited to strawbale houses, because the roof load is evenly spread around all the walls and (...) you don't have unprotected gables exposed to bad weather." (→B061:70;■379)
Perimeter walls carry the whole roof weight, but only 1/3 of the floor weight (1/6 on west wall, 1/6 on east wall), while the remaining 2/3 are carried by the timber-framed wall. (→■378) The roof plate directs roof load where straw is. Braun comments that "the total operating load might be taken by straw-bale walls, nevertheless at 69 kN/m we are close to the ultimate load (80–90 kN/m), at which buckling might occur. Therefore, window boxes have been sized in order to withstand a load of about 170 kN each. In case of local failure of straw bales and/or render, these boxes will be charged. Thus the building has a satisfactory reserve factor" (the global safety factor is close to 2 or perhaps higher). (→B045:118-119) Furthermore, a reinforcing post might be added at each corner of the ground floor in case further displacement is observed. Anyhow, during five years of service

„Die Berechnungen waren meine Aufgabe, aber Werner musste auch genug darüber verstehen, um während der Bauphase auf eventuell auftretende Ungereimtheiten reagieren zu können," erinnert sich Peter Braun. „Ausgehend von der Risikoanalyse, hatten wir eine experimentelle Annäherung entwickelt, die die verschiedensten Eingreifszenarien definierte für mögliche, unvorhergesehene Zwischenfälle beim Verhalten der Konstruktion."
„Wir haben schnell die Idee aufgegeben, die Lasten vollkommen über die Strohballen abzutragen: die Lasten waren mehr als doppelt so hoch wie in Disentis, außerdem mussten die inneren Trennwände in jedem Fall errichtet werden und so ausgebildet sein, dass sie eine tragende Funktion übernehmen konnten". (→B023) Braun und Schmidt konzipierten ein System, bei dem das Zusammenspiel verschiedener Teile – L-förmige Eckwände aus Jumboballen, seitliche Fensterlaibungen aus Holzplatten und Innenwände aus Backsteinen – es erlaubten, eine beträchtliche Höhe zu erreichen: wahrscheinlich ist dies das höchste lasttragende Strohballenhaus, zumindest in Europa. (→■381) Schließlich, setzt Braun mit seiner Erklärung fort, „Das Dach musste steil sein, mindestens 45° – damit der Schnee abrutschen konnte." (→B045:112) In der Tat wird berichtet, dass „die frühesten Strohballenhäuser Walmdächer hatten. (...) Dies ist eine sehr stabile Bauweise, gut geeignet für Strohballenhäuser, da die Dachlasten gleichmäßig auf alle Wände verteilt werden und (...) es gibt keine ungeschützten Giebelflächen, die dem schlechten Wetter ausgesetzt sind." (→B061:70;■379)
Die Außenwände tragen das ganze Gewicht des Daches, aber nur 1/3 des Gewichtes der Böden (1/6 auf der westlichen Wand, 1/6 auf der Ostwand), während die restlichen 2/3 über die Backsteinwände abgeführt werden. (→■378) Die Deckenplatte lenkt die Dachlasten auf das Stroh ab. Braun erklärt, dass „die gesamte Betriebslast durch die Strohballenwände aufgenommen werden könnte, jedoch sind wir bei 69 kN/m nahe an der maximalen Traglast (80–90 kN/m), bei dem ein

381

Strohpolis in Sieben Linden/SAW
is probably the second-tallest
straw-bale building in Europe ⌣
Strohpolis in Sieben Linden/
SAW ist wahrscheinlich das zweit
höchste Strohballenhaus in
Europa

**SCALE ⌣ MASSSTAB
1:200**

382

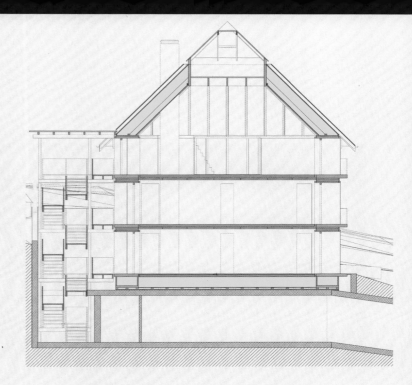

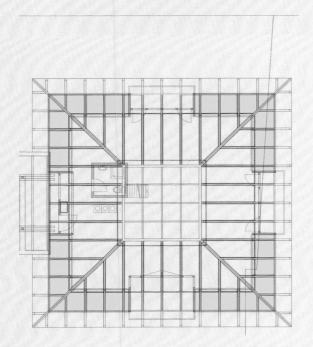

383

384

the straw-bale walls have withstood loads of about 50 kN/m without major problems.

Peter Braun concludes that "one must take maximum advantage of load-bearing straw-bale construction, but this approach should not be a religion. When a timber reinforcement is more practical, or when a window box is needed anyhow, one should take advantage of the situation, and integrate such element into the structural concept." (→B045:119)

Paradoxically, this virtuoso accomplishment may in the future encounter serious problems because of an issue totally different from structural safety – rain water. In fact, the client wanted downpipes to be embedded in straw-bale walls. Straw bales were imported from southern Bavaria – these days, almost exclusively round bales are produced in Northern Italy. Windows and doors, both internal and external, were produced locally and are of larch wood. Floors are glue-free timber decks, produced in the Pitztal. Partition walls

Ausbeulen auftreten könnte. Daher wurden die seitlichen Fensterlaibungen, die nachträglich eingebracht wurden, so dimensioniert, dass sie einer Last von ungefähr 170 kN standhalten können. Im Falle eines lokalen Versagens der Strohballen und/oder des Putzes, werden die Fensterlaibungen belastet. So verfügt das Gebäude über eine zuverlässige Absicherung" (der gesamte Sicherheitsfaktor ist nahe bei 2 oder vielleicht größer). (→B045:118-119) Darüber hinaus kann an jeder Ecke des Erdgeschosses ein Verstärkungspfosten angebracht werden, falls eine weitere Verschiebung beobachtet werden sollte. Jedenfalls haben die Strohballenwände seit fünf Jahren Betriebszeiten Lasten von etwa 50 kN/m ohne größere Probleme überstanden. Die Schlussfolgerung von Peter Braun ist, dass "man den maximalen Nutzen aus der lasttragenden Strohballenbauweise ziehen sollte, aber dieser Ansatz nicht zur Religion erhoben werden darf. Wenn eine Holzkonstruktion praktischer ist oder eine Fensterkiste sowieso benötigt wird,

386

are built with unfired bricks. Wall internal surfaces are coated with a ready-to-use Claytec mix, containing straw to enrich the texture. (→■390) The outdoor staircase is structurally independent from the building (→■386) – which implies a number of advantages, among which making sound insulation easier, preventing vertical draughts, and above all avoiding gaps in the floors, which would have implied concentrating loads in certain points. The staircase was built after creep had finished, from local timber: larch for structures and Swiss pine for parapets.

Superinsulation and large glazed surfaces provide exceptional passive thermal performances, enhanced by the thermal mass composed by brick walls and tiled floors.

sollte man die Situation entsprechend nutzen und solche Elemente in das statische Konzept integrieren." (→B045:119) Paradoxerweise muss sich diese virtuose Errungenschaft in der Zukunft vielleicht noch ganz anderen Herausforderungen stellen, gänzlich anders als die statische Sicherheit – das Regenwasser. In der Tat wollte der Bauherr gerne die Fallrohre in den Strohballenwänden einbetten.

Die Strohballen wurden aus Südbayern importiert. Die Fenster und die Innen- und Außentüren, wurden in der Nähe produziert und sind aus Lärchenholz. Die Böden wurden im Pitztal produziert und bestehen aus einer unverleimten Holzstapeldecke. Die Trennwände sind aus Backsteinen gemauert. Die Oberflächen der Innenwände wurden mit einer Fertigputz-

388

389

390

Nevertheless – also because for three weeks in winter the sun never rises above the facing mountain – a pre-existing chipped wood-burning boiler, located in the farmstead, has been connected to the new building to deliver hot water for sanitary uses and to three radiators located in the bathrooms. In addition, there is a fireplace in each apartment, which I think might have been skipped: During our early March 2012 visit, when at night the outdoor temperature always fell below 0°C, to sleep we had to shut off the radiators and leave the French windows ajar, and we still felt too warm. The atelier on the top floor makes up more than 40% of the building's out-of-grade volume; (→■388) there, the winter temperature is lower (15°C at the time of our visit) due to the high ceiling. In the skylight, a walk-in, triple-pane glass creates a buffer zone, separating the exterior and interior environments.

mischung von Claytec beschichtet und mit Stroh vermischt um die Textur zu verstärken. (→■390) Die Außentreppen sind statisch unabhängig vom Gebäude (→■386) – was einige Vorteile mit sich bringt, zum Beispiel gute Schalldämmung, keine vertikale Zugluft und vor allem vermeidet sie Lücken zwischen den Etagen, was an bestimmten Stellen zu konzentrierten Lasten geführt hätte. Die Treppe wurde aus heimischer Lärche (Konstruktion) und Schweizer Kiefer (Geländer) gefertigt und aufgestellt, nachdem der Setzungsprozess beendet war. Die Superisolierung und die großen Glasflächen bieten außergewöhnliche, passive thermische Leistung, die verstärkt wird durch die thermische Masse der Innenwände und gefliesten Böden. Da im Winter für drei Wochen die Sonne nicht über den gegenüberliegenden Berghang steigt, wurde eine bereits bestehende Hackschnitzelanlage, die im Bestandsgebäude der Bauherren steht, an das neue Gebäude angeschlossen, um es mit Warmwasser auszustatten und je einen Handtuchradiator in den drei Badezimmern zu wärmen. Darüber hinaus gibt es einen Holzofen in jeder Wohnung, die meiner Meinung nach überflüssig sind: während unseres Aufenthalts im März 2012, als über Nacht die Außentemperatur unter 0°C fiel, wir die Heizkörper ausschalteten und die französischen Fenster öffneten, war es immer noch sehr warm im Zimmer. Das Atelier im Dachgeschoss macht mehr als 40% des gesamten Gebäudevolumens aus; (→■388) dort ist im Winter auf Grund der hohen Decken die Temperatur niedriger (15° bei unserem Besuch). In der Dachluke bildet jedoch die begehbare Glasfläche mit ihrer Dreifachverglasung und die Glasspitze mit Isolierverglasung eine Art Pufferzone, die die Außenluft abhält.

BRAUN-DUBUIS HOUSE ⌐ HAUS BRAUN-DUBUIS

ADDRESS ⌐ ADRESSE:
Casa Tscheppa,
CH-7180 Disentis-Acletta/GR

ALTITUDE ⌐ HÖHE: 1289 m

DEGREE-DAYS ⌐ GRADTAGE: 4291

PROJECT ⌐ ENTWURF: 2001

CONSTRUCTION ⌐ BAU: 2002

**MAIN BUILDING FIRMS ⌐
WICHTIGEN BAUFIRMEN:**
Berther, Disentis
(general contractor ⌐ Baumeister);
Bearth, Rabius
(wood construction ⌐ Holzbau)
Atelier Werner Schmidt + Firma Flepp
(Straw Bale Construction ⌐ Strohbau)

**PROJECT MANAGER ⌐
PROJEKTLEITUNG:**
Werner Schmidt

PLOT AREA ⌐ GRUNDSTÜCKFLÄCHE:
322 m²

**HEATED FLOOR AREA ⌐
GEHEIZTE BODENFLÄCHE:**
110 m²

**MAIN GLAZED AREA (SW) ⌐
FENSTERFLÄCHE HAUPTFASSADE:**
27 m²

BUILDING COST ⌐ BAUKOSTEN (BKP2):
485,000 CHF (4,409 CHF/m²)

What became the very first straw-bale house built by Schmidt was initially intended as a small retreat, about 30 m². However, Urs Braun later asked for a family-size project. The client was soon caught by the idea of always finding his holiday home warm, without remote-controlled heating and other technological paraphernalia. Peter Braun expressed his confidence in the design and became the structural consultant for this project.

In order to allow future extensions by way of enclosing the space beneath it, the house was from the beginning as high as the maximum permitted. The building stands on a reinforced concrete floor slab, which sits on a foundation wall on the slope side, and on piers on the downhill side. Lacinski and Bergeron are correct when they say that "a house on piers tends to look rickety and disconnected from its site. This effect is exacerbated in the case of a plastered bale building; a structure with such a massive feel really wants to be anchored to the ground." (→B069:109) Schmidt deliberately wanted the massiveness of house Braun to starkly contrast with the slenderness of the piers it sits on, and this feature makes it stand out of its reassuring context. (→■391,398)

As the house is detached from the ground, a high-performance envelope was detailed on the lower side too. In fact, the ground floor slab (U = 0.095 W/m²K) is insulated with a 70-cm straw-bale layer, and is pierced at about 1 m centres to let out any occasional moisture. Between reinforced concrete and straw layers, there is a gravel drainage layer. The ground floor is paved with dark slate on a floating screed (10–12 cm thick).

Als das erste Strohballenhaus von Schmidt erbaut werden sollte, war es zunächst als kleiner Rückzugsort von etwa 30 m² geplant. Jedoch wollte Urs Braun schließlich ein großes, familientaugliches Haus. Der Bauherr hatte auch den Wunsch, sein Ferienhaus immer warm vorzufinden, ohne eine Fernsteuerung für Heizung und andere technische Utensilien. Peter Braun, zeigte sich zuversichtlich, was die Gestaltung anbelangte und wurde der statische Berater für das Projekt. Das Gebäude steht auf einer Stahlbetonplatte auf Stützen (talseits) und ist zur Hangseite auf einer Fundamentwand aufgelagert. Um das Haus bei Bedarf aufstocken zu können, wurde es von vorne herein auf der maximal zugelassenen Höhe platziert. Lacinski und Bergeron sind der Meinung, dass "ein Haus auf Pfeilern klapprig und vom Boden abgehoben wirkt. Dieser Effekt wird durch die verputzten Strohballen noch verstärkt; eine Struktur mit einer so massiven Wirkung, muss im Boden gut verankert sein" (109) In der Tat steht die Massivität des Hauses Braun, ganz bewusst und auch so von Schmidt beabsichtigt, in starkem Kontrast zu der Schlankheit der Pfeiler und es tritt umso selbstbewusster aus seinem sicheren Kontext heraus. (→■391,398)

Da das Haus Braun-Dubuis nicht direkt im Erdreich platziert ist, wurde die Unterseite mit einer hochleistungsfähigen Hülle aus 70 cm hohen Strohballen versehen. Tatsächlich ist die Grundplatte mit einer dicken Strohballenschicht isoliert (U = 0,095 W/m²K), und in der Betonplatte sind im Abstand von 1 m kleine, runde Öffnungen eingelassen, um jeglichen Feuchtigkeitsstau im Stroh zu vermeiden. Zwischen der Stahlbetonplatte und der

Walls are built with jumbo straw bales.
(→■392-393) Walls bear the roof and snow
load – with a roof area of 150 m², this means
over 100 tonnes maximum – and at the same
time, make an excellently insulating envelope (U = 0.037 W/m²K). (→■394) Straw bales
are stacked stretcher-bond-wise and are
tightened to the base plate by plastic straps.
These were drawn through plastic tubes that
had previously been inserted in the concrete
curb at the base of the wall. A ring wall-plate
made of timber bearers connected by 3-ply
boards sits on top of the walls.
After placing the trusses, and covering the
roof, the structure was left to set. During
this time plastic straps were constantly
tensioned to stabilise the walls and prevent
buckling. After four weeks, the house
stopped setting – it was now 30 cm shorter.
Outer and inner surfaces were then plastered with a lime-cement mix, 20–50 mm
thick; some of the sand was substituted by

Strohballenschicht wurden circa 7 cm Kies
als eine Art Drainageschicht eingebracht,
darüber kam eine dampfoffene Folie. Auf
den Strohballen im Erdgeschoss liegt eine
‚schwimmende' Betonplatte (10-12 cm) mit
einem Überzug und dunklen Schieferplatten.
Die Wände wurden aus Jumbostrohballen
errichtet. (→■392-393) Sie tragen die Dach-
und Schneelast – mit einer Dachfläche von
150 m² bedeutet dies mehr als 100 Tonnen
maximale Belastung – und gleichzeitig dienen sie als hervorragende Isolationsschicht
(U = 0,037 W/m²K). (→■394) Die Strohballen
wurden im Versatz aufeinandergesetzt, und
auf der letzten Ballenreihe wurde ein Holzkranz aufgelegt, der mittels Spanngurten mit
der Grundplatte verbunden ist. Hierfür wurden im Überzug Kunststoffröhren eingelegt,
durch die die Gurte gezogen werden konnten.
Nach dem Platzieren der Träger und dem Ab-
decken des Daches wartete man, bis sich das
Stroh gesetzt hatte. Während dieser Zeit

-2.0 °C	0.0 °C	2.0 °C	4.0 °C	6.0 °C

394

395

perlite to obtain a vapour-permeable mix. If the house had been plastered earlier that autumn, the mix would have contained less cement. Peter Braun and Werner Schmidt agree that it would have been better to use an ancient lime-plaster recipe, which would have required a long time though – traditionally, buildings were plastered one year after construction. The plaster has excellently withstood stress and weather: after more than ten years of service there is no crack. Windows (U = 0.7 W/m²K) are triple-glazed: two glass panes and a plastic sheet between them; the space between the layers is filled with xenon.

To keep the heated volume as compact as possible, the plan is very close to a square, and the straw-bale insulation layer has been positioned on the top floor (U = 0.072 W/m²K), under the gabled roof. (→■395) The roof's structure is made of solid wood trusses, and is covered with corrugated steel sheets.

wurden die Spanngurte immer wieder nachgespannt, um die Wände zu stabilisieren. Nach vier Wochen hatte sich das Dach um circa 30 cm gesetzt. Die Außen- und Innenflächen wurden anschließend mit einer Kalkputzmischung, mit geringem Zementanteil, 2 bis 5 cm dick verputzt. Ein Teil des Sandes wurde durch Perlite ersetzt, um ein dampfdurchlässiges Gemisch zu erhalten. Weil das Gebäude erst im Herbst verputzt wurde, fiel die Wahl auf einen Verputz mit kleinem Zementgehalt. Peter Braun und Werner Schmidt waren sich einig, dass es besser gewesen wäre, stattdessen ein altes Kalkputzrezept zu verwenden, was jedoch mehr Zeit erfordert hätte – traditionelle Gebäude wurden in der Regel erst ein Jahr nach dem Bau verputzt. Der Putz hat Belastungen und Wetter gut überstanden: Nach mehr als zehn Jahren ist noch kein Riss zu sehen.

Die Fenster (U = 0,7 W/m²K) sind dreifach verglast: zwei Glasscheiben umschließen

The wood-burning stove is reportedly used 5–6 times per year; its chimney runs externally, on the main façade. (→■396) The cooker has no hood – air is sucked downwards. (→■397) The ground floor toilet is provided with an air intake to allow the opening of the door. Air is sucked from the toilet bowl only, not from the room; moisture produced by the shower is absorbed by the render. The total thermal energy consumption (space + water heating) has been assessed as low as 1.4 kWh/m²a. (→B051)

eine Kunststofffolie und sind in den Zwischenräumen mit Edelgas gefüllt. Um das beheizte Volumen so kompakt wie möglich zu halten, ist der Grundriss nahezu quadratisch, und auf der obersten Etage unter dem Satteldach ist ebenfalls eine Isolationsschicht aus Strohballen (U = 0,072 W/m²K) platziert. (→■395) Die Dachstruktur ist aus massiven Holzbindern hergestellt und mit Wellblechplatten abgedeckt worden. Der Stückholzofen kommt jährlich 5 bis 6 mal zum Einsatz, dessen Kamin läuft außen an der Hauptfassade hoch. (→■396) Der Küchenherd hat eine

Abzugshaube – die Luft wird jedoch nach unten abgesaugt. (→■397) Die Toilette der WC-Box im Erdgeschoss ist mit einem Aktivkohlefilter ausgestattet, um ein Entlüften der Box über den Innenraum zu ermöglichen. Die Feuchtigkeit, die durch die Dusche entsteht, wird vom Kalkputz absorbiert. Der gesamte Verbrauch an thermischer Energie (Raum + Warmwasser) liegt bei 1,4 kWh/m²a berechnet. (→B051)

RENOVATION ⌣ RENOVIERUNG

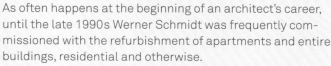

399

400

As often happens at the beginning of an architect's career, until the late 1990s Werner Schmidt was frequently commissioned with the refurbishment of apartments and entire buildings, residential and otherwise.

Apart from various interventions in Disentis abbey, (→p34-36,72-73) a number of projects deserve to be mentioned, characterised by an uncompromisingly anti-imitative approach. House Monn-Desax, in a three-family building from the 1960s in Disentis, was the result of merging two apartments into a larger one. (→■399) Schmidt created a rift cutting across the upper two stories and the garret, to break up the cramped spaces of the house. The new, curved walls intentionally cross existing, perpendicular lines both in plan and elevation. An interesting contrast is therefore created both inside and in respect of the building's rigidly geometric enclosure – from the outside, only the large portion of the roof that was glazed to let light flow into the house marks the transformation.

Both as a result of process and design choices, here we have an example of 'excavated' space as ontologically opposed

Wie es oft zu Beginn der Karriere eines Architekten der Fall ist, wurde auch Werner Schmidt bis in die späten 1990er Jahre mit Sanierungen von Wohnungen und ganzen Gebäuden beauftragt.

Abgesehen von verschiedenen Interventionen im Kloster Disentis, (→S.34-36,72-73) sollte eine Reihe von Projekten genannt werden, die von einem kompromisslosen, eigenständigen Ansatz geprägt sind.

Haus Monn-Desax, Disentis, ein Dreifamilienhaus aus den 1960er Jahren, wurde zu zwei großen Wohnungen zusammengeschlossen. (→■399) Schmidt legte einen Schlitz durch das Dachgeschoss und die oberen beiden Stockwerke, um die engen Räume des Hauses aufzubrechen. Die neuen, geschwungenen Wände durchkreuzen gewollt die bestehenden, geraden Linien sowohl im Grundriss als auch an den Wänden. So entsteht ein interessanter Kontrast im Inneren des Hauses, wie auch in Bezug auf die starre, geometrische Außenhülle – von Außen deutet nur der große, verglaste Bereich im Dach die Transformation an, welche Licht ins Haus fließen lässt.

401

ATELIER SIMON JACOMET

address ⌐ Adresse: CH-7173 Sumvitg-Surrein/GR
altitude ⌐ Höhe: 890 m
degree-days ⌐ Gradtage: 4013
project ⌐ Entwurf: 1986
construction ⌐ Bau: 1988
self-build ⌐ selbstbau
plot area ⌐ Grundstückfläche: 1,940 m²
heated floor area ⌐ Geheizte Bodenfläche: 100 m²
building cost ⌐ Baukosten: 200,000 CHF (2,000 CHF/m²)

to 'built' space. Of course curvy spaces exist which are not closed in themselves: besides more or less regularly-shaped 'eggs,' (→§01) also more open, fluent forms can be found in Schmidt's work. Unlike buildings just visually conceived, those designed with the users' movement inside them in mind have smooth forms, and tend to be generated by curved, solid lines.

The contrast between pre-existing forms and extension could not be more conspicuous and successful than in the atelier of Simon Jacomet, the renowned artist and ski designer. The old barn at the edge of a small, traditional Graubünden village was transformed as the result of the cooperation between Werner Schmidt and the artist himself, and adapted to new needs. Because of its singular appearance, the Municipality rejected the project for two years, but finally a new building commission took over and issued the permit.
Both Jacomet and Schmidt wanted to maintain the relation of the barn to its surroundings. The concept was therefore the intersection of two solids: the required additional volume

Sowohl als ein Ergebnis von Prozess- als auch von Design-entscheidungen, haben wir hier ein Beispiel von ‚neu generiertem' Raum, der selbstverständlich dem ‚gebauten' Raum gegenübergestellt ist. Natürlich gibt es kurvige Berei-che, die nicht in sich selbst geschlossen sind: neben mehr oder weniger regelmäßig geformten ‚Eiern' (→§01) können in Schmidts Arbeiten auch immer wieder offene, fließende Formen gefunden werden. Im Unterschied zu Gebäuden, die rein optisch erdacht sind, haben jene, die den Bewegungsab-lauf der Bewohner im Inneren berücksichtigen, geschmeidige Formen, und neigen dazu, aus gebogenen, durchgehenden Linien erzeugt worden zu sein.

Der Kontrast zwischen bereits bestehenden Formen und der Erweiterung könnte nicht auffälliger und gelungener sein, als im Atelier von Simon Jacomet, einem renommierten Künstler und Ski-Designer. Die alte Scheune am Rande eines kleinen, traditionellen Bündner Dorfes, hat Werner Schmidt in Zu-sammenarbeit mit dem Künstler Simon Jacomet umgestaltet

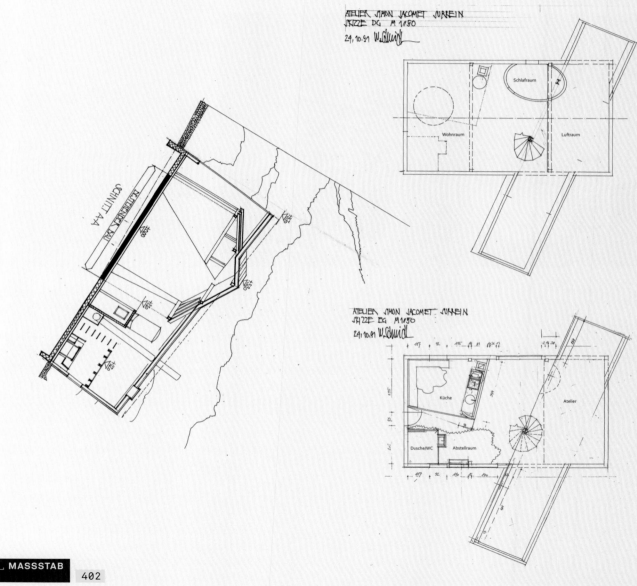

410

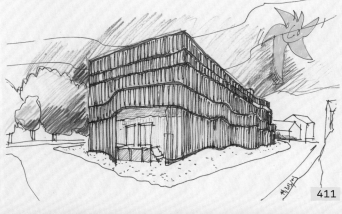

411

412

the building to catch warm air, which is sucked underground into a 1½ meter deep, gravel heat storage.

House Bühler-Seiz is a listed Engadine farmhouse which would have been insulated and whose interiors would have been renovated. (→■415-416) To make the building envelope comply with regulations, an additional timber construction, ventilated and insulated with 50 cm of straw, would have been installed on the interior face of the perimeter masonry walls. The large cattleshed would have been left as an open space containing egg-shaped volumes. (→§01)

energetische Altbausanierung ausgerichtet werden sollten, anstatt auf die Entwicklung hervorragender, leistungsstarker neuer Gebäude.

Werner Schmidt hat das Thema energetische Sanierung fünf Mal aufgegriffen – zwei Projekte wurden bereits realisiert, eines nicht und zwei weitere sind zur Zeit in Bearbeitung. Eines dieser Projekte ist bei weitem das bislang größte: es handelt sich um den Hauptsitz der Firma Complemedis AG, ein Unternehmen das chinesische Gesundheitsprodukte herstellt, dessen Gebäudehülle soll mit Holzelemente, die mit 50 cm dicken

413

414

Strohballen gefüllt sind, isoliert werden; als Beschattung dient eine umlaufende Hülle aus Bambusstäben. (→■410-412) Chronologisch gesehen war das Haus Neff im Kanton Appenzell (1997) die erste Gebäudesanierung. (→■413-414) Der bestehende Bauernhof wurde renoviert und zwei zusätzliche Wohneinheiten wurden geschaffen. Die Südwestseite des Giebeldaches des ehemaligen Stalls, der an das bestehende Haupthaus anschließt, wurde komplett verglast. Als Sonnenschutz dienen einstellbare Metalllamellen. Zwei vertikale, Pyramidenstumpf förmige Kanäle wurden in das offene Dachgeschoss gesetzt und sorgen somit für natürliches Licht in den darunter liegenden Räumen. Ein breites Rohr wurde unter dem First über die gesamte Gebäudelänge angebracht, welches die warme Luft ansaugt und sie nach unten ins Erdreich in einen 1,5 m hohen Kiesspeicher abführt. Beim Haus Bühler-Seiz handelt es sich um ein Engadiner Bauernhaus, welches isoliert und dessen Innenräume saniert werden sollten. (→■415-416) Um den Bauvorschriften zu genügen ('schützenswerte Baute') war geplant, die Gebäudehülle aus Naturstein von innen mit einer hinterlüfteten Holzkonstruktion zu ergänzen, und diese mit 50 cm dicken Strohballen zu füllen. Der große Stall sollte als offener Raum beibehalten und durch eierförmige Volumen ergänzt werden. (→§01)

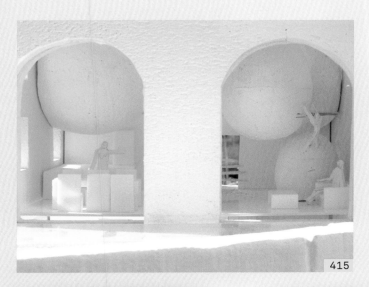

415

416

417

ERVIN JACOMET'S HOUSE ⌐ HAUS ERVIN JACOMET

ADDRESS ⌐ ADRESSE:
CH-7173 Sumvitg-Surrein/GR

ALTITUDE ⌐ HÖHE:
890 m

DEGREE-DAYS ⌐ GRADTAGE:
4013

PROJECT ⌐ ENTWURF:
2011

CONSTRUCTION ⌐ BAU:
2011

SELF-BUILD ⌐ SELBSTBAU

EXTENSION ⌐ ANBAU:
Fussenegger Holzbau GmbH,
Dornbirn (wood construction ⌐
Holzbau)

**PROJECT MANAGER ⌐
PROJEKTLEITUNG:**
Andrea Jacomet

**HEATED FLOOR AREA ⌐
GEHEIZTE BODENFLÄCHE:**
235 m²

**MAIN GLAZED AREA (S) ⌐
FENSTERFLÄCHE HAUPTFASSADE:**
17 m²

BUILDING COST ⌐ BAUKOSTEN (BKP2):
300,000 CHF (1,300 CHF/m²)

The three-storey building dates from 1883 and has 65 cm thick stone walls. A timber shed abuts on the east side. The owners – Ervin Jacomet, his wife Andrea, and their children – wanted to improve the thermal resistance of the building envelope. The decision to use straw came naturally, as Andrea is an employee of Atelier Werner Schmidt.
The existing roof framework was conserved; on the rafters is a 5 cm boarding, above which an insulation layer of 50 cm bales was placed between vertically positioned OSB panels. (→■418) The roof was then covered with a waterproof membrane and tiled.
Concrete which joined wall to balcony was demolished, and gaps were filled with insulation – therefore, the thermal bridge is now limited to reinforcing bars. To make room for the straw-bale insulation, external stairs were demolished too, and later rebuilt using the same stones.
Straw bales rest on a foam glass and XPS curb which isolates them from the ground. 45-mm OSB boards were fixed to the outer side of perimeter walls at 50 cm centres, using L-shaped metal brackets and wall plugs. This was somewhat tricky, because it is not always easy to drill stones and obtain a good grip. Next, straw bales were stacked between OSB boards, creating a 35 cm-thick insulation layer; chicken wire was laid to prevent the cracking of a 2–5 cm-thick lime plaster coat. (→■423)
Some windows were replaced by timber boxes and triple glazing (U = 0.7 W/m²K). To light up the living area, a new large window with triple glazing filled with a noble gas (U = 0.5 W/m²K) was created merging two smaller windows.

Das dreigeschossige Gebäude stammt aus dem Jahr 1883 und hat 65 cm dicke Natursteinmauern. Die Eigentümer, Ervin Jacomet, seine Frau Andrea und ihre Kinder, wollten die Wärmebeständigkeit der Gebäudehülle verbessern. Die Entscheidung Stroh zu verwenden war beinahe selbstverständlich, da Andrea Jacomet im Atelier von Werner Schmidt arbeitet.
Der bestehende Dachstuhl wurde beibehalten; über der Sparrenlage wurde eine 5 cm dicke Doppelnut- und Kammschalung angebracht und eine Isolierschicht aus 50 cm hohen Strohballen, die zwischen OSB Platten liegen. (→■418) Das Dach wurde dann mit der alten Dachschalung, einer wasserdichten Membran und Ziegeln eingedeckt.
Betonflächen, die an die Hauswand grenzten wurden abgerissen und die Lücken mit Isolation gefüllt, so wurden die Wärmebrücken über die Armierungseisen beschränkt. Um Platz für die Strohballenisolation zu schaffen wurde die bestehende Außentreppe abgerissen und später wieder aus den gleichen Steinen aufgemauert.
Die Strohballen liegen auf Foamglasschotter und XPS Platten auf, welche als Isolation gegen das Erdreich dienen. 19 mm dicke OSB Platten wurden mit einem Befestigungsabstand von 50 cm und unter Verwendung von L-förmigen Metallwinkeln in das Bruchsteinmauerwerk gedübelt. Die Befestigung dieser Winkel war sehr zeitintensiv, weil es nicht immer einfach war, in dem bestehenden Mauerwerk eine homogene Stelle für mehrere Bohrlöcher gleichzeitig zu finden. Danach wurden die Strohballen zwischen die OSB Platten gestapelt, wodurch eine 35 cm

279

Annex to ⌐ Anbau
Raiffeisen Bank,

1996

Disentis GR (Glass construction consultant ⌐ Glasbauingenieur Ingenieurbüro Duppentaler und Wälchli, Ernst Wälchli, CH-Langenau)

Renovation ⌐ Umbau
Atelier Schmidt,

1996-2001

Trun GR

Renovation ⌐ Umbau
Bauernhaus Neff,

1997

Steinegg AI

Extension ⌐ Erweiterung
Haus Maissen-Petschen,

1997

Trun GR

Installations ⌐ Einbau
Salomon-Station,

1997

*Engelberg OW
(in cooperation with ⌐ in Zusammenarbeit mit Simon Jacomet)*

Extension ⌐ Erweiterung
Haus Staubli,

1997

Disentis-Acletta GR

New building ⌐ Neubau
Haus Schmid-Cavegn,

1998

Tujetsch-Camischolas GR

New building ⌐ Neubau
Haus Gartmann-Sgier,

2000

Sevgein GR (Structural engineer ⌐ Bauingenieur Walter Deplazes, CH-Surrein; Heating and ventilation systems consultant ⌐ Heizungs-Lüftungsingenieur Reto Schmid, CH-Maienfeld)

New building ⌐ Neubau
Haus Wolf-Bearth,

2000

Untervaz GR (Structural engineer ⌐ Bauingenieur Walter Deplazes, CH- Surrein; Heating and ventilation systems consultant ⌐ Heizungs-Lüftungsingenieur Reto Schmid, CH-Maienfeld)

Connecting passage ⌐ Verbindungsgang

2000

Fabrikgelände Ferrari,
Maranello MO

Concept study of an autarchic hall of residence ⌐ Konzept-Studie Energieautarkes Studentenheim

2000

Klosterschule,
Disentis GR

Wind objects etc ⌐ Windobjekte usw,

2001

Bozen BZ

New building ⌐ Neubau
Haus Braun-Dubuis,

2002

Disentis-Acletta GR (Structural engineer ⌐ Bauingenieur Peter Braun, CH-Fribourg)

Straw-bale tower ⌐ Strohballenturm,

2002

*Bozen BZ
(Bauingenieur Benno Barth, I-Brixen)*

2003 **Architektur und Wasser,**
La Habana

New building ⌐ Neubau
Haus Dalsant-Pernter,

2003

Kurtatsch BZ (in cooperation with ⌐ in Zusammenarbeit mit Margareta Schwarz, I-Sankt Martin in Passeier)

Meranflora,
Meran BZ (Structural engineer ⌐ Bauingenieur Benno Barth, I-Brixen; students ⌐ Studenten HTW Chur; Gartenbauamt Meran, Anni Schwarz)

2004

New building ⌐ Neubau
Haus Schmidlin-Jeker,
Wahlen BL (Structural engineer ⌐ Bauingenieur Walter Deplazes, CH-Surrein; site management ⌐ örtliche Bauleitung Rainer Hettenbach (Architekturbüro Degen Hettenbach Müller, CH-Therwil))

2004

New building ⌐ Neubau
Haus Rüesch,

2005

Sevelen SG

2005-07

New building ⌐ Neubau
Bauernhaus Niederkofler,

Mühlbach BZ
(in cooperation with ⌐ in
Zusammenarbeit mit Margareta
Schwarz, I-Sankt Martin in Passeier)

2006

Renovation ⌐ Umbau
Haus Bühler-Seiz,

Bever GR

2006

New building ⌐ Neubau
„Wellenhaus",

Freienbach SZ

2006

New building ⌐ Neubau
Ferienwohnungen Esserhof,

Lana BZ
(in cooperation with ⌐ in
Zusammenarbeit mit Margareta
Schwarz, I-Sankt Martin in Passeier)

2007

Meranflora,
Meran BZ

2007

New building ⌐ Neubau
Ferienwohnungen Fliri-Aschoff,
Graun im Vinschgau-Langtaufers BZ
(structural engineer ⌐ Bauingenieur
Peter Braun, CH-Fribourg; site
management⌐ örtliche Bauleitung
Richard Fliri)

2008-10

New building ⌐ Neubau
Mehrfamilienhaus Häring-Braschler,

Freienbach SZ

2008

New building ⌐ Neubau
Haus Wegmann-Gasser,
Glarus GL (structural engineer ⌐
Bauingenieur Walter Deplazes,
CH-Surrein; site management ⌐
örtliche Bauleitung Erich Leuzinger,
CH-Glarus)

2009

New building ⌐ Neubau
Haus Schmid-Hermanutz,

Langenau UL (structural engineer⌐
Bauingenieur Peter Braun, CH-
Fribourg; site management ⌐
örtliche Bauleitung Ralph Schmidle,
D-Erbach)

2009

Extension ⌐ Erweiterung
Haus Bigliel-Wahrenberger,

Disentis GR

2009

New building ⌐ Neubau
Bauhof Berther,

Disentis-Segnas GR

2009

New building ⌐ Neubau
Resort La Donaira,

Ronda MA (in cooperation with ⌐
in Zusammenarbeit mit Margareta
Schwarz, I-Sankt Martin in Passeier)

2010

New building ⌐ Neubau
**vonRoll Hydro Ausstellungs- und
Ausbildungshallte,**

Oensingen SO (structural engineering
for timber ⌐ Statik Holz: Lauber
Ingenieure Holzbau, Tobias Knüsel,
CH-Luzern; structural engineering
for concrete ⌐ Statik Beton: BSB +
Partner, Martin Bussmann, CH-
Oensingen; structural engineering for
the membrane ⌐ Statik Membran:
Tentex Energieering GmbH, Hubert
Schällibaum, CH-Kerns)

2010

New building ⌐ Neubau
Haus Ochoa-de Battisti,
Faoug VD

2010

New building ⌐ Neubau
Haus Oetterli-Portmann,

Oltingen BL (site management ⌐
örtliche Bauleitung Lüthy Bauplanung
GmbH, CH-Oltingen)

2011

New building ⌐ Neubau
Haus Dora,

Merenschwand AG (structural
engineer ⌐ Bauingenieur Iso
Mazzetta, CH-Trun; site management
⌐ örtliche Bauleitung Langenegger
Architekten AG, Yves Siegrist, CH-Muri)

2011

New building ⌐ Neubau
Bauernhaus Gliott-Bucher,

Laax-Pardatsch GR (structural
engineer ⌐ Bauingenieur Iso
Mazzetta, CH-Trun; Electrical system
design ⌐ Elektroplaner: Elektro
Deflorin, CH-Flims; Sanitary system
design ⌐ Sanitärplaner: Hesaplan
AG, CH-Ilanz)

Retrofit ⌐ Umbau
Haus Ervin Jacomet,

2011

Sumvitg-Surrein GR (structural engineer ⌐ Bauingenieur Walter Deplazes, CH-Surrein)

New building ⌐ Neubau
Zwillinghäuser Forster + Pfyl,

2011

Dürnten ZH (structural engineer ⌐ Bauingenieur Iso Mazzetta, CH-Trun; site management ⌐ örtliche Bauleitung: H. Baumgartner AG, Stefan Baumgartner, CH-Rüti)

Renovation of a ⌐ Umbau eines
Maiensäss,
Rueun GR

2011

New building ⌐ Neubau
Bauernhaus Küng,

2012

Muri AG (structural engineer ⌐ Bauingenieur Iso Mazzetta, CH-Trun; site management ⌐ örtliche Bauleitung Langenegger Architekten AG, Yves Siegrist, CH-Muri, and ⌐ und Beat Küng)

New building ⌐ Neubau
Guesthouse Maya,

2012

Mont Noble-Nax VS

New building ⌐ Neubau
Haus Bühlmann,
Knutwil LU (site management ⌐ örtliche Bauleitung: CAS Architekten, CH-Willisau)

2012

New building ⌐ Neubau
Haus Camenzind,
Gersau SZ (timber structures consultant ⌐ Holzbauingenieur: Lauber Ingenieurbüro, CH-Luzern)

2013

New building ⌐ Neubau
Haus Mathis-Hirt,

2013

Amden SG (structural engineer for sprayed concrete ⌐ Bauingenieur Spritzbeton: Gauss & Merz AG, CH-Geroldswil; acoustics consultant ⌐ Akustik: Imhof Akustik AG, Thomas Imhof, CH-Speicher)

Renovation ⌐ Umbau
Bürogebäude Complemedis AG,
Trimbach SO

New building ⌐ Neubau
Bauernhaus von Erffa,
Osterwieck HZ

New development ⌐ Neubau
Zero Carbon Village „Lewari Dorf",
Traismauer NÖ (in cooperation with ⌐ in Zusammenarbeit mit GrAT, A-Wien, and ⌐ und Georg Scheicher, A-Adnet)

Extension ⌐ Anbau
Werkstätte Hug-Ackle,
Densbüren AG

Retrofit ⌐ Termische Sanierung
Haus Wydler-Piontek,
Susch GR

Renovation ⌐ Umbau
Haus Maissen,
Disentis GR

New building ⌐ Neubau
Haus Jürg Brand,
Faoug VD

realized ⌐ realisiert

unrealized ⌐ nicht realisiert

ongoing ⌐ laufend

AG = Kanton Aargau
AI = Halbkanton Appenzell-Innenrhoden
BE = Kanton Bern
BL = Halbkanton Basel-Land
BZ = Autonome Provinz Bozen-Südtirol
GL = Kanton Glarus
GR = Kanton Graubünden
HZ = Landkreis Harz
LU = Kanton Luzern
MA = Provincia de Málaga
MO = Provincia di Modena
NÖ = Land Niederösterreich
OW = Halbkanton Obwalden
SG = Kanton Sankt Gallen
SO = Kanton Solothurn
SZ = Kanton Schwyz
TG = Kanton Thurgau
UL = Alb-Donau Landkreis (Ulm)
VD = Canton Vaud
VS = Canton Valais
ZH = Kanton Zürich

Writings on Werner Schmidt's work ⌐ Schriften über Werner Schmidts Arbeit

Books ⌐ Bücher

Werner Schäfke; Thomas Schleper; Max Tauch (Hrsg.), *Aluminium. Das Metall der Moderne*, Köln: Kölnische Stadtmuseum, 1991, p. 189-190.

John Zukowsky; Ian Wardropper, *Austrian Architecture and Design, Beyond Tradition in the 1990s*, Berlin: Ernst & Sohn, 1991, p. 57-58 + 142-145

Sigrid Barten, *Starke Falten*, Zürich: Museum Bellerive Zürich, 1995, p. 45

Anton Graf, *Das Passivhaus – Wohnen ohne Heizung. Aktuelle Beispiele aus Deutschland, Österreich und der Schweiz*, München: Verlag Georg D.W. Callwey, 2000, p. 88-91

Anton Graf, *Wohnen und Arbeiten unter einem Dach, Beispiele für Büro, Atelier und Werkstatt im Einfamilienhaus*, München: Verlag Georg D.W. Callwey, 2000, p. 126-129

Hans Weidinger, *Treppen in Einfamilienhaus, Neue Beispiele der Raumgestaltung*, München: Verlag Georg D.W. Callwey, 2000, p.148-149

Hans Batz, *Die Kirchen und Kapellen des Kantons Graubünden*, Chur: Casanova Druck und Verlag, 2003, p. 58-60

Anton Graf, *Neue Passivhäuser. 24 Beispiele für den Energiestandard der Zukunft, Deutschland - Österreich - Schweiz*, München: Verlag Georg D.W. Callwey, 2003, p. 68-71

AXOR; Hansgrohe, *Aqua-Tektur 2, Architektur und Wasser - Havanna 2003, 19 Architekturbüros und Hansgrohe denken vor*, Leinfelden-Echterdingen: Verlagsanstalt Alexander Koch, 2004, p. 91-95.

Gernot Minke; Friedemann Mahlke, *Der Strohballenbau. Ein Konstruktionshandbuch*, Staufen bei Freiburg: Ökobuch Verlag, 2004, p. 101-102

Gernot Minke; Friedemann Mahlke, *Building with straw, Design and Technology of a Sustainable Architecture*, Basel: Birkhäuser, 2005, p. 96-97

Daniela Enz; Robert Hastings, *Innovative Wandkonstruktionen für Minergie-P und Passivhäuser*, Heidelberg: C.F. Müller Verlag, 2006, p. 42-51

Christian Hanus; Robert Hastings, *Bauen mit Solarenergie, Wegweisende Wohnbauten - heutige Rahmenbedingungen - Entwicklungstendenzen*, Zürich: vdf Hochschulverlag AG an der ETH Zürich, 2007, p. 36-37

Norbert Lantschner, *CasaClima, vivere nel Più. Klima Haus*, Bolzano: Edition Raetia, 2007, p. 176-181

Andrea Deplazes (Hrsg.), *Architektur konstruiren von Rohmaterial zum Bauwerk. Ein Handbuch*, Basel: Birkhäuser, 2008, p. 142-144

Herbert Gruber; Astrid Gruber; Helmuth Santler, *Neues Bauen mit Stroh*, Staufen bei Freiburg: Ökobuch Verlag, 2008, p. 35, 61

Catherine Collin (coordinatore editoriale), *Architecture, earth*, Terzo: Edizioni Gribaudo, 2009, p. 76-81

Sergi Costa Duran; Mariana R. Eguaras, *1000 Ideas by 100 Architects*, Beverly, Ma.: Rockport Publishers, 2009, p. 238-241

Gernot Minke; Benjamin Krick, *Handbuch Strohballenbau, Grundlagen/Konstruktion/Beispiele*, Staufen bei Freiburg: Ökobuch Verlag, 2009, p. 92-93, 104-107

Carmelia Maissen, "Obere Surselva: Von Himmelsleitern und Bergbauern", in: Köbi Gantenbein; Marco Guetg; Ralph Feiner (Hrsg.), *Himmelsleiter und Felsentherme. Architekturwandern in Graubünden*, Zürich: Rotpunktverlag, 2009, p. 404-408

Architettando (a cura di), *Equi vivere per un'architettura sostenibile*, Padova: Il Poligrafo, 2010, p. 154-161

Christjan Ladurner, *Mystische und stille Orte in Südtirol. Eine Reise durch ursprüngliche Welten*, Lana: Tappeiner, 2010, p. 13

Gernot Minke, *Manual de Construcción con Bambú*, Cali: Merlín S.E., 2010, p. 142-143 = Germot Minke, *Building with Bamboo. Design and Technology of a Sustainable Architecture*, Basel: Birkhäuser, 2012, p. 144-145

Simone K. Schleifer, *1000 Details in Architecture*, Antwerp: Booqs Publishers bvba, 2010, p. 293

Margareta Schwarz; Werner Schmidt, "Le case in paglia, Sistemi costruttivi alternativi", in: Giovanni Marucci (direttore editoriale), *Natura/Architettura. Ecologia dell'ambiente costruito 2010*, Milano: Di Baio editore, 2010, p. 174-179

Catherine Wanek, *The Hybrid House. Designing with Sun, Wind, Water, and Earth*, Layton: Gibbs Smith, 2010, p. 132-139

Luc Floissac, *La construction en paille. Principes fondamentaux. Techniques de mise en œuvre. Exemples de réalisations*, Mens: Terre vivante, 2012, p. 107-120

Herbert Gruber; Astrid Gruber; Helmuth Santler, *Neues Bauen mit Stroh. IN EUROPA*, Staufen bei Freiburg: Ökobuch Verlag, 2012, p. 33

Lore Kelly, „Wenn ein Stahlkonzern mit Stroh baut…", in: Roland Köhler (Herausgeber), *Schweizer Energiefachbuch 2013. 30. Jahrgang*, Sankt Gallen: Kömedia, s.d. [2012?], p. 116-118

Ulrich Pfammatter, *Bauen im Kultur- und Klimawandel. Green traditions - clean future*, Zürich: vdf Hochschulverlag AG an der ETH Zürich, 2012, p. 247

Magazines and Newspapers ⌐ Zeitschriften und Zeitungen

Rita Cathomas-Bearth, "Architektur, die irritiert", *Terra Grischuna*, 6, Juni 1997, p. 38-41

Benedikt Loderer, "Das Autoabwehrugewächs von Disentis", *Blick*, 12.8.1998, p. 12

Be. K., "Evangelische Kirche Cazis, Cazis/CH. Ab ovo", *Deutsche Bauzeitschrift*, 6, 6./1999, p. 69-74

Michele Rüegg; Thomas von Pufendorf, "Kisten ade", *transSuisse*, 5, 10.1999, p. 112-113

"Werner Schmidt, Eglise protestante, Cazis, Suisse", *L'architecture d'aujourd'hui*, 325, 12./1999, p. 105

Detlef Wittkuhn, "Tolle Blasen", *Häuser*, 4, April 2000, p. 80-85

Thomas Steinbeck; Helmuth Zipperlen, "Werner Schmidt - Architekt und Künstler", *Gemeindeblatt der Reformierten Kirchgemeinde Solothurn*, 9, 9.2000, p. 4-7

Werner Schmidt, "Curriculum dies", *Massiv*, 1, 2001, p. 32-36

Anna Schindler, "Geld und Geist", *Hochparterre*, 14, 1-2, 1.-2.2001, p. 20-21

Roman Rutkowski, "Kamienie skupienia", *Architektura & Biznes*, 12, 12.2002, p. 48-55

Kaoru Takigawa," Sustainable Design Report from Suisse", *Confort Interior Magazine*, 63, 4.2003, p. 114-117

Carolien Steenbruggen, "Kergebouw Cazis, de unvoltooide", *Detail in architectuur*, 5.2003, p. 18-21

Lore Kelly, "Bauen mit Stroh", *Baublatt*, 1.5.2003, p. 5

283

Köbi Gantenbein, "Cazis GR: Drei Steine", *Facts*, 35, 8.2003, p. 97

Lore Kelly, "Bauen mit Stroh", *Applica*, 9, September 2003, p. 4-6

Andreas Thomann, "Von gepresstem Stroh und plattgedrückten Nasen", *Bulletin - Credit Suisse Spezial*, 9, Herbst 2003, p. 14 = Andreas Thomann, "Von gepresstem Stroh und plattgedrückten Nasen", *Bulletin - Credit Suisse*, 5, Okt.-Nov./2003, p. 20

Lore Kelly, "Aus Stroh gebaut", *Leben & Glauben*, 43, 10.2003, p.35-37

Sibylle Stillhart, "Moderne Höhlenmenschen", *Beobachter. Ratgeber Bauen* [Beilage zum *Beobachter* Nr. 21], 17. Oktober 2003, p.13-16

Margareta Schwarz, "Neue Heimat", *Architektur & Technik*, 7, 2004, p. 30-32

Eveline Dudda, "«Als Bauer würde ich ein Strohhaus bauen»", *Die grüne*, 21, 10.2004, p. 40-43

Eveline Dudda, "Leben im Stroh", *St. Galler Tagblatt*, 11.10.2004 [www.tagblatt.ch]

Eveline Dudda, "Stroh - der Baustoff, der vor der Haustür wächst", *Casanostra*, 75, 3.2005, p. 4-6

Collin Klostermeier, "Strohburg, Bauen mit Strohballen: Passiv-Ferienhaus in Disentis", *Bauhandwerk*, 4, 4./2005, p.34-39

Adriano Oddo, "Vetrina a Bolzano", *Costruire*, 265, 6./2005, p. 124-127

Andrin C. Willi, "«Innenräume entstehen aus Ehrlichkeit, Wahrheit und Wahrhaftigkeit»", *SonntagsZeitung*, 46, 13.11.2005, p. 101

"Des maisons chaudes et bon marché en paille", *La Revue Durable*, 19, 2.-3.2006, p. 30-32

Eveline Dudda, "Die Zukunft beginnt hier", *Neue Zürcher Zeitung am Sonntag*, 9.4.2006, p. 25

„Die Zukunft gehört dem Teamspielern", *Schreinerzeitung*, 20, 18.5.2006, p. 14-16

Monika Knoll, "Architekturwettbewerb", *Dolomiten Journal. Bauen*, 91, 4.2007, p. 54-60

Lioba Schneemann, "Genial einfach, Strohballen: Ein Baustoff mit Zukunft", *Zeitpunkt*, 89, Mai-Juni 2007, p. 46-47

Lioba Schneemann, "Bauen mit Stroh", *Leben & Glauben*, 23, 6.2007, p. 36-37

Reto Westermann, "So sparen Sie standardmässig", *SonntagsZeitung*, 10.6.2007, p. 125

A. Lenz; C. Manek, "Werner Schmidt", *ar/t/chitecture*, 2, 8.-9.2007, p. 14-22

Andrea Rinaldi, "Naturalmente. Un'architettura in balle di paglia", *L'ufficio tecnico*, 9, 9.2007, p. 38-43

Beatrice Spirandelli, "Atelier W. Schmidt + Margareta Schwarz, Appartamenti per vacanze a Lana", *L'architettura naturale*, 10, 36, settembre 2007, p. 4-11

André de Bouter, "Construire une maison en paille sans ossature bois: La paille sans la poutre", *Habitat Naturel. Construire & Vivre sain*, 16, 10.2007, p. 44-47

Annette Rübesamen, "Ferien auf dem Bauernhof", *Geo Saison Extra*, „Südtirol für Geniesser 2008", 2008, p. 46-55

Collin Klostermeier, "Gute Erholung, Ferienhäuser aus lastabtragenden Strohballen in Lana/Südtirol", *Bauhandwerk*, 3, März 2008, p. 28-35

Gwenaëlle Reyt, "Paille qui vaille", *Le Temps*, 17.3.2008, p. 32

Susanne Stacher, "Vom Klappstuhl zum Strohhaus = From folding chair to straw house", *Architektur aktuell*, 340-341, 7.-8.2008, p. 124-132

Marc Bernard, Susanne Stacher, "Experimenter la paille", *Le Moniteur architecture*, 181, 9.2008, p. 101-104

"Maison en paille, c'est du solide", *La Maison écologique*, 48, décembre 2008-janvier 2009, p. 23-33

Benjamin Krick, "Gut gedämmt", *Zeno. Zeitschrift für nachhaltiges Bauen*, 4, 2009, p. 54-55

Josef Chybík, "Ako stavajú, pasívne v zahraničí", *Nízkoenergetické. EKO bývanie*, marec 2009, p. 132-135

Anton Nothegger, "Lasttragender Strohballenbau in der Praxis", *Wohnung + Gesundheit*, 131, 6.2009, p. 9-11

H. Menzing, "Ferienhausanlage aus Strohballen im Passivhausstandard, Lana (I). Aus Stroh gebaut", *Greenbuilding*, 7.-8.2009, p. 32-35

Pierre Cauderay, "De la paille pour construire", *Tracés*, 135, 17 septembre 2009, p. 7-13

Olivier Namias, "Les habits neufs des maisons paille", *À vivre*, 51, 11.-12.2009, p.106-115

Jano Felice Pajarola, "Von Strohhäusern und Wunderboxen", *die Südostschweiz am Sonntag*, 71, 14.3.2010, p. 13

Ariane Löbert, "Haus aus Stroh", *ff Bauen*, 18, 5.2010, p. 40-43

Jörg Krummenacher, "Der Architekt, der auf Stroh baut", *Neue Zürcher Zeitung*, 122, 31.5.2010, p. 8

Thomas Compagno, "Strohhaus: Heizen ohne Ofen", *Coopzeitung*, 22, 1.6.2010, p. 8-9

Florencia Figueroa, "Wohnen im Stroh", *Baublatt*, 26, 7.2010, p. 10-13

Robert Alder, "Ein Haus ohne Heizung bauen wird realistisch", *Schweizer Bauer*, 10.7.2010, p. 8

Andreas Krebs, "Der Strohmann", *Natürlich leben*, 09, 9.2010, p. 60-62

Anna Schindler, "Geballte Kraft in Strohbauten", *Sonntagszeitung*, 12.9.2010, p. 115-116

"Schmidt baut mit Stroh", *Architektur + Technik*, 10, 2010, p. 11

Marcin Mateusz Kołakowski; Maciej Jagielak, "Słoma? Słoma... Słoma!", *Architektura & Biznes*, 220, 11.2010, p. 22-23

Dierk Jensen, "Vom Acker in die Wand", *Deutsche Bauzeitung*, 1, Januar 2011, p. 64-65

Erika Bühler, "Stroh - der Baustoff der Zukunft?", *Traumhaus. Das Schweizer Magazin für Planen, Bauen, Wohnen*, 6, 1.-2.2011, p. 46-47

Andrea Bocco Guarneri, "vonRoll Pavillon, Oensingen, Schweiz – Wieder aus dem Ei geschlüpft", *Architektur aktuell*, 372, 3.2011, p. 114-124

Bosco Büeler, "Ökologische Produkte und Konzepte", *Baubiologie*, 3.2011, p. 8

Karin Oetterli-Portmann, "Ein Haus aus Stroh", *Haus Magazin*, 2, März 2011, p. 9-12

David Höner, "Das Strohhaus", *Cigar*, 2, Juni 2011, p. 29-30

Heinz Abegglen, "Stroh ist unschlagbar", *Bauern Zeitung*, 24, 17.6.2011, p.23

Andrea Bocco Guarneri, "Werner Schmidt, vonRoll pavilion", *Kenchiku to Toshi* [*Architecture and Urbanism*], 490, 7.2011, p. 64-71

Susanne Gutknecht, "Aus Stroh gebaut", *Zürcher Oberländer*, 186, 12.8.2011, p. 3

John Chilton, "Heinz Isler: Shells for two Churches", *Journal of the international association for shell and spatial structures*, 52, 3, September 2011, p. 173-183

Татьяна Зимина, "Соломенная гостиница", *Наука И Жизнь*, 10, 2011, p. 28

"Die besten Öko-Häuser", *Das Haus*, 11.2011, p. 46

Andreas Seeholzer, „Gersauer Holzhaus mit Stroh isoliert", *Bote der Urschweiz*, 8.3.2012, p. 7

Jörg Clavadetscher, "Strohballenbau Surselva", *Bündner Wald*, 2, April 2012, p. 47-51

René Küng, „Aussergewöhnlicher Neubau", *Wochen-Zeitung*, 47, 23.11.2012, p. 21

Olga Yurkina, "Quand Maya a plus d'un tour dans sa botte", *Hotel Revue*, 51-52, 20.12.2012, p. 24

Juho Nyberg, „Vom Staub zum Stein zur Kirche", *Caminada*, 1, Winter/Frühling 2012/13, p. 6-12

Texts quoted by Andrea Bocco Guarneri ⌴
Texte von Andrea Bocco Guarneri zitiert

001 → Franco Agostini; Nicola Alberto De Carlo, *Giochi dell'intelligenza*, Torino: Bollati Boringhieri, 1985

002 → http://www.akdn.org/2005_december_bulletin.asp

003 → http://www.akdn.org/pakistan

004 → http://www.akdn.org/photos_show.asp?Sid=90

005 → http://www.akdn.org/press_release.asp?ID=152

006 → http://www.akdn.org/rural_development/pakistan.asp

007 → Leon Battista Alberti, *Della architettura, libri dieci*, 1485 (as quoted in Aldo Castellano, *L'architettura rurale in Italia*, Milano: Electa, 1986, p. 96)

008 → Andrew Alcorn, *Embodied Energy and CO2 Coefficients for NZ Building Materials*, Victoria University of Wellington - Centre for Building Performance Research, March 2003

009 → Christopher Alexander; Sara Ishikawa; Murray Silverstein, *A Pattern Language. Towns – Buildings – Construction*, New York: Oxford University Press, 1977

010 → Architecture for humanity (editor), *Design Like You Give a Damn. Architectural Responses to Humanitarian Crises*, New York: Metropolis Books, 2006

011 → Rudolf Arnheim, *The Dynamics of Architectural Form*, Berkeley: University of California Press, 1977

012 → Nishat Awan; Tatjana Schneider; Jeremy Till, *Spatial Agency. Other Ways of Doing Architecture*, London: Routledge, 2011

013 → Gaston Bachelard, *La poétique de l'espace*, Paris: PUF, 1957

014 → Reyner Banham, *The Architecture of the Well-Tempered Environment*, London: Architectural Press, 1969

015 → Werner Bätzing, *Die Alpen. Geschichte und Zukunft einer europäischen Kulturlandschaft*, München: C.H. Beck, 20032

016 → Bjørn Berge, *The Ecology of Building Materials*, London: Architectural Press, 20092

017 → Bjørn Berge, "The engine is not responding. A critique of the automatic energy-saving home", *Arkitektur*, 1, 2011

018 → *Big-Bale-Solution*, Berrien: BBS, 2010 [grey literature]

019 → Peter Blundell Jones, *Peter Hübner. Bauen als ein sozialer Prozeß*,

Stuttgart: Axel Menges, 2007

020 → Andrea Bocco Guarneri, "Però, le balle di paglia portanti!", *Il giornale dell'architettura*, 98, ottobre 2011, p. 23

021 → Andrea Bocco Guarneri; Gianfranco Cavaglià, *Flessibile come di pietra. Tattiche di sopravvivenza e pratiche di costruzione nei villaggi montani*, Torino: CELID, 2008

022 → Godfrey Boyle; Peter Harper; the editors of Undercurrents (editors), *Radical Technology*, London: Wildwood House, 1976

023 → Peter Braun, *La botte de paille comme élément porteur*, février 2012 (unpublished manuscript)

024 → conversation with Peter Braun, Fribourg, 17 May 2012

025 → BRE, *Green Guide to Specification*, available on line at http://www.bre.co.uk/greenguide/podpage.jsp?id=2126

026 → http://users.design.ucla.edu/~djvmc/24/bucky/bathroom.html

027 → www.bfi.org (Buckminster Fuller Institute)

028 → Jean Chevalier; Alain Gheerbrant, *Dictionnaire des symboles*, Paris: Robert Laffont / Jupiter, 1969

029 → John Chilton, *Heinz Isler. The Engineer's Contribution to Contemporary Architecture*, London: Thomas Telford Publishing, 2000

030 → John Chilton, "Heinz Isler: Shells for Two Churches", *Journal of the International Association for Shell and Spatial Structures* (J.IASS), LII, 3, September 2011, p. 173-183

031 → *Conradin Clavuot Architekt*, Sulgen: Niggli, 2008

032 → Matthew Crawford, *Shop Class as Soulcraft*, New York: The Penguin Press, 2009

033 → *El Croquis*, 156, 2011 ("Valerio Olgiati 1996-2011")

034 → *Darco magazine*, 15, 2011 ("Bearth & Deplazes Architects")

035 → Christopher Day, *Places of the Soul*, Wellingborough: The Aquarian Press, 1990

036 → Christopher Day, *Spirit and Place*, Oxford: Architectural Press, 2002

037 → http://www.designcommunity.com/discussion/9518.html

038 → http://www.designcommunity.com/discussion/15101.html

039 → David Dickson, *The politics of alternative technology*, New York: Universe Books, 1974

040 → Lynne Elizabeth; Cassandra Adams (editors), *Alternative Construction. Contemporary Natural Building Methods*, Hoboken: John Wiley and Sons, 2005

041 → www.fasba.de

042 → Hassan Fathy, *Construire avec le peuple. Histoire d'un village d'Égypte: Gourna*, Paris: Sindbad, 1971

043 → Wolfgang Feist, *Einfluss der Lüftungsstrategie auf die Schadstoffkonzentration und -ausbreitung im Raum*, Berichte des Arbeitskreises Kostengünstige Passivhäuser, Protokollband 23, 2003

044 → Beppe Finessi, *Su Mangiarotti*, Milano: Abitare Segesta, 2002

045 → Luc Floissac, *La construction en paille. Principes fondamentaux, Techniques de mises en oeuvre, Exemples de réalisations*, Mens: Terre Vivante, 2012

046 → Yona Friedman, *L'architecture de survie. Où s'invente aujourd'hui le monde de demain*, Paris: Casterman, 1978

047 → Marcel Gloor, *Strohballenhäuser Schweiz. Ökobilanz Haus Glarus*

[Umwelttechnik und -management Master Thesis], Muttenz: Fachhochschule Nordwestschweiz – Hochschule für Life Sciences, 2009

048 → Max Gschwend, *Schweitzer Bauernhäuser*, Bern: Haupt, 1971

049 → Geoff Hammond; Craig Jones, *Inventory of carbon & energy. Version 1.6a*, University of Bath, 2008 (www.bath.ac.uk/mech-eng/sert/embodied/)

050 → Karsten Harries, *The Ethical Function of Architecture*, Cambridge: The MIT Press, 1997

051 → Robert Hastings; Christian Hanus, *Kolloquiumsdokumentation [Gebäudedokumentationskolloquium Nachhaltige Solarwohnbauten, 20. Oktober 2005]*, Zürich: Departement Architektur ETH Zürich, 2005 (Roman Loretan, „Strohballenhaus Braun, Disentis", S. 8-9)

052 → Barrett Hazeltine; Christopher Bull, Appropriate *Technology: Tools, Choices, and Implications*, New York: Academic Press, 1999

053 → Manfred Hegger, „Von der passiven Nutzung zu einer smarten Solararchitektur", in: Christian Schittich (Herausgeber), *Solares Bauen: Strategien Visionen Konzepte*, München: Edition Detail – Institut für internationale Architektur-Dokumentation, 2003, S. 12-25

054 → Sepp Holzer, *Der Agrar-Rebell*, Graz: Leopold Stocker Verlag, 2002

055 → HTW Chur, *Strohballendruckversuche*, [2003] (grey literature)

056 → HTW Chur, *KTI – Projekt Nr.: 6594.2 FHS-ES „Autarkes Wohnen"*, [2006] (graue Literatur)

057 → Johan Huizinga, *Homo ludens. Versuch einer Bestimmung des Spielelmentes der Kultur*, Amsterdam: Pantheon Akademische Verlagsanstalt, 939

058 → Ivan Illich, *Toward a History of Needs*, New York: Pantheon Books, 1978

059 → Karl Jaspers, *Von der Wahrheit*, München: Piper & Co. Verlag, 1947

060 → Hans Jonas, *Das Prinzip Verantwortung*, Frankfurt am Main: Insel Verlag, 1979

061 → Barbara Jones, *Building with Straw Bales: A Practical Guide for the UK and Ireland*, Totnes: Green Books, 2009[2]

062 → Carl Gustav Jung, *Der Mensch und seine Symbole*, Walter: Olten, 1968

063 → Bruce King, *Design of Straw Bale Buildings. The State of the Art*, San Rafael: Green Building Press, 2006

064 → Claudia Kohlus, Interview mit Werner Schmidt, www.nachhaltigkeit.org (7.1.2009)

065 → Leopold Kohr, *The Breakdown of Nations*, London: Routledge and Kegan Paul, 1957

066 → Bancha Kongtragool, Somchai Wongwises, "A review of solar-powered Stirling engines and low temperature differential Stirling engines", *Renewable and Sustainable Energy Reviews*, 7, 2003, p. 131-154

067 → Leonard Koren, *Wabi-Sabi: for Artists, Designers, Poets and Philosophers*, Berkeley: Stone Bridge Press, 1994

068 → Benjamin Krick, *Untersuchung von Strohballen und Strohballenkonstruktionen hinsichtlich ihrer Anwendung für ein Energie sparendes Bauen unter besonderer Berücksichtigung der Lasttragenden Bauweise*, (Dissertation Universität Kassel), 2008

069 → Paul Lacinski; Michel Bergeron, *Serious Straw Bale. A Home Construction Guide for All Climates*, White River Junction: Chelsea Green Publishing, 2000

070 → Bryan Lawson, *The Language of Space*, Oxford: Architectural Press, 2001

071 → Nils Larsson, "Bumpy Road ahead", in: Greg Foliente et al. (editors), *Proceedings of the World Conference SB08*, Melbourne, 2008, vol. 3, p. 33-44

072 → Primo Levi, *La chiave a stella*, Torino: Einaudi, 1978

073 → John McKean, *Von Segal lernen*, Basel: Birkhäuser, 1989

074 → Enzo Mari, *Progetto e passione*, Torino: Bollati Boringhieri, 2001

075 → Robert W. Marks, *The Dymaxion World of Buckminster Fuller*, New York: Reinhold, 1960

076 → Edward Mazria, *The passive solar energy book. A complete guide to passive solar home, greenhouse, and building design*, Emmaus: Rodale Press, 1979

077 → Gernot Minke; Benjamin Krick, *Handbuch Strohballenbau. Grundlagen Konstruktion Beispiele*, Staufen bei Freiburg: Ökobuch, 2009

078 → Gernot Minke, *Handbuch Lehmbau. Baustoffkunde, Techniken, Lehmarchitektur*, Staufen bei Freiburg : Ökobuch, 2009[7]

079 → www.modcell.com

080 → Bruno Munari, *Da cosa nasce cosa*, Roma: Laterza, 1981, p. 160-177

081 → Anton Nothegger, „Lasttragende Strohballenbau in der Praxis", *Wohnung + Gesundheit*, 131, 6. 2009, S. 9-11

082 → Paul Oliver, *Built to Meet Needs. Cultural Issues in Vernacular Architecture*, Oxford: Architectural Press, 2006

083 → Andrea Oppenheimer Dean, *Rural Studio: Samuel Mockbee and an Architecture of Decency*, New York: Princeton Architectural Press, 2002

084 → PAKSBAB (http://nees.unr.edu/projects/straw_bale_house.html)

085 → Victor Papanek, *Design for the Real World. Human Ecology and Social Change*, New York: Pantheon Books, 1971

086 → Carlo Petrini, *Buono, pulito e giusto. Principî di una nuova gastronomia*, Torino: Einaudi, 2011

087 → Ekkehard Ramm; Eberhard Schunk, *Heinz Isler Schalen*, Zürich: vdf Hochschulverlag, 2002

088 → Michael Reynolds, *Earthship: How to Build Your Own*, Taos: Solar Survival Press, 1990

089 → Enrichetta Ritter (a cura di), *I pieghevoli. Raccolta di oggetti progettati per ridurre il loro ingombro*, Bologna: Zanichelli, 1980

090 → Richard Rosentreter, "Oil, Profits, and the Question of Alternative Energy", *Humanist*, 60, 5, September/October 2000, p. 8

091 → Bernard Rudofsky, *Architecture without Architects: A short introduction to non-pedigreed architecture*, New York: The Museum of Modern Art, 1964

092 → Bernard Rudofsky, *Behind the Picture Window*, New York: Oxford University Press, 1955

093 → Bernard Rudofsky, *The Prodigious Builders: Notes toward a natural history of architecture with special regard to those species that are traditionally neglected or downright ignored*, New York: Harcourt Brace Jovanovich, 1977

094 → Floriana Sabba, *Legno, mattone e terra: tecnologie a confronto* (tesi di laurea magistrale in Architettura Costruzione Città, Politecnico di Torino), dicembre 2012

095 → Bettina Schlorhaufer (herausgegeben von), *Cul zuffel e l'aura dado. Gion A. Caminada*, Luzern: Quart Verlag, 2005

096 → Daniela Schmid; Jennifer Sprunger; Nicole Scheidegger, *Strohballenhaus vs. konventionelles Haus*, 07.03.2008 (graue Literatur)
097 → Friedrich Schmidt-Bleek; Willy Bierter, *Das MIPS-Konzept. Weniger Naturverbrauch, mehr Lebensqualität durch Faktor 10*, München: Knaur, 2000
098 → Ernst Friedrich Schumacher, *Small Is Beautiful. Economics as if People Mattered*, New York: Harper & Row, 1975
099 → Richard Sennett, *The Craftsman*, New Haven: Yale University Press, 2008
100 → Luigi Sertorio, *Vivere in nicchia e pensare globale*, Torino: Bollati Boringhieri, 2005
101 → John Seymour, *The New Complete Book of Self-Sufficiency*, London: Dorling Kindersley, 2002
102 → Christoph Simonett, *Die Bauernhäuser des Kantons Graubünden*, Basel: Krebs, 1. Band 1965, 2. Band 1968
103 → Peter Sloterdijk, *Sphären I. Mikrosphärologie*, Frankfurt am Main: Suhrkamp, 1998
104 → Cynthia E. Smith, *Design for the Other 90%*, New York: Smithsonian, 2007
105 → William F. Smith, *Foundations of Material Science and Engineering*, Boston: McGrawHill, 1993^2
106 → www.sunvention.com
107 → Athena Swentzell Steen et al., *The Straw Bale House*, White River Junction: Chelsea Green Publishing, 1994
108 → Thomas Thiis-Evensen, *Archetypes in Architecture*, Oslo: Norwegian University Press, 1987
109 → Nancy Jack Todd; John Todd, *Bioshelters, Ocean Arks, City Farming: Ecology as the Basis of Design*, San Francisco: Sierra Club Books, 1984
110 → Martin Treberspurg, *Neues Bauen mit der Sonne: Ansätzen zu einer klimagerechten Architektur*, Wien: Springer Verlag, 1999
111 → John F.C. Turner, *Housing by people*, London: Marion Boyars Publishers, 1976
112 → Brenda Vale; Robert Vale, *The Autonomous House. Design and planning for self-sufficiency,* London: Thames & Hudson, 1975
113 → Brenda Vale; Robert Vale, *The New Autonomous House,* London: Thames & Hudson, 2000
114 → Robert Vale; Brenda Vale, *Time to Eat the Dog? The Real Guide to Sustainable Living*, London: Thames & Hudson, 2009
115 → Alexander von Vegesack et al. (editors), *Jean Prouvé. The poetics of Technical Objects*, Weil am Rhein: Vitra Design Museum, 2005
116 → Erhard Wagner; Christoph Schubert-Weller, *Earth and Cave Architecture Peter Vetsch*, Sulgen: Verlag Niggli, 1994
117 → conversation with Pete Walker, 29 October 2012
118 → *Allan Wexler*, Barcelona: Gustavo Gili, 1998
119 → www.allanwexlerstudio.com
120 → *Preamble to the Constitution of the World Health Organization* as adopted by the International Health Conference, New York, 19 June - 22 July 1946; signed on 22 July 1946 by the representatives of 61 States (Official Records of the World Health Organization, 2, p. 100) and entered into force on 7 April 1948
121 → Andrin C. Willi, "«Innenräume entstehen aus Ehrlichkeit, Wahrheit und Wahrhaftigkeit»", *SonntagsZeitung*, 46, 13.11.2005, S. 101

122 → http://de.wikipedia.org/wiki/Steinkirche_Cazis
123 → http://en.wikipedia.org/wiki/Appropriate_technology
124 → http://en.wikipedia.org/wiki/Stirling_engine
125 → *Wohnung + Gesundheit* magazine
126 → Tom Woolley, *Natural building. A guide to materials and techniques*, Ramsbury: The Crowood Press, 2006
127 → David Wright, *Natural solar architecture. A passive primer*, New York: Van Nostrand Reinhold, 1978
128 → Nobuyuki Yoshida (editor), *Peter Zumthor*, Tokyo: a+u, February 1998
129 → John Zukowsky; Ian Wardropper, *Austrian Architecture and Design. Beyond Tradition in the 1990s*, Chicago: The Art Institute of Chicago / Berlin: Ernst & Sohn, 1991

CREDITS

Yvonne Aschoff:
196, 197, 389, 390

Atelier Werner Schmidt:
cover; all in front flyleaves; 002, 004, 006, 007, 009, 010, 012, 014, 015, 016, 017, 018, 019, 020, 021, 022, 023, 024, 025, 028, 030, 032, 035, 040, 041, 049, 050, 103, 106, 107, 108, 109, 110, 118, 119, 120, 125, 128, 129, 130, 133, 135, 145, 146, 147, 148, 156, 157, 158, 159, 160, 162, 163, 165, 166, 167, 168, 169, 170, 171, 172, 186, 187, 198, 199, 200, 201, 204, 206, 208, 209, 210, 222, 224, 225, 226, 227, 228, 229, 230, 231, 232, 233, 243, 244, 245, 246, 247, 248, 249, 250, 251, 252, 253, 254, 267, 268, 269, 270, 272, 274, 275, 276, 277, 278, 279, 280, 281, 282, 283, 284, 285, 286, 287, 288, 289, 290, 291, 292, 293, 294, 295, 296, 297, 298, 299, 300, 301, 302, 303, 304, 305, 306, 307, 308, 309, 310, 311, 312, 313, 314, 315, 316, 317, 318, 319, 320, 321, 322, 323, 324, 325, 326, 327, 328, 329, 330, 331, 332, 333, 334, 336, 338, 340, 341, 342, 343, 345, 346, 347, 348, 349, 353, 355, 356, 358, 370, 382, 383, 384, 385, 387, 391, 392, 393, 394, 395, 397, 398, 401, 403, 404, 410, 412, 415, 416, 417, 418, 419, 420, 421; all at p. 190-195; in catalogue (numbering from top down, then from left to right): 8, 13, 15, 18, 19, 20, 21, 23, 25, 26, 27, 28, 29, 31, 32, 34, 36, 37, 38, 40; in back flyleaves (numbering from left to right, and from top down, first on left page and then on right page): 2, 3, 4, 5, 6, 8, 9, 13, 14, 15, 16, 17, 19, 20, 21, 22, 23, 24, 25, 27, 29, 32

Anna Rita Bertorello:
013, 396, 405, 407, 422; in catalogue: 3

Andrea Bocco Guarneri:
001, 003, 011, 027, 033, 037, 042, 043, 046, 047, 093, 100, 131, 136, 137, 138, 139, 149, 150, 151, 153, 154, 155, 192,

193, 194, 195, 203, 205, 211, 271, 335, 337, 339, 350, 351, 352, 381, 386, 388, 406; in catalogue: 9, 11, 13, 17

**from Peter Braun /
Luc Floissac: (→ B045)**
371, 372, 373, 374, 375, 376, 378, 379, 380

Rolf Bucher:
202, 207; in catalogue: 35

Familie Bühlmann:
in back flyleaves: 10

Noé Cauderay:
369

Lucia Degonda:
026, 031, 036, 038, 039, 044, 045, 048, 060, 061, 062, 063, 064, 066, 067, 068, 069, 070, 071, 072, 073, 074, 075, 076, 078, 079, 080, 081, 082, 083, 084, 085, 087, 088, 089, 090, 091, 092, 094, 152, 213, 223, 399, 400, 408, 409, 413, 414; in catalogue: 1, 3, 4, 5, 6, 7, 10, 12, 14, 16; in back flyleaves: 30

**from Development Center for
Appropriate Technology, 2009:**
368

Familie Esser:
in back flyleaves: 12, 18, 31

**Ignazia Favata /
Studio Joe Colombo, Milano:**
219

Frank Huster:
220

Impact, Flims:
099, 104; in catalogue: 2

Familie Ervin Jacomet:
in back flyleaves: 28

Familie Simon Jacomet:
in back flyleaves: 1

Karl Ernst Osthaus Museum, Hagen:
221

Familie Küng:
212; in back flyleaves: 7

ModCell ltd:
266

from Bruno Munari: (→ B080)
215, 216, 217, 218

Ginevra Puppo:
132, 134, 142, 164

PVGIS © European Union, 2001-2012:
105

from Enrichetta Ritter: (→ B089)
051

Philipp Rohner:
005

Werner Schmidt:
008, 029, 034, 057, 058, 059, 065, 077, 086, 098, 101, 102, 111, 112, 113, 114, 115, 116, 117, 121, 122, 123, 124, 126, 140, 141, 143, 144, 161, 173, 174, 175, 176, 177, 178, 179, 180, 181, 182, 183, 184, 185, 188, 189, 190, 191, 234, 235, 236, 237, 238, 239, 240, 241, 242, 273, 344, 354, 357, 359, 360, 361, 362, 363, 367, 377, 402, 411, 423; in catalogue: 22, 24, 30, 33, 39

Schweizerbrot, Bern:
127

Studio Aisslinger, Berlin:
095, 096

University of Bath:
255, 256, 257, 258, 259, 260, 261, 262,

263, 264, 265

U.S. Patent # 2,220,482:
214

Catherine Wanek:
in back flyleaves: 11, 26

lucky clients!